U0912026

新曲綫 New Curves | 用心雕刻每一本......

http://site.douban.com/110283/
http://weibo.com/nccpub

用心字里行间　雕刻名著经典

Management

Tenth Edition

O.C. Ferrell
University of New Mexico

Geoffrey A. Hirt
DePaul University

Linda Ferrell
University of New Mexico

管　理

第 10 版

双语教学版

O.C. 费雷尔
［美］杰弗里·赫特　著
琳达·费雷尔

人民邮电出版社
北　京

图书在版编目（CIP）数据

管理：第 10 版：双语教学版：汉、英 /（美）O.C. 费雷尔等著 . -- 北京：人民邮电出版社，2018.3

商务英语 / 工商管理双语教学教材系列

ISBN 978-7-115-47635-7

Ⅰ . ①管… Ⅱ . ① O… Ⅲ . ①管理学—双语教学—教材—汉、英 Ⅳ . ① C93

中国版本图书馆 CIP 数据核字（2018）第 004118 号

O.C. Ferrell, Geoffrey A. Hirt, Linda Ferrell

Management, 10th Edition

ISBN 978-1-259-17939-6

管理（第 10 版，双语教学版）

◆ 著　　　[美] O.C. 费雷尔　杰弗里·赫特　琳达·费雷尔
策　　划 刘　力　陆　瑜
责任编辑　王润秋
装帧设计　陶建胜

◆ 人民邮电出版社出版发行　北京市丰台区成寿寺路 11 号
邮编　100164　电子邮件　315@ptpress.com.cn
网址　http://www.ptpress.com.cn
电话（编辑部）010-84937150　（市场部）010-84937152
三河市少明印务有限公司印刷
新华书店经销

◆ 开本：850 × 1092　1 /16
印张：10.75
字数：265 千字
2018 年 3 月第 1 版　　2018 年 3 月第 1 次印刷

定价：48.00 元

本书如有印装质量问题，请与本社联系　电话：(010) 84937150

内容提要

《管理》（第 10 版，双语教学版）摘选自 *Business: A Changing World*（10e）一书，该书是美国同类书市场领导品牌。第一作者 O.C. 费雷尔教授，曾担任美国营销协会学术委员会主席，其研究领域包括全球商业、市场营销和商业伦理。本书主要讲述企业的创办与发展以及运营管理等商学知识，具体内容包括企业的组织形式，小企业、创业企业和特许经营，管理的本质，组织、团队和沟通，服务与生产运营管理。本书保留了原版书中全部英文及其教材要素，编者对目录以及部分专业词汇进行了翻译，书中还引用了一些新鲜有趣的商业案例、习题，语言简练，通俗易懂。

本书可作为高等院校财经类及商务英语专业的双语课适用教材，也适用于 MBA 学员、企业管理者以及对该领域感兴趣的普通读者。

Authors 作者简介

O.C. FERRELL

O.C. Ferrell is University Distinguished Professor of Marketing and Bill Daniels Professor of Business Ethics in the Anderson School of Management at the University of New Mexico. He served as the Bill Daniels Distinguished Professor of Business Ethics at the University of Wyoming and the Chair of the Department of Marketing at Colorado State University. He also has held faculty positions at the University of Memphis, University of Tampa, Texas A&M University, Illinois State University, and Southern Illinois University, as well as visiting positions at Queen's University (Ontario, Canada), University of Michigan (Ann Arbor), University of Wisconsin (Madison), and University of Hannover (Germany). He has served as a faculty member for the Master's Degree Program in Marketing at Thammasat University (Bangkok, Thailand). Dr. Ferrell received his B.A. and M.B.A. from Florida State University and his Ph.D. from Louisiana State University. His teaching and research interests include business ethics, global business, and marketing.

Dr. Ferrell is widely recognized as a leading teacher and scholar in business. He has published more than 100 articles in leading journals. He has co-authored more than 20 books. In addition to *Business: A Changing World,* he has two other textbooks, *Marketing* and *Business Ethics: Ethical Decision Making and Cases,* that are market leaders in their respective areas. He also has co-authored other textbooks for marketing, management, business and society, and other business courses, as well as a trade book on business ethics. He chaired the American Marketing Association (AMA) ethics committee that developed its current code of ethics. He is past president of the Academic Council for the AMA. Currently he is Vice President of Publications for the Academy of Marketing Science and is a Distinguished Fellow with AMS and is the AMS, Cutco-Vector Distinguished Marketing Educator.

Dr. Ferrell's major focus is teaching and developing teaching resources for students and faculty to better understand the increasing complex global business environment. He has taught the introduction to business course using this textbook. This gives him the opportunity to develop, improve, and test the book and ancillary materials on a firsthand basis. He has traveled extensively to work with students and understands the needs of instructors of introductory business courses. He lives in Albuquerque, New Mexico, and enjoys skiing, golf, and international travel.

GEOFFREY A. HIRT

Geoffrey A. Hirt of DePaul University previously taught at Texas Christian University and Illinois State University where he was Chairman of the Department of Finance and Law. At DePaul, he was Chairman of the Finance Department from 1987 to 1997 and held the title of Mesirow Financial Fellow. He developed the MBA program in Hong Kong and served as Director of International Initiatives for the College of Business, supervising overseas programs in Hong Kong, Prague, and Manama and was awarded the Spirit of St. Vincent DePaul award for his contributions to the university. Dr. Hirt directed the Chartered Financial Analysts (CFA) study program for the Investment Analysts Society of Chicago from 1987 to 2003. He has been a visiting professor at the University of Urbino in Italy, where he still maintains a relationship with the economics department. He received his Ph.D. in Finance from the University of Illinois at Champaign–Urbana, his M.B.A. at Miami University of Ohio, and his B.A. from Ohio Wesleyan University.

Dr. Hirt is currently on the Dean's Advisory Board and Executive Committee of DePaul's School of Music and is on the Board of the James Tyree Foundation. The Tyree Foundation funds innovative education programs in Chicago, and Dr. Hirt also serves on the Grant Committee. Dr. Hirt is past president and a current member of the Midwest Finance Association, a former editor of the *Journal of Financial Education,* and also a member of the Financial Management Association. He belongs to the Pacific Pension Institute, an organization of public pension funds, private equity firms, and international organizations such as the Asian Development Bank, the IMF, and the European Bank for Reconstruction and Development.

Dr. Hirt is widely known for his textbook *Foundations of Financial Management* published by McGraw-Hill/Irwin. This book in its fifteenth edition has been used in more than 31 countries and translated into more than 14 different languages. Additionally, Dr. Hirt is well known for his textbook, *Fundamentals of Investment Management,* also published by McGraw-Hill/Irwin and now in its tenth edition. Dr. Hirt enjoys golf, swimming, music, and traveling with his wife, who is a pianist and opera coach.

LINDA FERRELL

Dr. Linda Ferrell is Professor of Marketing and Bill Daniels Professor of Business Ethics in the Anderson School of Management at the University of New Mexico. She completed her Ph.D. in Business Administration, with a concentration in management, at the University of Memphis. She has taught at the University of Tampa, Colorado State University, University of Northern Colorado, University of Memphis, and the University of Wyoming. She also team teaches a class at Thammasat University in Bangkok, Thailand, as well as an online Business Ethics Certificate course through the University of New Mexico.

Her work experience as an account executive for McDonald's and Pizza Hut's advertising agencies supports her teaching of advertising, marketing management, marketing ethics, and marketing principles. She has published in the *Journal of Public Policy & Marketing, Journal of Business Research, Journal of the Academy of Marketing Science, Journal of Business Ethics, AMS Review, Journal of Academic Ethics, Journal of Marketing Education, Marketing Education Review, Journal of Teaching Business Ethics,* and *Case Research Journal,* and is co-author of *Business Ethics: Ethical Decision Making and Cases* (10th edition) and *Business and Society* (5th edition). She co-leads the Daniels Fund business ethics initiative at the University of New Mexico.

Dr. Ferrell is the President of the Academy of Marketing Science and a past president for the Marketing Management Association. She is a member of the college advisory board for Cutco Vector. She is on the NASBA Center for the Public Trust Board of Directors, University of Central Florida-Nicholson School of Communication Board of Visitors, University of Tampa-Sykes College of Business, Board of Fellows, and the Direct Selling Education Foundation Board and Executive Committee. She frequently speaks to organizations on "Teaching Business Ethics," including the Direct Selling Education Foundation's training programs, Ethics & Compliance Officer Association, NASBA Center for the Public Trust Ethical Leadership Conference, as well as others. She has served as an expert witness in cases related to advertising, business ethics, and consumer protection.

Contents 目录

Management

1

Options for Organizing Business
企业的组织形式

Learning Objectives

After reading this chapter, you will be able to:

- **LO 1-1** Define and examine the advantages and disadvantages of the sole proprietorship form of organization.
- **LO 1-2** Identify two types of partnership and evaluate the advantages and disadvantages of the partnership form of organization.
- **LO 1-3** Describe the corporate form of organization and cite the advantages and disadvantages of corporations.
- **LO 1-4** Define and debate the advantages and disadvantages of mergers, acquisitions, and leveraged buyouts.
- **LO 1-5** Propose an appropriate organizational form for a startup business.

Chapter Outline

- Introduction
- Sole Proprietorships
  - *Advantages of Sole Proprietorships*
  - *Disadvantages of Sole Proprietorships*
- Partnerships
  - *Types of Partnership*
  - *Articles of Partnership*
  - *Advantages of Partnerships*
  - *Disadvantages of Partnerships*
  - *Taxation of Partnerships*
- Corporations
  - *Creating a Corporation*
  - *Types of Corporations*
  - *Elements of a Corporation*
  - *Advantages of Corporations*
  - *Disadvantages of Corporations*
- Other Types of Ownership
  - *Joint Ventures*
  - *S Corporations*
  - *Limited Liability Companies*
  - *Cooperatives*
- Trends in Business Ownership: Mergers and Acquisitions

进入商业世界

Enter the World of Business

股东激进主义

Shareholder Activism

Corporations are owned by investors, who receive shares of stock and are called shareholders. Investors are increasingly clashing with board members of major corporations. Shareholder activism occurs when shareholders use their ownership to put pressure on management. The majority of activist campaigns are centered on getting corporations to increase dividends or change their boards of directors. Shareholders are also demanding more transparency about operations related to sustainability, human rights, and other social issues. Investors target firms with large cash reserves to release this cash in the form of preferred stock or dividends. Apple Inc. received a blow when investor David Einhorn filed a lawsuit demanding that Apple decrease its $137 billion cash stockpile by issuing preferred stock. Although the lawsuit was dropped, investor pressure on Apple continues.

Another reason for shareholder activism is dissatisfaction with the board. Proxy battles, in which shareholders use their proxy votes to change board members or managers, are increasing. Hess shareholder Elliot Management launched a large fight against the company, accusing its board of weak discipline and accountability. The battle ended when Hess agreed to give Elliot three board seats if the fund would support five of Hess's directors.

Shareholder activism can be beneficial and problematic. On the one hand, activism allows owners to participate in the company, and firms have acknowledged that activists sometimes have good ideas that benefit the firms. However, proxy battles and lawsuits cost money, and some managers claim they are spending more time with shareholders and less on managing.[1]

引言
Introduction

The legal form of ownership taken by a business is seldom of great concern to you as a customer. When you eat at a restaurant, you probably don't care whether the restaurant is owned by one person (a sole proprietorship), has two or more owners who share the business (a partnership), or is an entity owned by many stockholders (a corporation); all you want is good food. If you buy a foreign car, you probably don't care whether the company that made it has laws governing its form of organization that are different from those for businesses in the United States. You are buying the car because it is well made, fits your price range, or appeals to your sense of style. Nonetheless, a business's legal form of ownership affects how it operates, how much taxes it pays, and how much control its owners have.

connect*

Need help understanding Forms of Business Ownership? Visit your Connect ebook video tab for a brief animated explanation.

This chapter examines three primary forms of business ownership—sole proprietorship, partnership, and corporation—and weighs the advantages and disadvantages of each. These forms are the most often used whether the business is a traditional bricks and mortar company, an online-only one, or a combination of both. We also take a look at S corporations, limited liability companies, and cooperatives and discuss some trends in business ownership. You may wish to refer to Table 1.1 to compare the various forms of business ownership mentioned in the chapter.

独资企业
Sole Proprietorships

LO 1-1

独资企业
sole proprietorships businesses owned and operated by one individual; the most common form of business organization in the United States

Sole proprietorships, businesses owned and operated by one individual, are the most common form of business organization in the United States. Common examples include many restaurants, hair salons, flower shops, dog kennels, and independent grocery stores. Many sole proprietors focus on services—small retail stores, financial counseling, appliance repair, child care, and the like—rather than on the manufacture of goods, which often requires large sums of money not available to most small businesses. As you can see in Figure 1.1, proprietorships far outnumber corporations, but they net far fewer sales and less income.

TABLE 1.1 Various Forms of Business Ownership

Structure	Ownership	Taxation	Liability	Use
Sole Proprietorship	One owner	Individual income taxed	Unlimited	Owned by a single individual and is the easiest way to conduct business
Partnership	Two or more owners	Individual owners' income taxed	Somewhat limited	Easy way for two individuals to conduct business
Corporation	Any number of shareholders	Corporate and shareholder taxed	Limited	A legal entity with shareholders or stockholders
S Corporation	Up to 100 shareholders	Taxed as a partnership	Limited	A legal entity with tax advantages for restricted number of shareholders
Limited Liability Company	Unlimited number of shareholders	Taxed as a partnership	Limited	Avoid personal lawsuits

* 注：有需要 Connect 等在线资源的读者请致电麦格劳－希尔教育集团北京办公室 010-57997618。

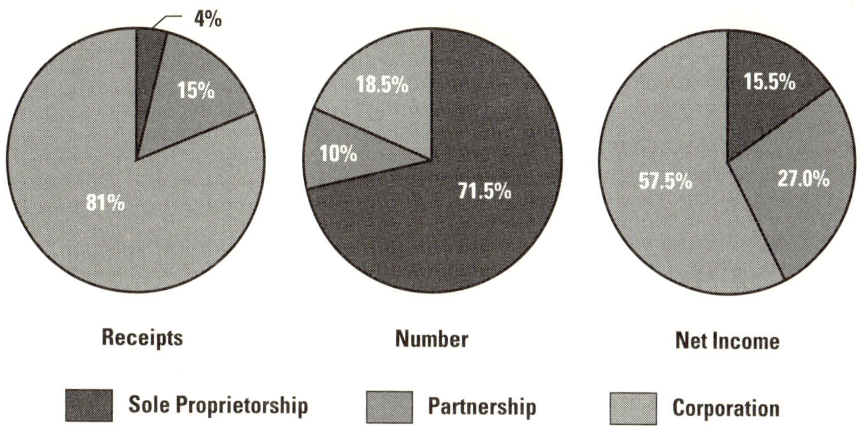

FIGURE 1.1
Comparison of Sole Proprietorships, Partnerships, and Corporations

Source: U.S. Bureau of the Census, *The 2012 Statistical Abstract*.

Sole proprietorships are typically small businesses employing fewer than 50 people. (We'll look at small businesses in greater detail in Chapter 2.) Sole proprietorships constitute approximately three-fourths of all businesses in the United States. It is interesting to note that men are twice as likely as women to start their own business.[2] In many areas, small businesses make up the vast majority of the economy.

独资企业的优势

Advantages of Sole Proprietorships

Sole proprietorships are generally managed by their owners. Because of this simple management structure, the owner/manager can make decisions quickly. This is just one of many advantages of the sole proprietorship form of business.

容易成立且费用低

Ease and Cost of Formation. Forming a sole proprietorship is relatively easy and inexpensive. In some states, creating a sole proprietorship involves merely announcing the new business in the local newspaper. Other proprietorships, such as barber shops and restaurants, may require state and local licenses and permits because of the nature of the business. The cost of these permits may run from $25 to $100. No lawyer is needed to create such enterprises, and the owner can usually take care of the required paperwork without outside assistance.

Of course, an entrepreneur starting a new sole proprietorship must find a suitable site from which to operate the business. Some sole proprietors look no farther than their garage or a spare bedroom when seeking a workshop or office. Among the more famous businesses that sprang to life in their founders' homes are Google, Walt Disney, Dell, eBay, Hewlett-Packard, Apple, and Mattel.[3] Computers, personal copiers, scanners, and other high-tech gadgets have been a boon for home-based businesses, permitting them to interact quickly with customers, suppliers, and others. Many independent salespersons and contractors can perform their work using a smartphone or tablet computer as they travel. E-mail and social networks have made it possible for many proprietorships to develop in the services area. Internet connections also allow small businesses to establish websites to promote their products and even to make low-cost long-distance phone calls with voice-over Internet protocol (VoIP) technology. One of the most famous services using VoIP is Skype, which allows people to make free calls over the Internet.

Many local restaurants are sole proprietorships.

保密性

Secrecy. Sole proprietorships make possible the greatest degree of secrecy. The proprietor, unlike the owners of a partnership or corporation, does not have to discuss publicly his or her operating plans, minimizing the possibility that competitors can obtain trade secrets. Financial reports need not be disclosed, as do the financial reports of publicly owned corporations.

利润的分配与使用

Distribution and Use of Profits. All profits from a sole proprietorship belong exclusively to the owner. He or she does not have to share them with any partners or stockholders. The owner decides how to use the funds—for expansion of the business, or salary increases, for travel to purchase additional inventory, or to find new customers.

企业的灵活性和控制力

Flexibility and Control of the Business. The sole proprietor has complete control over the business and can make decisions on the spot without anyone else's approval. This control allows the owner to respond quickly to competitive business conditions or to changes in the economy. The ability to quickly change prices or products can provide a competitive advantage for the business.

政府监管

Government Regulation. Sole proprietorships have the most freedom from government regulation. Many government regulations—federal, state, and local—apply only to businesses that have a certain number of employees, and securities laws apply only to corporations that issue stock. Nonetheless, sole proprietors must ensure that they follow all laws that do apply to their business. For example, sole proprietorships must be careful to obey employee and consumer protection regulation.

税负

Taxation. Profits from sole proprietorships are considered personal income and are taxed at individual tax rates. The owner, therefore, pays one income tax that includes the business and individual income. Another tax benefit is that a sole proprietor is allowed to establish a tax-exempt retirement account or a tax-exempt profit-sharing account. Such accounts are exempt from current income tax, but payments taken after retirement are taxed when they are received.

关闭企业

Closing the Business. A sole proprietorship can be dissolved easily. No approval of co-owners or partners is necessary. The only legal condition is that all financial obligations must be paid or resolved.

独资企业的劣势
Disadvantages of Sole Proprietorships

What may be seen as an advantage by one person may turn out to be a disadvantage to another. For profitable businesses managed by capable owners, many of the following factors do not cause problems. On the other hand, proprietors starting out with little management experience and little money are likely to encounter many of the disadvantages.

无限责任

Unlimited Liability. The sole proprietor has unlimited liability in meeting the debts of the business. In other words, if the business cannot pay its creditors, the owner may be forced to use personal, nonbusiness holdings such as a car or a home to pay off the debts. There are only a few states in which houses and homesteads cannot be taken by creditors, even if the proprietor declares bankruptcy. The more wealth an individual has, the greater is the disadvantage of unlimited liability.

Sole proprietorships often have greater difficulty attracting talented employees because of competition from larger companies.

资金来源有限

Limited Sources of Funds. Among the relatively few sources of money available to the sole proprietorship are banks, friends, family, the Small Business Administration, or his or her own funds. The owner's personal financial condition determines his or her credit standing. Additionally, sole proprietorships may have to pay higher interest rates on funds borrowed from banks than do large corporations because they are considered greater risks. Often, the only way a sole proprietor can borrow for business purposes is to pledge a car, a house, other real estate, or other personal assets to guarantee the loan. If the business fails, the owner may lose the personal assets as well as the business. Publicly owned corporations, in contrast, can not only obtain funds from commercial banks but can sell stocks and bonds to the public to raise money. If a public company goes out of business, the owners do not lose personal assets.

技能水平有限

Limited Skills. The sole proprietor must be able to perform many functions and possess skills in diverse fields such as management, marketing, finance, accounting, bookkeeping, and personnel management. Specialized professionals, such as accountants or attorneys, can be hired by businesses for help or advice. Sometimes, sole proprietors need assistance with certain business functions. For instance, Barrett Business Services provides businesses with staffing and management consulting. The 50-year-old company has refined personnel placement skills, ensuring good matches between employee and employer, while having a strong management knowledge base that serves to strengthen the foundation of any business. Many businesses take advantage of these kinds of services to gain a competitive advantage.[4] In the end, however, it is up to the business owner to make the final decision in all areas of the business.

缺乏持续性

Lack of Continuity. The life expectancy of a sole proprietorship is directly linked to that of the owner and his or her ability to work. The serious illness of the owner could result in failure of the business if competent help cannot be found.

It is difficult to arrange for the sale of a proprietorship and at the same time assure customers that the business will continue to meet their needs. For instance, how

Entrepreneurship in Action

Smashing Its Way to Success: Smashburger

Smashburger
Founder: Tom Ryan
Founded: 2007, in Denver, Colorado
Success: Since its founding, Smashburger has opened 200 locations with annual profits of $250 million.

Smashburger differentiates itself from fast-food competitors with its unique approach to operations and service. When he opened Smashburger, founder Tom Ryan was aiming to create a "better burger" with fresh-quality ingredients and unique healthy options—including flash-fried green beans and carrot sticks—to appeal to all food lovers. To make Smashburger further stand out from competitors, stores have a gallery-like atmosphere complete with murals and real silverware. Local twists on certain product offerings inspire customer loyalty, such as the Brooklyn Burger offered in Brooklyn, New York.

A year after its creation, Smashburger was incorporated as a limited liability company. This means that the owners have limited liability for debt, but the organization is taxed like a partnership. Smashburger became a subsidiary of Burger Development LLC. It made the decision to become a franchise, allowing entrepreneurs to license the Smashburger name and open their own restaurants. According to Ryan, Smashburger views its franchisees as investors and important partners in the company. Strong partnership, quality food offerings, and customer engagement may be the edge Smashburger needs to propel it toward its goals and keep the competition at bay. The company has been included in *Inc.* magazine's 500 fastest-growing private companies.[5]

---

does one sell a veterinary practice? A veterinarian's major asset is patients. If the vet dies suddenly, the equipment can be sold, but the patients will not necessarily remain loyal to the office. On the other hand, a veterinarian who wants to retire could take in a younger partner and sell the practice to the partner over time. One advantage to the partnership is that some of the customers are likely to stay with the business, even if ownership changes.

缺少合格员工
Lack of Qualified Employees. It is usually difficult for a small sole proprietorship to match the wages and benefits offered by a large competing corporation because the proprietorship's profits may not be as high. In addition, there is little room for advancement within a sole proprietorship, so the owner may have difficulty attracting and retaining qualified employees. On the other hand, the trend of large corporations downsizing and outsourcing tasks has created renewed opportunities for small businesses to acquire well-trained employees.

合伙企业
partnership
a form of business organization defined by the Uniform Partnership Act as "an association of two or more persons who carry on as co-owners of a business for profit"

税负
Taxation. Although we listed taxation as an advantage for sole proprietorships, it can also be a disadvantage, depending on the proprietor's income. Under current tax rates, sole proprietors pay a higher marginal tax rate than do small corporations on income of less than $75,000. However, sole proprietorships avoid the double taxation that occurs with corporations. The tax effect often determines whether a sole proprietor chooses to incorporate his or her business.

合伙企业
Partnerships

LO 1-2

One way to minimize the disadvantages of a sole proprietorship and maximize its advantages is to have more than one owner. Most states have a model law governing partnerships based on the Uniform Partnership Act. This law defines a **partnership** as "an association of two or more persons who carry on as co-owners of a business for

TABLE 1.2
Keys to Success in Business Partnerships

1. Keep profit sharing and ownership at 50/50, or you have an employer/employee relationship.
2. Partners should have different skill sets to complement one another.
3. Honesty is critical.
4. Must maintain face-to-face communication in addition to phone and e-mail.
5. Maintain transparency, sharing more information over time.
6. Be aware of funding constraints, and do not put yourself in a situation where neither you nor your partner can secure additional financial support.
7. To be successful, you need experience.
8. Whereas family should be a priority, be careful to minimize the number of associated problems.
9. Do not become too infatuated with "the idea" as opposed to implementation.
10. Couple optimism with realism in sales and growth expectations and planning.

Source: Abstracted from J. Watananbe, "14 Reasons Why 80% of New Business Partnerships Would Fail Within Their First 5 Years of Existence".

profit." Partnerships are the least used form of business (see Figure 1.1). They are typically larger than sole proprietorships but smaller than corporations.

Partnerships can be a fruitful form of business, as long as you follow some basic keys to success, which are outlined in Table 1.2.

合伙企业的类型
Types of Partnership

There are two basic types of partnership: general partnership and limited partnership. A **general partnership** involves a complete sharing in the management of a business. In a general partnership, each partner has unlimited liability for the debts of the business. For example, Webco, a military retail service provider, is a general partnership that has four locations in the United States. These four locations are strategic business units that focus on many product categories at once. This strategy has allowed the company to become a leader in category management in the military retail market, sustaining its business for more than 50 years.[6] Professionals such as lawyers, accountants, and architects often join together in general partnerships.

普通合伙
general partnership
a partnership that involves a complete sharing in both the management and the liability of the business

A **limited partnership** has at least one general partner, who assumes unlimited liability, and at least one limited partner, whose liability is limited to his or her investment in the business. Limited partnerships exist for risky investment projects where the chance of loss is great. The general partners accept the risk of loss; the limited partners' losses are limited to their initial investment. Limited partners do not participate in the management of the business but share in the profits in accordance with the terms of a partnership agreement. Usually the general partner receives a larger share of the profits after the limited partners have received their initial investment back. Popular examples are oil-drilling partnerships and real estate partnerships.

有限合伙
limited partnership
a business organization that has at least one general partner, who assumes unlimited liability, and at least one limited partner, whose liability is limited to his or her investment in the business

合伙条款
Articles of Partnership

Articles of partnership are legal documents that set forth the basic agreement between partners. Most states require articles of partnership, but even if they are not

合伙条款
articles of partnership
legal documents that set forth the basic agreement between partners

Going Green

Sustainably Organized: Crimson Renewable Energy

Crimson Midstream Limited Liability Corporation (LLC) is a holding company specializing in petroleum pipelines, the shipping of petro-chemicals, and specialty asphalt products. The LLC designation allows the company to have as many members or owners as it pleases of all different types (i.e., individuals, corporations, partnerships, and so on). It also gives the company the ability to choose how much and when to pay distributions to stockholders, giving it more control over its finances.

As a holding company, it is able to generate independent business units with slightly different functions within the same industry. Denver-based Crimson Renewable Energy Limited Partnership (LP) is one such business unit that produces oil and gas with a focus on biodiesel fuels. As an LP, Crimson Renewable Energy has limited its liability to its own business, while Crimson Midstream LLC serves as the general partner that holds unlimited liability for the LP.

Crimson Renewable Energy produces 25 million gallons of biodiesel per year. It invests heavily in its ability to transform natural materials such as used cooking oil waste, vegetable oils, algae oils, animal fats, and waste corn oil derived from ethanol production into biofuels. With more than 20 years of experience, the firm oversees the quality of its operations in-house through testing and has the capacity to customize fuel for customers to meet certain price points, function requirements, or climate considerations. Crimson Renewable Energy's supply chain consists of those who are dedicated to sustainable practices. The company also sources locally when possible.[7]

Discussion Questions

1. Crimson Midstream organized as a limited liability corporation. What are some of the advantages of an LLC?
2. What protections does Crimson Renewable receive by organizing as a limited partnership?
3. What does it mean that Crimson Midstream holds unlimited liability for Crimson Renewable LP?

required, it makes good sense for partners to draw them up. Articles of partnership usually list the money or assets that each partner has contributed (called *partnership capital*), state each partner's individual management role or duty, specify how the profits and losses of the partnership will be divided among the partners, and describe how a partner may leave the partnership as well as any other restrictions that might apply to the agreement. Table 1.3 lists some of the issues and provisions that should be included in articles of partnership.

In 1996, Stanford students Sergey Brin and Larry Page partnered to form the search engine Google as part of a research project. The company was incorporated in 1998 and is now the world's top search engine.

合伙企业的优势

Advantages of Partnerships

Law firms, accounting firms, and investment firms with several hundred partners have partnership agreements that are quite complicated in comparison with the partnership agreement among two or three people owning a computer repair shop. The advantages must be compared with those offered by other forms of business organization, and not all apply to every partnership.

成立相对简单

Ease of Organization. Starting a partnership requires little more than drawing up articles of partnership. No legal charters have to be granted, but the name of the business should be registered with the state.

TABLE 1.3
Issues and Provisions in Articles of Partnership

1. Name, purpose, location
2. Duration of the agreement
3. Authority and responsibility of each partner
4. Character of partners (i.e., general or limited, active or silent)
5. Amount of contribution from each partner
6. Division of profits or losses
7. Salaries of each partner
8. How much each partner is allowed to withdraw
9. Death of partner
10. Sale of partnership interest
11. Arbitration of disputes
12. Required and prohibited actions
13. Absence and disability
14. Restrictive covenants
15. Buying and selling agreements

资本和信用的可得性

Availability of Capital and Credit. When a business has several partners, it has the benefit of a combination of talents and skills and pooled financial resources. Partnerships tend to be larger than sole proprietorships and therefore have greater earning power and better credit ratings. Because many limited partnerships have been formed for tax purposes rather than for economic profits, the combined income of all U.S. partnerships is quite low, as shown in Figure 1.1. Nevertheless, the professional partnerships of many lawyers, accountants, and banking firms make quite large profits. For instance, the partners in the international law firm Davis Polk & Wardwell LLP take home an average of nearly $3 million a year.[8]

知识与技能相结合

Combined Knowledge and Skills. Partners in the most successful partnerships acknowledge each other's talents and avoid confusion and conflict by specializing in a particular area of expertise such as marketing, production, accounting, or service. The diversity of skills in a partnership makes it possible for the business to be run by a management team of specialists instead of by a generalist sole proprietor. Co-founders Justin Wetherill, Edward Trujillo, and David Reiff credit diversity as being a key component to the success of their company uBreakiFix, an iPhone repair service. In just six years, the startup has grown to 47 locations, generating $8.5 million in revenue. They have also embarked upon a franchising strategy, which is sure to spur further growth.[9] Service-oriented partnerships in fields such as law, financial planning, and accounting may attract customers because clients may think that the service offered by a diverse team is of higher quality than that provided by one person. Larger law firms, for example, often have individual partners who specialize in certain areas of the law—such as family, bankruptcy, corporate, entertainment, and criminal law.

决策制定

Decision Making. Small partnerships can react more quickly to changes in the business environment than can large partnerships and corporations. Such fast reactions are possible because the partners are involved in day-to-day operations and can make decisions quickly after consultation. Large partnerships with hundreds of partners in many states are not common. In those that do exist, decision making is likely to be slow. However, some partnerships have been successful despite their large size. The accounting firm PricewaterhouseCoopers LLP (PwC) is the third largest accounting and advisory firm in the United States with more than 9,500 partners and principals and more than 174,000 personnel. The company has gross revenues of more than $32 billion. Some have attributed PwC's success to its strong diversification techniques and the ability to operate in different market niches.[10]

法规限制

Regulatory Controls. Like a sole proprietorship, a partnership has fewer regulatory controls affecting its activities than does a corporation. A partnership does not have to file public financial statements with government agencies or send out quarterly financial statements to several thousand owners, as do corporations such as Apple and Ford Motor Co. A partnership does, however, have to abide by all laws relevant to the industry or profession in which it operates as well as state and federal laws relating to hiring and firing, food handling, and so on, just as the sole proprietorship does.

合伙企业的劣势
Disadvantages of Partnerships

Partnerships have many advantages compared to sole proprietorships and corporations, but they also have some disadvantages. Limited partners have no voice in the management of the partnership, and they may bear most of the risk of the business while the general partner reaps a larger share of the benefits. There may be a change in the goals and objectives of one partner but not the other, particularly when the partners are multinational organizations. This can cause friction, giving rise to an enterprise that fails to satisfy both parties or even forcing an end to the partnership. Many partnership disputes wind up in court or require outside mediation. A partnership can be jeopardized when two business partners cannot resolve disputes. For instance, Evan Spiegel and Bobby Murphy, co-founders of photo sharing mobile application Snapchat, are being sued by an earlier founder, Reggie Brown, for one-third of the value of the company. Brown claims that the business is founded on his idea, which Spiegel and Murphy stole from him. Despite a few settlement talks, an agreement is still pending at this time.[11] In some cases, the ultimate solution may be dissolving the partnership. Major disadvantages of partnerships include the following.

无限责任

Unlimited Liability. In general partnerships, the general partners have unlimited liability for the debts incurred by the business, just as the sole proprietor has unlimited liability for his or her business. Such unlimited liability can be a distinct disadvantage to one partner if his or her personal financial resources are greater than those of the others. A potential partner should check to make sure that all partners have comparable resources to help the business in time of trouble. This disadvantage is eliminated for limited partners, who can lose only their initial investment.

企业责任

Business Responsibility. All partners are responsible for the business actions of all others. Partners may have the ability to commit the partnership to a contract without approval of the other partners. A bad decision by one partner may put the other partners' personal resources in jeopardy. Personal problems such as a divorce can eliminate a significant portion of one partner's financial resources and weaken the financial structure of the whole partnership.

合伙企业的寿命

Life of the Partnership. A partnership is terminated when a partner dies or withdraws. In a two-person partnership, if one partner withdraws, the firm's liabilities would be paid off and the assets divided between the partners. Obviously, the partner who wishes to continue in the business would be at a serious disadvantage. The business could be disrupted, financing would be reduced, and the management skills of the departing partner would be lost. The remaining partner would have to find another or reorganize the business as a sole proprietorship. In very large partnerships such as those found in law firms and investment banks, the continuation of the partnership may be provided for in the articles of partnership. The provision may simply state the terms for a new partnership agreement among the remaining partners. In such cases, the disadvantage to the other partners is minimal.

Selling a partnership interest has the same effect as the death or withdrawal of a partner. It is difficult to place a value on a partner's share of the partnership. No public value is placed on the partnership, as there is on publicly owned corporations. What is a law firm worth? What is the local hardware store worth? Coming up with a fair value that all partners can agree to is not easy. Selling a partnership interest is easier if the articles of partnership specify a method of valuation. Even if there is not a procedure for selling one partner's interest, the old partnership must still be dissolved and a new one created. In contrast, in the corporate form of business, the departure of owners has little effect on the financial resources of the business, and the loss of managers does not cause long-term changes in the structure of the organization.

利润分配

Distribution of Profits. Profits earned by the partnership are distributed to the partners in the proportions specified in the articles of partnership. This may be a disadvantage if the division of the profits does not reflect the work each partner puts into the business. You may have encountered this disadvantage while working on a student group project: You may have felt that you did most of the work and that the other students in the group received grades based on your efforts. Even the perception of an unfair profit-sharing agreement may cause tension between the partners, and unhappy partners can have a negative effect on the profitability of the business.

资金来源有限

Limited Sources of Funds. As with a sole proprietorship, the sources of funds available to a partnership are limited. Because no public value is placed on the business (such as the current trading price of a corporation's stock), potential partners do not know what one partnership share is worth. Moreover, because partnership shares cannot be bought and sold easily in public markets, potential owners may not want to tie up their money in assets that cannot be readily sold on short notice. Accumulating enough funds to operate a national business, especially a business requiring intensive investments in facilities and equipment, can be difficult. Partnerships also may have to pay higher interest rates on funds borrowed from banks than do large corporations because partnerships may be considered greater risks.

合伙企业的税负
Taxation of Partnerships

Partnerships are quasi-taxable organizations. This means that partnerships do not pay taxes when submitting the partnership tax return to the Internal Revenue Service. The tax return simply provides information about the profitability of the organization and the distribution of profits among the partners. Partners must report their share of profits on their individual tax returns and pay taxes at the income tax rate for individuals.

LO 1-3

公司
Corporations

公司
corporation
a legal entity, created by the state, whose assets and liabilities are separate from its owners

When you think of a business, you probably think of a huge corporation such as General Electric, Procter & Gamble, or Sony because a large portion of your consumer dollars go to such corporations. A **corporation** is a legal entity, created by the state, whose assets and liabilities are separate from its owners. As a legal entity, a corporation has many of the rights, duties, and powers of a person, such as the right to receive, own, and transfer property. Corporations can enter into contracts with individuals or with other legal entities, and they can sue and be sued in court.

Corporations account for the majority of all U.S. sales and income. Thus, most of the dollars you spend as a consumer probably go to incorporated businesses (see Figure 1.1). Most corporations are not mega-companies like General Mills or Ford Motor Co.; even small businesses can incorporate. As we shall see later in the chapter, many smaller firms elect to incorporate as "S Corporations," which operate under slightly different rules and have greater flexibility than do traditional "C Corporations" like General Mills.

股份
stock
shares of a corporation that may be bought or sold

股息
dividends
profits of a corporation that are distributed in the form of cash payments to stockholders

Corporations are typically owned by many individuals and organizations who own shares of the business, called **stock** (thus, corporate owners are often called *shareholders* or *stockholders*). Stockholders can buy, sell, give or receive as gifts, or inherit their shares of stock. As owners, the stockholders are entitled to all profits that are left after all the corporation's other obligations have been paid. These profits may be distributed in the form of cash payments called **dividends.** For example, if a corporation earns $100 million after expenses and taxes and decides to pay the owners $40 million in dividends, the stockholders receive 40 percent of the profits in cash dividends. However, not all after-tax profits are paid to stockholders in dividends. Some corporations may retain profits to expand the business. For example, Berkshire Hathaway has always retained its earnings and reinvested them for the shareholders. This has resulted in an average 20 percent increase in per share investment over a 40-year period.[12]

公司的创建
Creating a Corporation

A corporation is created, or incorporated, under the laws of the state in which it incorporates. The individuals creating the corporation are known as *incorporators.* Each state has a specific procedure, sometimes called *chartering the corporation,* for incorporating a business. Most states require a minimum of three incorporators; thus, many small businesses can be and are incorporated. Another requirement is that the new corporation's name cannot be similar to that of another business. In most states, a corporation's name must end in "company," "corporation," "incorporated," or "limited" to show that the owners have limited liability. (In this text, however, the word *company* means any organization engaged in a commercial enterprise and can refer to a sole proprietorship, a partnership, or a corporation.)

The incorporators must file legal documents generally referred to as *articles of incorporation* with the appropriate state office (often the secretary of state). The articles of incorporation contain basic information about the business. The following 10 items are found in the Model Business Corporation Act, issued by the American Bar Association, which is followed by most states:

1. Name and address of the corporation.
2. Objectives of the corporation.
3. Classes of stock (common, preferred, voting, nonvoting) and the number of shares for each class of stock to be issued.

4. Expected life of the corporation (corporations are usually created to last forever).
5. Financial capital required at the time of incorporation.
6. Provisions for transferring shares of stock between owners.
7. Provisions for the regulation of internal corporate affairs.
8. Address of the business office registered with the state of incorporation.
9. Names and addresses of the initial board of directors.
10. Names and addresses of the incorporators.

Based on the information in the articles of incorporation, the state issues a **corporate charter** to the company. After securing this charter, the owners hold an organizational meeting at which they establish the corporation's bylaws and elect a board of directors. The bylaws might set up committees of the board of directors and describe the rules and procedures for their operation.

公司执照
corporate charter
a legal document that the state issues to a company based on information the company provides in the articles of incorporation

公司的类型
Types of Corporations

If the corporation does business in the state in which it is chartered, it is known as a *domestic corporation.* In other states where the corporation does business, it is known as a *foreign corporation.* If a corporation does business outside the nation in which it is incorporated, it is called an *alien corporation.* A corporation may be privately or publicly owned.

私营公司
private corporation
a corporation owned by just one or a few people who are closely involved in managing the business

A **private corporation** is owned by just one or a few people who are closely involved in managing the business. These people, often a family, own all the corporation's stock, and no stock is sold to the public. Many corporations are quite large, yet remain private, including Cargill, a farm products business. It is the nation's largest private corporation with annual revenues of well over $100 billion. Founded at the end of the Civil War, descendents of the original founder have owned equity in the company for more than 140 years.[13] The fifth largest privately held company in the United States is Mars, founded by Frank C. Mars, who spent time in Switzerland learning to create chocolate confectionaries. Mars grew significantly through the acquisition of the Wm. Wrigley Jr. Company. Founded in Tacoma, Washington, in 1911, Mars is now the world's leading confectionary company and a leader in pet care products with Pedigree and Whiskas.[14] The business was successful early on because it paid employees three times the normal wage for the time. The company remains successful to this day, largely because of its established brands, such as M&Ms, and healthy snack lines for kids, like Generation Max.[15] Other well-known privately held companies include HJ Heinz, Publix Supermarkets, Toys 'R' Us, and Amway.[16] Privately owned corporations are not required to disclose financial information publicly, but they must, of course, pay taxes.

上市公司
public corporation
a corporation whose stock anyone may buy, sell, or trade

A **public corporation** is one whose stock anyone may buy, sell, or trade. Table 1.4 lists 10 U.S. corporations with more than half of their revenue coming from outside of the United States. Despite its high revenue, Amazon had negative profits in 2013.[17] Thousands of smaller public corporations in the United States have sales under $10 million. In large public corporations such as AT&T, the stockholders are often far removed from the management of the company. In other public corporations, the managers are often the founders and the major shareholders. Moelis & Co., for example, became a public corporation under the terms that the founder, chairman, and CEO would remain in his position and control more than 50 percent of the company.[18] *Forbes'* Global 2000 companies generate around $38 trillion in revenues, $2.4 trillion

TABLE 1.4
American Companies with More than Half of Their Revenues from Outside the United States

Company	Description
Caterpillar Inc.	Designs, manufactures, markets, and sells machinery, engines, and financial products
Dow Chemical	Manufactures chemicals, with products including plastics, oil, and crop technology
General Electric	Operates in the technology infrastructure, energy, capital finance, and consumer and industrial fields, with products including appliances, locomotives, weapons, lighting, and gas
General Motors	Sells automobiles with brands including Chevrolet, Buick, Cadillac, and Isuzu
IBM	Conducts technological research, develops intellectual property including software and hardware, and offers consulting services
Intel	Manufactures and develops semiconductor chips and microprocessors
McDonald's	Operates second-largest chain of fast-food restaurants worldwide after Subway
Nike	Designs, develops, markets, and sells athletic shoes and clothing
Procter & Gamble	Sells consumer goods with brands including Tide, Bounty, Crest, and Iams
Yum! Brands	Operates and licenses restaurants including Taco Bell, Kentucky Fried Chicken, and Pizza Hut

in profits, and $159 trillion in assets. They are worth $39 trillion in market value.[19] Asia-Pacific companies account for the majority of the Global 2000 companies, but other nations are catching up. The rankings of the Global 2000 span across 63 countries.[20] Publicly owned corporations must disclose financial information to the public under specific laws that regulate the trade of stocks and other securities.

首次公开募股
initial public offering (IPO) selling a corporation's stock on public markets for the first time

A private corporation that needs more money to expand or to take advantage of opportunities may have to obtain financing by "going public" through an **initial public offering (IPO),** that is, becoming a public corporation by selling stock so that it can be traded in public markets. Digital media companies are leading a surge in initial public offerings. Twitter, Marketo (a cloud-based marketing services company), Rocket Fuel (a digital advertising company), and Veeva Systems (an enterprise cloud provider for life sciences companies) all released IPOs in 2013.[21]

Also, privately owned firms are occasionally forced to go public with stock offerings when a major owner dies and the heirs have large estate taxes to pay. The tax payment may only be possible with the proceeds of the sale of stock. This happened to the brewer Adolph Coors Inc. After Adolph Coors died, the business went public and his family sold shares of stock to the public in order to pay the estate taxes.

On the other hand, public corporations can be "taken private" when one or a few individuals (perhaps the management of the firm) purchase all the firm's stock so that it can no longer be sold publicly. Taking a corporation private may be desirable when owners want to exert more control over the firm or they want the flexibility to make decisions for restructuring operations. For example, Michael Dell took his company private in order to set a new direction as PC sales continue to decline. Becoming a private company again allows Mr. Dell to focus on the needs of the company more fully than having to worry about the stock price for investors.[22] Taking a corporation private is also one technique for avoiding a takeover by another corporation.

Quasi-public corporations and nonprofits are two types of public corporations. **Quasi-public corporations** are owned and operated by the federal, state, or local government. The focus of these entities is to provide a service to citizens, such as mail delivery, rather than earning a profit. Indeed, many quasi-public corporations operate at a loss. Examples of quasi-public corporations include the National Aeronautics and Space Administration (NASA) and the U.S. Postal Service.

准公营公司
quasi-public corporations
corporations owned and operated by the federal, state, or local government

Like quasi-public corporations, **nonprofit corporations** focus on providing a service rather than earning a profit, but they are not owned by a government entity. Organizations such as the Sesame Workshop, the Elks Clubs, the American Lung Association, the American Red Cross, museums, and private schools provide services without a profit motive. To fund their operations and services, nonprofit organizations solicit donations from individuals and companies and grants from the government and other charitable foundations.

非营利性公司
nonprofit corporations
corporations that focus on providing a service rather than earning a profit but are not owned by a government entity

公司要素
Elements of a Corporation

董事会
The Board of Directors. A **board of directors,** elected by the stockholders to oversee the general operation of the corporation, sets the long-range objectives of the corporation. It is the board's responsibility to ensure that the objectives are achieved on schedule. Board members are legally liable for the mismanagement of the firm or for any misuse of funds. An important duty of the board of directors is to hire corporate officers, such as the president and the chief executive officer (CEO), who are responsible to the directors for the management and daily operations of the firm. The role and expectations of the board of directors took on greater significance after the accounting scandals of the early 2000s and the passage of the Sarbanes-Oxley Act.[23] As a result, most corporations have restructured how they compensate board directors for their time and expertise.

董事会
board of directors
a group of individuals, elected by the stockholders to oversee the general operation of the corporation, who set the corporation's long-range objectives

However, some experts now speculate that Sarbanes-Oxley did little to motivate directors to increase company oversight. Founder and former chairman of Best Buy Richard Schulze found this out firsthand. He resigned after a probe revealed he had known about an inappropriate relationship between the Best Buy CEO and an employee but failed to inform the board. Schulze later returned to Best Buy under a new title, chairman emeritus.[24] At the same time, the pay rate of directors is rising. On average, corporate directors are paid around $250,000. Over the past several years, the trend of increasing directors' pay continues to reach higher and higher limits. Although such pay is meant to attract top-quality directors, concerns exist over whether excessive pay will have unintended consequences. Some believe that this trend is contributing to the declining effectiveness in corporate governance.[25]

Directors can be employees of the company *(inside directors)* or people unaffiliated with the company *(outside directors)*. Inside directors are usually the officers responsible for running the company. Outside directors are often top executives from other companies, lawyers, bankers, even professors. Directors today are increasingly chosen for their expertise, competence, and ability to bring diverse perspectives to strategic discussions. Outside directors are also thought to bring more independence to the monitoring function because they are not bound by past allegiances, friendships, a current role in the company, or some other issue that may create a conflict of interest. Many of the corporate scandals uncovered in recent years might have been prevented if each of the companies' boards of directors had been better qualified, more knowledgeable, and more independent.

There is a growing shortage of available and qualified board members. Boards are increasingly telling their own CEOs that they should be focused on serving their company, not serving on outside boards. Because of this, the average CEO sits on less than one outside board. This represents a decline from a decade ago when the average was two. Because many CEOs are turning down outside positions, many companies have taken steps to ensure that boards have experienced directors. They have increased the mandatory retirement age to 72 or older, and some have raised it to 75 or even older. Minimizing the amount of overlap between directors sitting on different boards helps to limit conflicts of interest and provides for independence in decision making.

优先股
preferred stock
a special type of stock whose owners, though not generally having a say in running the company, have a claim to profits before other stockholders do

普通股
common stock
stock whose owners have voting rights in the corporation, yet do not receive preferential treatment regarding dividends

股份所有权

Stock Ownership. Corporations issue two types of stock: preferred and common. Owners of **preferred stock** are a special class of owners because, although they generally do not have any say in running the company, they have a claim to profits before any other stockholders do. Other stockholders do not receive any dividends unless the preferred stockholders have already been paid. Dividend payments on preferred stock are usually a fixed percentage of the initial issuing price (set by the board of directors). For example, if a share of preferred stock originally cost $100 and the dividend rate was stated at 7.5 percent, the dividend payment will be $7.50 per share per year. Dividends are usually paid quarterly. Most preferred stock carries a cumulative claim to dividends. This means that if the company does not pay preferred-stock dividends in one year because of losses, the dividends accumulate to the next year. Such dividends unpaid from previous years must also be paid to preferred stockholders before other stockholders can receive any dividends.

Owners of preferred stock have first claim to profits.

Although owners of **common stock** do not get such preferential treatment with regard to dividends, they do get some say in the operation of the corporation. Their ownership gives them the right to vote for members of the board of directors and on other important issues. Common stock dividends may vary according to the profitability of the business, and some corporations do not issue dividends at all, but instead plow their profits back into the company to fund expansion.

Common stockholders are the voting owners of a corporation. They are usually entitled to one vote per share of common stock. During an annual stockholders' meeting, common stockholders elect a board of directors. Some boards find it easier than others to attract high profile individuals. For example, the board of Procter & Gamble consists of Ernesto Zedillo, former president of Mexico; Kenneth I. Chenault, CEO of the American Express Company; Scott D. Cook, founder of Intuit Inc.; Patricia A. Woerte, CEO of Archer Daniels Midland; W. James McNerney Jr., CEO of Boeing; Margaret C. Whitman, CEO of Hewlett-Packard; and a few others.[26] Because they can choose the board of directors, common stockholders have some say in how the company will operate. Common stockholders may vote by *proxy,* which is a written authorization by which stockholders assign their voting privilege to someone else, who then votes for his or her choice at the stockholders' meeting. It is a normal practice for management to request proxy statements from shareholders who are not planning to attend the annual meeting. Most owners do not attend annual meetings of the very large companies, such as Westinghouse or Boeing, unless they live in the city where the meeting is held.

Common stockholders have another advantage over preferred shareholders. In most states, when the corporation decides to sell new shares of common stock in the marketplace, common stockholders have the first right, called a *preemptive right,* to purchase new shares of the stock from the corporation. A preemptive right is often included in the articles of incorporation. This right is important because it allows stockholders to purchase new shares to maintain their original positions. For example, if a stockholder owns 10 percent of a corporation that decides to issue new shares, that stockholder has the right to buy enough of the new shares to retain the 10 percent ownership.

公司的优势
Advantages of Corporations

Because a corporation is a separate legal entity, it has some very specific advantages over other forms of ownership. The biggest advantage may be the limited liability of the owners.

有限责任

Limited Liability. Because the corporation's assets (money and resources) and liabilities (debts and other obligations) are separate from its owners', in most cases the stockholders are not held responsible for the firm's debts if it fails. Their liability or potential loss is limited to the amount of their original investment. Although a creditor can sue a corporation for not paying its debts, even forcing the corporation into bankruptcy, it cannot make the stockholders pay the corporation's debts out of their personal assets. Occasionally, the owners of a private corporation may pledge personal assets to secure a loan for the corporation; this would be most unusual for a public corporation.

容易转移所有权

Ease of Transfer of Ownership. Stockholders can sell or trade shares of stock to other people without causing the termination of the corporation, and they can do this without the prior approval of other shareholders. The transfer of ownership (unless it is a majority position) does not affect the daily or long-term operations of the corporation.

无期限寿命

Perpetual Life. A corporation usually is chartered to last forever unless its articles of incorporation stipulate otherwise. The existence of the corporation is unaffected by the death or withdrawal of any of its stockholders. It survives until

Volkswagen is the eighth-largest corporation in the world.

the owners sell it or liquidate its assets. However, in some cases, bankruptcy ends a corporation's life. Bankruptcies occur when companies are unable to compete and earn profits. Eventually, uncompetitive businesses must close or seek protection from creditors in bankruptcy court while the business tries to reorganize.

外部筹资

External Sources of Funds. Of all the forms of business organization, the public corporation finds it easiest to raise money. When a corporation needs to raise more money, it can sell more stock shares or issue bonds (corporate "IOUs," which pledge to repay debt), attracting funds from anywhere in the United States and even overseas. The larger a corporation becomes, the more sources of financing are available to it.

扩张潜力

Expansion Potential. Because large public corporations can find long-term financing readily, they can easily expand into national and international markets. And, as a legal entity, a corporation can enter into contracts without as much difficulty as a partnership.

公司的劣势
Disadvantages of Corporations

Corporations have some distinct disadvantages resulting from tax laws and government regulation.

双重税收

Double Taxation. As a legal entity, the corporation must pay taxes on its income just like you do. When after-tax corporate profits are paid out as dividends to the stockholders, the dividends are taxed a second time as part of the individual owner's income. This process creates double taxation for the stockholders of dividend paying corporations. Double taxation does not occur with the other forms of business organization.

成立公司

Forming a Corporation. The formation of a corporation can be costly. A charter must be obtained, and this usually requires the services of an attorney and payment of legal fees. Filing fees ranging from $25 to $150 must be paid to the state that awards the corporate charter, and certain states require that an annual fee be paid to maintain the charter. Today, a number of Internet services such as LegalZoom.com and Business.com make it easier, quicker, and less costly to form a corporation. However, in making it easier for people to form businesses without expert consultation, these services have increased the risk that people will not choose the kind of organizational form that is right for them. Sometimes, one form works better than another. The business's founders may fail to take into account disadvantages, such as double taxation with corporations.

信息披露

Disclosure of Information. Corporations must make information available to their owners, usually through an annual report to shareholders. The annual report contains financial information about the firm's profits, sales, facilities and equipment, and debts, as well as descriptions of the company's operations, products, and plans for the future. Public corporations must also file reports with the Securities and Exchange Commission (SEC), the government regulatory agency that regulates securities such as stocks and bonds. The larger the firm, the more data the SEC requires. Because all reports filed with the SEC are available to the public, competitors can access them. Additionally, complying with securities laws takes time.

DID YOU KNOW? The first corporation with a net income of more than $1 billion in one year was General Motors, with a net income in 1955 of $1,189,477,082.[27]

员工与所有者分离

Employee–Owner Separation. Many employees are not stockholders of the company for which they work. This separation of owners and employees may cause employees to feel that their work benefits only the owners. Employees without an ownership stake do not always see how they fit into the corporate picture and may not understand the importance of profits to the health of the organization. If managers are part owners but other employees are not, management–labor relations take on a different, sometimes difficult, aspect from those in partnerships and sole proprietorships. However, this situation is changing as more corporations establish employee stock ownership plans (ESOPs), which give shares of the company's stock to its employees. Such plans build a partnership between employee and employer and can boost productivity because they motivate employees to work harder so that they can earn dividends from their hard work as well as from their regular wages.

其他的所有权形式
Other Types of Ownership

In this section we take a brief look at joint ventures, S corporations, limited liability companies, and cooperatives—businesses formed for special purposes.

合资企业
Joint Ventures

A **joint venture** is a partnership established for a specific project or for a limited time. The partners in a joint venture may be individuals or organizations.Control of a joint venture may be shared equally, or one partner may control decision making. Joint ventures are especially popular in situations that call for large investments, such as extraction of natural resources and the development of new products. Joint ventures are especially popular in situations that call for large investments and can even take place between businesses and governments. For example, Samsung and Venezuela formed a joint venture for the purpose of manufacturing electronics and appliances in the country. This partnership also serves to limit the amount of price manipulation that occurs in the country by smaller companies that import items and mark them up.[28]

合资企业
joint venture
a partnership established for a specific project or for a limited time

S 公司
S Corporations

An **S corporation** is a form of business ownership that is taxed as though it were a partnership. Net profits or losses of the corporation pass to the owners, thus

S 公司
S corporation
corporation taxed as though it were a partnership with restrictions on shareholders

REI is organized as a consumer cooperative.

eliminating double taxation. The benefit of limited liability is retained. Formally known as Subchapter S Corporations, they have become a popular form of business ownership for entrepreneurs and represent almost half of all corporate filings.[29] Vista Bank Texas is an S corporation, and the owners get the benefits of tax advantages and limited liability. Advantages of S corporations include the simple method of taxation, the limited liability of shareholders, perpetual life, and the ability to shift income and appreciation to others. Disadvantages include restrictions on the number (75) and types (individuals, estates, and certain trusts) of shareholders and the difficulty of formation and operation.

有限责任公司
Limited Liability Companies

有限责任公司
limited liability company (LLC) form of ownership that provides limited liability and taxation like a partnership but places fewer restrictions on members

A **limited liability company (LLC)** is a form of business ownership that provides limited liability, as in a corporation, but is taxed like a partnership. Although relatively new in the United States, LLCs have existed for many years abroad. Professionals such as lawyers, doctors, and engineers often use the LLC form of ownership. Many consider the LLC a blend of the best characteristics of corporations, partnerships, and sole proprietorships. One of the major reasons for the LLC form of ownership is to protect the members' personal assets in case of lawsuits. LLCs are flexible, simple to run, and do not require the members to hold meetings, keep minutes, or make resolutions, all of which are necessary in corporations. For example, Domino's Pizza, which sells and delivers pizza, is a limited liability company.[30]

合作社
Cooperatives

合作社
cooperative (co-op) an organization composed of individuals or small businesses that have banded together to reap the benefits of belonging to a larger organization

Another form of organization in business is the **cooperative** or **co-op,** an organization composed of individuals or small businesses that have banded together to reap the benefits of belonging to a larger organization. ARISE Food Co-op, for example, is a food cooperative based in Massachusetts;[31] Ocean Spray is a cooperative of cranberry farmers. REI operates a bit differently because it is owned by consumers rather than farmers or small businesses. A co-op is set up not to make money as an entity. It exists so that its members can become more profitable or save money. Co-ops are generally expected to operate without profit or to create only enough profit to maintain the co-op organization.

Many cooperatives exist in small farming communities. The co-op stores and markets grain; orders large quantities of fertilizer, seed, and other supplies at discounted prices; and reduces costs and increases efficiency with good management. A co-op can purchase supplies in large quantities and pass the savings on to its members. It

Responding to Business Challenges

The Evolution of Sears Holdings Company

Sears Holdings began as a sole proprietorship in 1886 known as R.W. Sears Watch Company in Minneapolis. As the name suggests, founder Richard W. Sears sold only watches. Sears wanted to establish his company in Chicago and needed a partner to do so. He put an advertisement in the local paper, and Alvah C. Roebuck responded. Together, they formed Sears, Roebuck, and Co. as a corporation and expanded the business's to offer more product lines through mail order catalogs.

Sears became a public corporation in 1901 to secure financing for growth. To manage its growth, the company developed a time scheduling system that ensured orders were accurate and shipped on time. Expansion continued with the introduction of retail stores in 1925. The company's Craftsman and Kenmore brands became popular, and soon retail sales outperformed mail order sales. Sears even sold arts and crafts for assembly on the customer's property. Foreign expansion, the building of the famous Sears Tower, and the installation of Sears.com solidified the retailer as a household name.

However, success can often breed complacency that results in a business' decline. Lack of investment has resulted in less-than-pristine retail locations that customers no longer frequent. In 2004, Kmart acquired Sears for $11 billion and adopted the name Sears Holdings Company. The merged company continues to struggle with losses and is selling off its best-known business units and underperforming stores.[32]

Discussion Questions

1. Why did Sears become a public corporation? What benefits does this form of organization have to offer Sears?
2. Describe some reasons for why the firm is struggling.
3. What is Sears doing to bounce back from its losses?

---

also can help distribute the products of its members more efficiently than each could on an individual basis. A cooperative can advertise its members' products and thus generate demand. Ace Hardware, a cooperative of independent hardware store owners, allows its members to share in the savings that result from buying supplies in large quantities; it also provides advertising, which individual members might not be able to afford on their own.

企业所有权的发展趋势：合并与收购
Trends in Business Ownership: Mergers and Acquisitions

LO 1-4

Companies large and small achieve growth and improve profitability by expanding their operations, often by developing and selling new products or selling current products to new groups of customers in different geographic areas. Such growth, when carefully planned and controlled, is usually beneficial to the firm and ultimately helps it reach its goal of enhanced profitability. But companies also grow by merging with or purchasing other companies.

A **merger** occurs when two companies (usually corporations) combine to form a new company. An **acquisition** occurs when one company purchases another, generally by buying most of its stock. The acquired company may become a subsidiary of the buyer, or its operations and assets may be merged with those of the buyer. The government sometimes scrutinizes mergers and acquisitions in an attempt to protect customers from monopolistic practices. For example, the decision to authorize Whole Foods' acquisition of Wild Oats was carefully analyzed, as was the merger of Sirius and XM Satellite Radio. In 2013, Google paid $3.2 billion for smart home company, Nest Labs.[33] The company was just one of many that Google acquired

合并
merger
the combination of two companies (usually corporations) to form a new company

收购
acquisition
the purchase of one company by another, usually by buying its stock

TABLE 1.5 Major Mergers and Acquisitions Worldwide 2000–2010

Rank	Year	Acquirer	Target	Transaction Value (in millions of U.S. dollars)
1	2000	America Online Inc. (AOL) (*Merger*)	Time Warner	$164,747
2	2000	Glaxo Wellcome Plc.	SmithKline Beecham Plc.	75,961
3	2004	Royal Dutch Petroleum Co.	Shell Transport & Trading Co.	74,559
4	2006	AT&T Inc.	BellSouth Corporation	72,671
5	2001	Comcast Corporation	AT&T Broadband & Internet Svcs.	72,041
6	2004	JP Morgan Chase & Co.	Bank One Corporation	58,761
7	2013	American Airlines	U.S. Airways	11,000
8	2008	Bank of America	Countrywide	4,000
9	2008	JP Morgan Chase & Co.	Bear Stearns Companies Inc.	1,100
10	2011	Southwest Airlines	AirTran Holdings	1,000

Unless noted, deal was an acquisition.

Sources: Institute of Mergers, Acquisitions and Alliances Research, Thomson Financial; *"JPMorgan Chase Completes Bear Stearns Acquisition," JPMorganChase News Release, May 31, 2008; "Southwest Completes Purchase of Orlando-Based AirTran,"* Orlando Sentinel, *May 2, 2011.*

during the year. While these acquisitions have the potential to diversify Google's service offerings and benefit it financially, some believe that Google might be investing in companies of which it has little knowledge. In these cases, acquisitions could end up harming the acquiring company.[34] Acquisitions sometimes involve the purchase of a division or some other part of a company rather than the entire company. The late 1990s saw a merger and acquisition frenzy, which is slowing in the 21st century (see Table 1.5).

When firms that make and sell similar products to the same customers merge, it is known as a *horizontal merger,* as when Martin Marietta and Lockheed, both defense contractors, merged to form Lockheed Martin. Horizontal mergers, however, reduce the number of corporations competing within an industry, and for this reason they are usually reviewed carefully by federal regulators before the merger is allowed to proceed.

When companies operating at different but related levels of an industry merge, it is known as a *vertical merger.* In many instances, a vertical merger results when one corporation merges with one of its customers or suppliers. For example, if Burger King were to purchase a large Idaho potato farm—to ensure a ready supply of potatoes for its french fries—a vertical merger would result.

A *conglomerate merger* results when two firms in unrelated industries merge. For example, the purchase of Sterling Drug, a pharmaceutical firm, by Eastman Kodak, best-known for its films and cameras, represents a conglomerate merger because the two companies are of different industries. (Kodak later sold Sterling Drug to a pharmaceutical company.)

Eli Lilly purchased Novartis' animal health unit for $5.4 billion.

When a company (or an individual), sometimes called a *corporate raider,* wants to acquire or take over another company, it first offers to buy some or all of the other company's stock at a premium over its current price in a *tender offer.* Most such offers are "friendly," with both groups agreeing to the proposed deal, but some are "hostile," when the second company does not want to be taken over. News Corp. adopted a poison pill plan to discourage challenges to Rupert Murdoch's family-controlled media empire, which split into two businesses. (A poison pill is an attempt to make a takeover less attractive to a potential acquirer.) News Corp.'s plan is set to go off if an outside company buys 15 percent or more of the companies' Class B voting shares. In this case, shareholders would have the option to buy new shares at a 50 percent discount. Because the Murdoch family owns many of the shares, this plan is a good way to maintain control of the firm.[35]

To head off a hostile takeover attempt, a threatened company's managers may use one or more of several techniques. They may ask stockholders not to sell to the raider; file a lawsuit in an effort to abort the takeover; institute a *poison pill* (in which the firm allows stockholders to buy more shares of stock at prices lower than the current market value) or *shark repellant* (in which management requires a large majority of stockholders to approve the takeover); or seek a *white knight* (a more acceptable firm that is willing to acquire the threatened company). In some cases, management may take the company private or even take on more debt so that the heavy debt obligation will "scare off" the raider.

In a **leveraged buyout (LBO),** a group of investors borrows money from banks and other institutions to acquire a company (or a division of one), using the assets of the purchased company to guarantee repayment of the loan. In some LBOs, as much as 95 percent of the buyout price is paid with borrowed money, which eventually must be repaid.

杠杆收购
leveraged buyout (LBO) a purchase in which a group of investors borrows money from banks and other institutions to acquire a company (or a division of one), using the assets of the purchased company to guarantee repayment of the loan

Because of the explosion of mergers, acquisitions, and leveraged buyouts in the 1980s and 1990s, financial journalists coined the term *merger mania.* Many companies joined the merger mania simply to enhance their own operations by consolidating them with the operations of other firms. Mergers and acquisitions enabled these companies to gain a larger market share in their industries, acquire valuable assets such as new products or plants and equipment, and lower their costs. Mergers also represent a means of making profits quickly, as was the case during the 1980s when many companies' stock was undervalued. Quite simply, such companies represent a bargain to other companies that can afford to buy them. Additionally, deregulation of some industries has permitted consolidation of firms within those industries for the first time, as is the case in the banking and airline industries.

Some people view mergers and acquisitions favorably, pointing out that they boost corporations' stock prices and market value, to the benefit of their stockholders. In many instances, mergers enhance a company's ability to meet foreign competition in an increasingly global marketplace. Additionally, companies that are victims of hostile takeovers generally streamline their operations, reduce unnecessary staff, cut costs, and otherwise become more efficient with their operations, which benefits their stockholders whether or not the takeover succeeds.

Critics, however, argue that mergers hurt companies because they force managers to focus their efforts on avoiding takeovers rather than managing effectively and profitably. Some companies have taken on a heavy debt burden to stave off a takeover, later to be forced into bankruptcy when economic downturns left them unable to handle the debt. Mergers and acquisitions also can damage employee morale and productivity, as well as the quality of the companies' products.

Many mergers have been beneficial for all involved; others have had damaging effects for the companies, their employees, and customers. No one can say whether mergers will continue to slow, but many experts say the utilities, telecommunications, financial services, natural resources, computer hardware and software, gaming, managed health care, and technology industries are likely targets.

So You'd Like to Start a Business

If you have a good idea and want to turn it into a business, you are not alone. Small businesses are popping up all over the United States, and the concept of entrepreneurship is hot. Entrepreneurs seek opportunities and creative ways to make profits. Business emerges in a number of different organizational forms, each with its own advantages and disadvantages. Sole proprietorships are the most common form of business organization in the United States. They tend to be small businesses and can take pretty much any form—anything from a hair salon to a scuba shop, from an organic produce provider to a financial advisor. Proprietorships are everywhere serving consumers' wants and needs. Proprietorships have a big advantage in that they tend to be simple to manage—decisions get made quickly when the owner and the manager are the same person and they are fairly simple and inexpensive to set up. Rules vary by state, but at most all you will need is a license from the state.

Many people have been part of a partnership at some point in their life. Group work in school is an example of a partnership. If you ever worked as a DJ on the weekend with your friend and split the profits, then you have experienced a partnership. Partnerships can be either general or limited. General partners have unlimited liability and share completely in the management, debts, and profits of the business. Limited partners, on the other hand, consist of at least one general partner and one or more limited partners who do not participate in the management of the company but share in the profits. This form of partnership is used more often in risky investments where the limited partner stands only to lose his or her initial investment. Real estate limited partnerships are an example of how investors can minimize their financial exposure, given the poor performance of the real estate market in recent years. Although it has its advantages, partnership is the least utilized form of business. Part of the reason is that all partners are responsible for the actions and decisions of all other partners, whether or not all of the partners were involved. Usually, partners will have to write up an Articles of Partnership that outlines respective responsibilities in the business. Even in states where it is not required, it is a good idea to draw up this document as a way to cement each partner's role and hopefully minimize conflict. Unlike a corporation, proprietorships and partnerships both expire upon the death of one or more of those involved.

Corporations tend to be larger businesses, but do not need to be. A corporation can consist of nothing more than a small group of family members. In order to become a corporation, you will have to file in the state under which you wish to incorporate. Each state has its own procedure for incorporation, meaning there are no general guidelines to follow. You can make your corporation private or public, meaning the company issues stocks, and shareholders are the owners. While incorporating is a popular form of organization because it gives the company an unlimited lifespan and limited liability (meaning that if your business fails, you cannot lose personal funds to make up for losses), there is a downside. You will be taxed as a corporation and as an individual, resulting in double taxation. No matter what form of organization suits your business idea best, there is a world of options out there for you if you want to be or experiment with being an entrepreneur.

Review Your Understanding

Define and examine the advantages and disadvantages of the sole proprietorship form of organization.

Sole proprietorships—businesses owned and managed by one person—are the most common form of organization. Their major advantages are the following: (1) They are easy and inexpensive to form, (2) they allow a high level of secrecy, (3) all profits belong to the owner, (4) the owner has complete control over the business, (5) government regulation is minimal, (6) taxes are paid only once, and (7) the business can be closed easily. The disadvantages include: (1) The owner may have to use personal assets to borrow money, (2) sources of external funds are difficult to find, (3) the owner must have many diverse skills, (4) the survival of the business is tied to the life of the owner and his or her ability to work, (5) qualified employees are hard to find, and (6) wealthy sole proprietors pay a higher tax than they would under the corporate form of business.

Identify two types of partnership and evaluate the advantages and disadvantages of the partnership form of organization.

A partnership is a business formed by several individuals; a partnership may be general or limited. Partnerships offer the following advantages: (1) They are easy to organize, (2) they may have higher credit ratings because the partners possibly have more combined wealth, (3) partners can specialize, (4) partnerships can make decisions faster than larger businesses, and (5) government regulations are few. Partnerships also have several disadvantages: (1) General partners have unlimited liability for the debts of the partnership, (2) partners are responsible for each other's decisions, (3) the death or termination of one partner requires a new partnership agreement to be drawn up, (4) it is difficult to sell a partnership interest at a fair price, (5) the distribution of profits may not correctly reflect the amount of work done by each partner, and (6) partnerships cannot find external sources of funds as easily as can large corporations.

Describe the corporate form of organization and cite the advantages and disadvantages of corporations.

A corporation is a legal entity created by the state, whose assets and liabilities are separate from those of its owners. Corporations are chartered by a state through articles of incorporation. They have a board of directors made up of corporate officers or people from outside the company. Corporations, whether private or public, are owned by stockholders. Common stockholders have the right to elect the board of directors. Preferred stockholders do not have a vote but get preferential dividend treatment over common stockholders.

Advantages of the corporate form of business include: (1) The owners have limited liability, (2) ownership (stock) can be easily transferred, (3) corporations usually last forever, (4) raising money is easier than for other forms of business, and (5) expansion into new businesses is simpler because of the ability of the company to enter into contracts. Corporations also have disadvantages: (1) The company is taxed on its income, and owners pay a second tax on any profits received as dividends; (2) forming a corporation can be expensive; (3) keeping trade secrets is difficult because so much information must be made available to the public and to government agencies; and (4) owners and managers are not always the same and can have different goals.

Define and debate the advantages and disadvantages of mergers, acquisitions, and leveraged buyouts.

A merger occurs when two companies (usually corporations) combine to form a new company. An acquisition occurs when one company buys most of another company's stock. In a leveraged buyout, a group of investors borrows money to acquire a company, using the assets of the purchased company to guarantee the loan. They can help merging firms to gain a larger market share in their industries, acquire valuable assets such as new products or plants and equipment, and lower their costs. Consequently, they can benefit stockholders by improving the companies' market value and stock prices. However, they also can hurt companies if they force managers to focus on avoiding takeovers at the expense of productivity and profits. They may lead a company to take on too much debt and can harm employee morale and productivity.

Propose an appropriate organizational form for a startup business.

After reading the facts in "Solve the Dilemma" on page 141 and considering the advantages and disadvantages of the various forms of business organization described in this chapter, you should be able to suggest an appropriate form for the startup nursery.

Revisit the World of Business

1. What are some of the major reasons for shareholder activism?
2. Do you feel that large shareholders such as David Einhorn are justified in filing lawsuits against corporations sitting on large cash reserves?
3. What are some of the benefits of shareholder activism? Disadvantages?

Learn the Terms

acquisition
articles of partnership
board of directors
common stock
cooperative (co-op)
corporate charter
corporation
dividends
general partnership
initial public offering (IPO)
joint venture
leveraged buyout (LBO)
limited liability company (LLC)
limited partnership
merger
nonprofit corporations
partnership
preferred stock
private corporation
public corporation
quasi-public corporations
S corporation
sole proprietorships
stock

Check Your Progress

1. Name five advantages of a sole proprietorship.
2. List two different types of partnerships and describe each.
3. Differentiate among the different types of corporations. Can you supply an example of each type?
4. Would you rather own preferred stock or common stock? Why?
5. Contrast how profits are distributed in sole proprietorships, partnerships, and corporations.
6. Which form of business organization has the least government regulation? Which has the most?
7. Compare the liability of the owners of partnerships, sole proprietorships, and corporations.
8. Why would secrecy in operating a business be important to an owner? What form of organization would be most appropriate for a business requiring great secrecy?
9. Which form of business requires the most specialization of skills? Which requires the least? Why?
10. The most common example of a cooperative is a farm co-op. Explain the reasons for this and the benefits that result for members of cooperatives.

Get Involved

1. Select a publicly owned corporation and bring to class a list of its subsidiaries. These data should be available in the firm's corporate annual report, *Standard & Poor's Corporate Records,* or *Moody Corporate Manuals.* Ask your librarian for help in finding these resources.
2. Select a publicly owned corporation and make a list of its outside directors. Information of this nature can be found in several places in your library: the company's annual report, its list of corporate directors, and various financial sources. If possible, include each director's title and the name of the company that employs him or her on a full-time basis.

Build Your Skills

LO 1-5

Selecting a Form of Business

Background

Ali Bush sees an opportunity to start her own website development business. Ali has just graduated from the University of Mississippi with a master's degree in computer science. Although she has many job opportunities outside the Oxford area, she wishes to remain there to care for her aging parents. She already has most of the computer equipment necessary to start the business, but she needs additional software. She is considering the purchase of a server to maintain websites for small businesses. Ali feels she has the ability to take this start-up firm and create a long-term career opportunity for herself and others. She knows she can hire Ole Miss students to work on a part-time basis to support her business. For now, as she starts the business, she can work out of the extra bedroom of her apartment. As the business grows, she'll hire the additional full- and/or part-time help needed and reassess the location of the business.

Task

1. Using what you've learned in this chapter, decide which form of business ownership is most appropriate for Ali. Use the tables provided to assist you in evaluating the advantages and disadvantages of each decision.

Sole Proprietorships	
Advantages	Disadvantages
•	•
•	•
•	•
•	•
•	•
•	•
•	•
Corporation	
Advantages	Disadvantages
•	•
•	•
•	•
•	•
•	•
•	•
•	•
Limited Liability Company	
Advantages	Disadvantages
•	•
•	•
•	•
•	•
•	•
•	•
•	•

Solve the Dilemma

To Incorporate or not to Incorporate

Thomas O'Grady and Bryan Rossisky have decided to start a small business buying flowers, shrubs, and trees wholesale and reselling them to the general public. They plan to contribute $5,000 each in startup capital and lease a 2.5-acre tract of land with a small, portable sales office.

Thomas and Bryan are trying to decide what form of organization would be appropriate. Bryan thinks they should create a corporation because they would have limited liability and the image of a large organization. Thomas thinks a partnership would be easier to start and would allow them to rely on the combination of their talents and financial resources. In addition, there might be fewer reports and regulatory controls to cope with.

Discussion Questions

1. What are some of the advantages and disadvantages of Thomas and Bryan forming a corporation?
2. What are the advantages and disadvantages of their forming a partnership?
3. Which organizational form do you think would be best for Thomas and Bryan's company and why?

Build Your Business Plan

Options for Organizing Business

Your team needs to think about how you should organize yourselves that would be most efficient and effective for your business plan. The benefits of having partners include having others to share responsibilities with and to toss ideas off of each other. As your business evolves, you will have to decide whether one or two members will manage the business while the other members are silent partners. Or perhaps you will all decide on working in the business to keep costs down, at least initially. However you decide on team member involvement in the business, it is imperative to have a written agreement so that all team members understand what their responsibilities are and what will happen if the partnership dissolves.

It is not too soon for you and your partners to start thinking about how you might want to find additional funding for your business. Later on in the development of your business plan, you might want to show your business plan to family members. Together, you and your partners will want to develop a list of potential investors in your business.

See for Yourself Videocase

PODS Excels at Organizing a Business

What happens when homeowners need to store their belongings temporarily? Before 1998, people would choose to either rent storage space, which can be costly and inconvenient, or store their belongings in their front yards. Yet, starting in 1998, another option was introduced: PODS.

PODS, short for Portable On Demand Storage, was founded after a group of firemen noticed the difficulties that many people faced when they needed to store their belongings for a short period. PODS delivers storage containers and leaves them in front of a house or business. A specially made hydraulic lift called Podzilla is able to place the container on ground level, which makes it easier for owners to store their belongings inside the container. PODS will then pick up the containers and move them to either its warehouses for storage or to anywhere else in the country.

When PODS was first started, banks and financial institutions were uncertain about how successful the moving and storage services company would be. Another issue was the expense of the actual containers. PODS containers, made of plywood over steel frames, cost between $2,200 and $2,500 each. If the company failed, the banks could repossess the containers. However, because PODS was a first-mover and there were no other comparable companies around, the banks feared that they would not be able to resell the containers. The risk for banks and financial institutions was high. This meant that PODS initially depended on venture capitalists for funding.

Once the company got started, however, PODS proved it was well worth the investment. More than a decade later, PODS can be found on three continents and has more than 200 million customers across the United States, Canada, the United Kingdom, and Australia. In addition to its convenience, PODS has also become known for its high-quality services and social responsibility. For instance, the company provided PODS containers to help recovery efforts in Hurricane Katrina. In 2011, PODS became a finalist in the National Association of Professional Organizers award for best service provider.

As PODS has expanded, its business organization has also undergone changes. Originally, PODS was formed as a sole proprietorship. Many businesses start off as sole proprietorships because of the benefits involved, such as ease of formation and greater control over operations. PODS's initial name was PODS LLC, meaning that it was a limited liability company. Limited liability companies provide more protection to owners so that their personal belongings will not be seized to pay the company's debts. It also frees owners from some of the restrictions that exist for corporations.

However, as businesses grow nationally, they become much more difficult for one or two individuals to handle. PODS soon realized that its rapid expansion required a new form of business organization. PODS decided to become a private corporation and renamed itself PODS Enterprises Inc. Although more people became involved in the ownership of the company, a small group of individuals maintains control over much of the general corporate operations. PODS stock is not issued publicly.

Eventually, PODS also decided to adopt a franchise model. The corporation began to allow other entrepreneurs, called franchisees, to license its name and products for a fee. This provided PODS with additional funding as well as the opportunity to expand into more areas. Because PODS is already successful, franchisees have a lower failure rate than starting their own businesses from scratch. Franchisees also understand their particular markets better than a corporation can.

"Franchisees bring another advantage, though, and that is their knowledge and connections in the local market, so they can take advantage of particularities in a market," said Ann Lehman, senior vice president of Franchise Operations. This increases PODS's adaptability when it expands into other areas.

On the other hand, because corporations are able to bring together several knowledgeable individuals, PODS corporate headquarters finds that it is better able to handle larger markets such as Los Angeles and Chicago. With this business model, PODS has figured out how to meet the needs of both local markets, through franchisees, and larger markets. Because of PODS's ability to understand the best ways of organizing its business, the company has been able to reap the benefits from all types of market sizes.[36]

Discussion Questions

1. What are some advantages of sole proprietorships for PODS? What are some disadvantages?
2. What are some advantages of private corporations for PODS? What are some disadvantages?
3. How has adopting a franchise model made PODS more adaptable?

You can find the related video in the Video Library in Connect. Ask your instructor how you can access Connect.

Team Exercise

Form groups and find examples of mergers and acquisitions. Mergers can be broken down into traditional mergers, horizontal mergers, and conglomerate mergers. When companies are found, note how long the merger or acquisition took, if there were any requirements by the government before approval of the merger or acquisition, and if any failed mergers or acquisitions were found that did not achieve government approval. Report your findings to the class, and explain what the companies hoped to gain from the merger or acquisition.

2 Small Business, Entrepreneurship, and Franchising 小型企业、创业企业和特许经营

Learning Objectives

After reading this chapter, you will be able to:

- **LO 2-1** Define *entrepreneurship* and *small business.*
- **LO 2-2** Investigate the importance of small business in the U.S. economy and why certain fields attract small business.
- **LO 2-3** Specify the advantages of small-business ownership.
- **LO 2-4** Summarize the disadvantages of small-business ownership, and analyze why many small businesses fail.
- **LO 2-5** Describe how you go about starting a small business and what resources are needed.
- **LO 2-6** Evaluate the demographic, technological, and economic trends that are affecting the future of small business.
- **LO 2-7** Explain why many large businesses are trying to "think small."
- **LO 2-8** Assess two entrepreneurs' plans for starting a small business.

Chapter Outline

Introduction
The Nature of Entrepreneurship and Small Business
- *What Is a Small Business?*
- *The Role of Small Business in the American Economy*
- *Industries That Attract Small Business*

Advantages of Small-Business Ownership
- *Independence*
- *Costs*
- *Flexibility*
- *Focus*
- *Reputation*

Disadvantages of Small-Business Ownership
- *High Stress Level*
- *High Failure Rate*

Starting a Small Business
- *The Business Plan*
- *Forms of Business Ownership*
- *Financial Resources*
- *Approaches to Starting a Small Business*
- *Help for Small-Business Managers*

The Future for Small Business
- *Demographic Trends*
- *Technological and Economic Trends*

Making Big Businesses Act "Small"

进入商业世界

Enter the World of Business

乔巴尼抢占酸奶市场

Chobani Yogurt Fights for Dominance in the Yogurt Market

For the founder of Chobani Yogurt, it took more than a good idea to propel the company into what it is today. It was almost by chance that Hamdi Ulukaya made it into the billion-dollar venture it is now. At one time, Greek yogurt accounted for less than 1 percent of the yogurt market in the United States; it now makes up 50 percent. With the help of a Small Business Administration loan, Ulukaya purchased a small yogurt plant Kraft was selling. Ulukaya decided to sell Greek yogurt, a product he knew was popular in other parts of the world.

When Chobani yogurt hit shelves in 2007, the product was an immediate success. Unlike his contemporaries, Ulukaya does not outsource but maintains control of the entire manufacturing process. Under his leadership, the company has become a challenger to the top yogurt makers in the industry in only a matter of years. It is for this reason that Hamdi Ulukaya has been nicknamed the "Steve Jobs of yogurt." Today, Chobani Yogurt is netting more than $1 billion in sales and controls 17 percent of the yogurt market.

Chobani Yogurt has recently faced some challenges. For instance, in fall 2013 the company had to recall its yogurt after reports that mold growing in the yogurt made consumers sick. Later that year, Whole Foods decided to drop Chobani Yogurt from its shelves. Chobani is also facing increased competition from more established rivals such as Danone's Oikos brand and Yoplait Greek.[1]

引言
Introduction

Although many business students go to work for large corporations upon graduation, others may choose to start their own business or to find employment opportunities in small organizations with 500 or fewer employees. Small businesses employ about half of all private-sector employees.[2] Each small business represents the vision of its owners to succeed through providing new or better products. Small businesses are the heart of the U.S. economic and social system because they offer opportunities and demonstrate the freedom of people to make their own destinies. Today, the entrepreneurial spirit is growing around the world, from Russia and China to India, Germany, Brazil, and Mexico. For instance, within eastern Europe, approximately 24 percent of the population is engaged in entrepreneurial activities. Within the BRIC countries (Brazil, Russia, India, and China), the average is only slightly less at 21 percent.[3]

This chapter surveys the world of entrepreneurship and small business. First we define entrepreneurship and small business and examine the role of small business in the American economy. Then we explore the advantages and disadvantages of small-business ownership and analyze why small businesses succeed or fail. Next, we discuss how an entrepreneur goes about starting a business and the challenges facing small businesses today. Finally, we look at entrepreneurship in larger organizations.

LO 2-1

创业企业和小型企业的实质
The Nature of Entrepreneurship and Small Business

创业
enterpreneurship
the process of creating and managing a business to achieve desired objectives

We defines an entrepreneur as a person who risks his or her wealth, time, and effort to develop for profit an innovative product or way of doing something. **entrepreneurship** is the process of creating and managing a business to achieve desired objectives. Many large businesses you may recognize (Levi Strauss and Co., Procter & Gamble, McDonald's, Dell Computers, Microsoft, and Google) all began as small businesses based on the visions of their founders. Some entrepreneurs who start small businesses have the ability to see emerging trends; in response, they create a company to provide a product that serves customer needs. For example, rather than inventing a major new technology, an innovative company may take advantage of technology to create new markets, such as Amazon.com. Or they may offer a familiar product that has been improved or placed in a unique retail environment, such as Starbucks and its coffee shops. A company may innovate by focusing on a particular market segment and delivering a combination of features that consumers in that segment could not find anywhere else. Tweezerman, which manufactures beauty tools, became successful after its founder, Dal LaMagna, developed diamond tweezers directed specifically for beauty salons. For many years, the company only sold tweezers but has since expanded to encompass a range of other beauty tools.[4]

Of course, smaller businesses do not have to evolve into such highly visible companies to be successful, but those entrepreneurial efforts that result in rapidly growing businesses gain visibility along with success. Entrepreneurs who have achieved success, like Michael Dell (Dell Computers), Bill Gates (Microsoft), Larry Page and Sergey Brin (Google), and the late Steve Jobs (Apple) are some of the most well known. Table 2.1 lists some of the greatest entrepreneurs of the past few decades.

The entrepreneurship movement is accelerating, and many new, smaller businesses are emerging. Technology once available only to the largest firms can now

TABLE 2.1
Great Entrepreneurs of Innovative Companies

Company	Entrepreneur
Hewlett-Packard	Bill Hewlett, David Packard
Walt Disney Productions	Walt Disney
Starbucks	Howard Schultz
Amazon.com	Jeff Bezos
Dell	Michael Dell
Microsoft	Bill Gates
Apple	Steve Jobs
Walmart	Sam Walton
Google	Larry Page, Sergey Brin
Ben & Jerry's	Ben Cohen, Jerry Greenfield
Ford	Henry Ford
General Electric	Thomas Edison

be obtained by a small business. Websites, podcasts, online videos, social media, cellular phones, and even expedited delivery services enable small businesses to be more competitive with today's giant corporations. Small businesses can also form alliances with other companies to produce and sell products in domestic and global markets.

Another growing trend among small businesses is social entrepreneurship. *Social entrepreneurs* are individuals who use entrepreneurship to address social problems. They operate by the same principles as other entrepreneurs but view their organizations as vehicles to create social change. Although these entrepreneurs often start their own nonprofit organizations, they can also operate for-profit organizations committed to solving social issues. CEO of TOMS Shoes Blake Mycoskie is an example of a social entrepreneur who founded the firm with the purpose of donating one pair of shoes to a child in need for every pair of shoes sold to consumers. Muhammad Yunus, founder of micro-lending organization Grameen Bank, is another example of a social entrepreneur. Yunus seeks to combat poverty by providing small loans to low-income individuals to start their own businesses.

什么是小型企业
What Is a Small Business?

This question is difficult to answer because smallness is relative. In this book, we will define a **small business** as any independently owned and operated business that is not dominant in its competitive area and does not employ more than 500 people. A local Mexican restaurant may be the most patronized Mexican restaurant in your community, but because it does not dominate the restaurant industry as a whole, the restaurant can be considered a small business. This definition is similar to the one used by the **Small Business Administration (SBA),** an independent agency of the federal government that offers managerial and financial assistance to small businesses. On its website, the SBA outlines the first steps in starting a small business and offers a wealth of information to current and potential small-business owners.

小型企业
small business
any independently owned and operated business that is not dominant in its competitive area and does not employ more than 500 people

小型企业管理局
Small Business Administration (SBA)
an independent agency of the federal government that offers managerial and financial assistance to small businesses

TABLE 2.2
Importance of Small Businesses to Our Economy

Small firms represent 99.7 percent of all employer firms.
Small firms have generated 63 percent of net new jobs.
Small firms hire approximately 37 percent of high-tech workers (such as scientists, engineers, computer programmers, and others).
Small firms produce 16 times more patents per employee than large patenting firms.
Small firms employ nearly half of all private-sector employees.
Small firms pay 42 percent of the total U.S. private payroll.

Source: Small Business Administration Department of Advocacy, "Frequently Asked Questions," March 2014.

小型企业在美国经济中扮演的角色
The Role of Small Business in the American Economy

No matter how you define a small business, one fact is clear: They are vital to the American economy. As you can see in Table 2.2, more than 99 percent of all U.S. firms are classified as small businesses, and they employ about half of private workers. Small firms are also important as exporters, representing 98 percent of U.S. exporters of goods and contributing 33 percent of the value of exported goods.[5] In addition, small businesses are largely responsible for fueling job creation and innovation. Small businesses also provide opportunities for minorities and women to succeed in business. Women-owned businesses are responsible for employing 7.7 million workers and contribute $1.3 trillion in sales. Women own more than 8 million businesses nationwide, with great success in the professional services, retail, communication, and administrative services areas.[6] Minority-owned businesses have been growing faster than other classifiable firms as well, representing 21.3 percent of all small businesses.[7] One successful business was started by a refugee from Belgrade, Serbia (formerly Yugoslavia). Although Marie Gray's early life was filled with hardship in WWII Yugoslavia, she immigrated to the United States and later used her passion for clothing to develop the women's dressmaker brand, St. John. Today, the company earns $346 million in annual revenue.[8]

提供就业机会

Job Creation. The energy, creativity, and innovative abilities of small-business owners have resulted in jobs for many people. About 63 percent of net new jobs annually were created by small businesses.[9] Table 2.3 indicates that 99.7 percent of all businesses employ fewer than 500 people. Businesses employing 19 or fewer people account for 89.8 percent of all businesses.[10]

Many small businesses today are being started because of encouragement from larger ones. Many new jobs are also created by big-company/small-company alliances. Whether through formal joint ventures, supplier relationships, or product or marketing cooperative projects, the rewards of collaborative relationships are creating many jobs for small-business owners and their employees. In India, many small information technology (IT) firms provide IT services to global markets. Because of lower costs, international companies often can find Indian businesses to provide their information processing solutions.[11]

创新

Innovation. Perhaps one of the most significant strengths of small businesses is their ability to innovate and to bring significant benefits to customers. Small firms produce more than half of all innovations. Among the important 20th-century innovations

TABLE 2.3
Number of Firms by Employment Size

Firm Size	Number of Firms	Percentage of All Firms
0–19 employees	5,104,014	89.8
20–99 employees	481,496	8.5
100–499 employees	81,243	1.4
500+ employees	17,671	0.3

Source: "Statistics of U.S. Businesses (SUSB)," Statistics of U.S. Businesses.

by U.S. small firms are the airplane, the audio tape recorder, fiber-optic examining equipment, the heart valve, the optical scanner, the pacemaker, the personal computer, soft contact lenses, the Internet, and the zipper. For instance, the founder and CEO of the small firm UniKey, Phil Dumas, invented a new way for consumers to keep their doors locked. Dumas invented Kevo, a motorized deadbolt lock that links to users' iPhones. With just the touch of a finger, consumers can lock and unlock their doors from remote locations. UniKey distributes products in major retailers such as Lowe's and Home Depot. This is just one example of a small company with the ability to innovate and contribute to the benefit of customers.[12]

The innovation of successful firms take many forms. For instance, small firms make up approximately 52 percent of home-based businesses and 2 percent of franchises. Many of today's largest businesses started off as small firms that used innovation to achieve success.[13] Small businessman Ray Kroc found a new way to sell hamburgers and turned his ideas into one of the most successful fast-food franchises in the world—McDonald's. Small businesses have become an integral part of our lives. J. Darius Bikoff founded Glaceau in 1996 to market enhanced water drinks. He built his small

Jeffrey Lubell founded premium apparel company True Religion in 2002. It has gone on to be listed among *Forbes'* best publicly traded small companies in America.

business offering slightly flavored drinks in health food stores into a nationally recognized company that Coca-Cola acquired in 2006. Its brands—including VitaminWater and SmartWater—are still popular today.[14] Travis Kalanick co-launched the successful company Uber, an app-based car service company rapidly growing in cities throughout the world. The Uber app allows consumers to rent a car or driver on demand. The cars arrive within a few minutes of the order. Much like Ray Kroc, Kalanick's innovative concept has the potential to change its industry—its low cost and convenience is making it a major player in the transportation rivaling traditional cab companies.[15] Entrepreneurs provide fresh ideas and usually have greater flexibility to change than do large companies.

吸引小型企业的行业
Industries That Attract Small Business

LO 2-2

Small businesses are found in nearly every industry, but retailing and wholesaling, services, manufacturing, and high technology are especially attractive to entrepreneurs. These fields are relatively easy to enter and require low initial financing. Small-business owners in these industries also find it easier to focus on specific groups of consumers; new firms in these industries initially suffer less from heavy competition than do established firms.

The retailing industry is particularly attractive to entrepreneurs. Pike's Perk Coffee & Tea House is a small locally owned coffee shop in Colorado Springs, Colorado.

零售与批发业

Retailing and Wholesaling. Retailers acquire goods from producers or wholesalers and sell them to consumers. Main streets and shopping centers and malls are generally lined with independent music stores, sporting-goods stores, dry cleaners, boutiques, drugstores, restaurants, caterers, service stations, and hardware stores that sell directly to consumers. Retailing attracts entrepreneurs because gaining experience and exposure in retailing is relatively easy. Additionally, an entrepreneur opening a new retail store does not have to spend the large sums of money for the equipment and distribution systems that a manufacturing business requires. All that a new retailer needs is a lease on store space, merchandise, money to sustain the business, knowledge about prospective customers' needs and desires, and basic management and marketing skills. However, it is important for entrepreneurs to anticipate the costs of opening a retail or wholesale business beforehand. When Patrick Leon Esquerré decided to open up a French bakery, he invested $100,000 into the bakery—all the money he had. He was able to raise more money from friends in France and Texas and opened up his first bakery, La Madeleine. After guests started asking for food, Esquerré used his mother's recipes to expand the menu. Eventually, the company began selling its products through stores such as Sam's Club. Esquerré's initial $100,000 investment has led to 63 restaurant locations today.[16]

Entrepreneurship in Action

From Farmer's Market to Franchiser: Auntie Anne's Soft Pretzels

Auntie Anne's Soft Pretzels
Founder: Anne Beiler
Founded: 1988, in Downingtown, Pennsylvania
Success: Auntie Anne's is the largest soft pretzel franchise in the world with sales of $410 million.

Auntie Anne's Soft Pretzels began as a weekend operation at a farmer's market in Downingtown, Pennsylvania, in February 1988. Founder Anne Beiler received a $6,000 loan from her husband's parents to buy a pretzel stand at the farmer's market. In the first weekend, the business earned close to $1,000. Beiler experimented with the pretzel recipes, and the final product was twice as profitable as the original. She bought more ovens, hired more employees, and was soon making $2,000 each weekend. The company used sampling to market the product.

In July 1988, Beiler opened a store in Harrisburg, Pennsylvania, and by the end of the year made approximately $100,000. Beiler received repeated requests from people wanting to sell her product, so she decided to allow friends and family to open 10 new stores under a licensing agreement. By 1990, there were 75 locations in several states. Now owned by Focus Brands, Auntie Anne's is the largest soft pretzel franchise in the world with 1,200 shops in 26 countries.[17]

Wholesalers supply products to industrial, retail, and institutional users for resale or for use in making other products. Wholesaling activities range from planning and negotiating for supplies, promoting, and distributing (warehousing and transporting) to providing management and merchandising assistance to clients. Wholesalers are extremely important for many products, especially consumer goods, because of the marketing activities they perform. Although it is true that wholesalers themselves can be eliminated, their functions must be passed on to some other organization such as the producer, or another intermediary, often a small business. Frequently, small businesses are closer to the final customers and know what it takes to keep them satisfied. Some smaller businesses start out manufacturing, but find their real niche as a supplier or distributor of larger firms' products.

服务业

Services. The service sector includes businesses that do not actually produce tangible goods. The service sector accounts for 80 percent of U.S. jobs, excluding farmworkers. Real-estate, insurance and personnel agencies, barbershops, banks, television and computer repair shops, copy centers, dry cleaners, and accounting firms are all service businesses. Services also attract individuals—such as beauticians, morticians, jewelers, doctors, and veterinarians—whose skills are not usually required by large firms. Many of these service providers are retailers who provide their services to ultimate consumers.

制造业

Manufacturing. Manufacturing goods can provide unique opportunities for small businesses. Consider Nashville-based specialty chocolate company Olive & Sinclair. Within four years of its founding, the company was selling chocolates in the United States, London, Singapore, and Japan. The manufacturing of the chocolate is distinctively "southern" in nature. Its varieties include two ingredients—buttermilk and brown sugar—commonly associated with the South and a grinding process used to make Southern-style grits. This association appeals to global consumers. Today, Olive & Sinclair manufactures 1,500 chocolate bars each day.[18] Small businesses sometimes have an advantage over large firms because they can customize products to meet specific customer needs and wants. Such products include custom artwork, jewelry, clothing, and furniture.

DID YOU KNOW? Small businesses hire 37 percent of high-tech workers in the United States?[19]

高科技行业

High Technology. *High technology* is a broad term used to describe businesses that depend heavily on advanced scientific and engineering knowledge. People who were able to innovate or identify new markets in the fields of computers, biotechnology, genetic engineering, robotics, and other markets have become today's high-tech giants. One innovative technology was developed by a teenager interested in virtual reality. Only a few years ago, virtual reality was considered a dead technology past its prime. However, when 19-year-old Palmer Luckey developed a virtual gaming headset, it caught the attention of programmer John Carmack. Together, they brought virtual reality to a new level for gamers. The company, Oculus Rift, was sold to Facebook for $2 billion.[20] In general, high-technology businesses require greater capital and have higher initial startup costs than do other small businesses. Many of the biggest, nonetheless, started out in garages, basements, kitchens, and dorm rooms.

LO 2-3

小型企业的优势
Advantages of Small-Business Ownership

There are many advantages to establishing and running a small business. These can be categorized into personal advantages and business advantages. Table 2.4 lists some of the traits that can help entrepreneurs succeed.

自主性
Independence

Independence is probably one of the leading reasons that entrepreneurs choose to go into business for themselves. Being a small-business owner means being your own boss. Many people start their own businesses because they believe they will do better for themselves than they could do by remaining with their current employer or by changing jobs. They may feel stuck on the corporate ladder and that no business would take them seriously enough to fund their ideas. Sometimes people who venture forth to start their own small business are those who simply cannot work for someone else. Such people may say that they just do not fit the "corporate mold."

More often, small-business owners just want the freedom to choose whom they work with, the flexibility to pick where and when to work, and the option of working in a family setting. The availability of the computer, copy machine, fax, and Internet has permitted many people to work at home. In the past, most of them would have needed the support that an office provides.

TABLE 2.4
10 Successful Traits of Young Entrepreneurs

Intuitive	Persistent
Creative	Innovative
Productive	Frugal
Patient	Friendly
Charismatic	Fearless

Source: Yan Susanto, "10 Successful Traits of Young Entrepreneurs," Retire @ 21, *April 10, 2009.*

成本
Costs

As already mentioned, small businesses often require less money to start and maintain than do large ones. Obviously, a firm with just 25 people in a small factory spends less money on wages and salaries, rent, utilities, and other expenses than does a firm employing tens of thousands of people in several large facilities. Rather than maintain the expense of keeping separate departments for accounting, advertising, and legal counseling, small businesses often hire other firms (sometimes small businesses themselves) to supply these services as they are needed. Additionally, small-business owners can sometimes rely on friends and family members to help them save money by volunteering to work on a difficult project.

灵活性
Flexibility

With small size comes the flexibility to adapt to changing market demands. Small businesses usually have only one layer of management—the owners. Decisions therefore can be made and executed quickly. In larger firms, decisions about even routine matters can take weeks because they must pass through multiple levels of management before action is authorized. When Taco Bell introduces a new product, for example, it must first research what consumers want, then develop the product and test it before introducing it nationwide—a process that sometimes takes years. An independent snack shop, however, can develop and introduce a new product (perhaps to meet a customer's request) in a much shorter time.

专注
Focus

Small firms can focus their efforts on a precisely defined market niche—that is, a specific group of customers. Many large corporations must compete in the mass market or for large market segments. Smaller firms can develop products for particular groups of customers or to satisfy a need that other companies have not addressed. For example, Hampton Creek, based in San Francisco, focuses on using technology to produce sustainable protein products. The company developed a new type of egg substitute made from plant materials. This concept is likely to attract vegetarians and consumers concerned with sustainability, but founder and CEO Josh Tetrick has bigger plans. His concept is not to focus solely on a niche industry; he believes the solutions discovered at Hampton Creek will eventually help solve food shortages through alternatives that do not place a strain on the environment.[21] By targeting small niches or product needs, businesses can sometimes avoid competition from larger firms, helping them to grow into stronger companies.

声誉
Reputation

Small firms, because of their capacity to focus on narrow niches, can develop enviable reputations for quality and service. A good example of a small business with a formidable reputation is W. Atlee Burpee and Co., which has the country's premier bulb and seed catalog. Burpee has an unqualified returns policy (complete satisfaction or your money back) that demonstrates a strong commitment to customer satisfaction.

小企业的劣势
Disadvantages of Small-Business Ownership

LO 2-4

The rewards associated with running a small business are so enticing that it's no wonder many people dream of it. However, as with any undertaking, small-business ownership has its disadvantages.

高压力
High Stress Level

A small business is likely to provide a living for its owner, but not much more (although there are exceptions as some examples in this chapter have shown). There are ongoing worries about competition, employee problems, new equipment, expanding inventory, rent increases, or changing market demand. In addition to other stresses, small-business owners tend to be victims of physical and psychological stress. The small-business person is often the owner, manager, sales force, shipping and receiving clerk, bookkeeper, and custodian. Having to multitask can result in long hours for most small-business owners. Many creative persons fail, not because of their business concepts, but rather because of difficulties in managing their business.

高失败率
High Failure Rate

Despite the importance of small businesses to our economy, there is no guarantee of success. Half of all new employer firms fail within the first five years.[22] Restaurants are a case in point. Look around your own neighborhood, and you can probably spot the locations of several restaurants that are no longer in business.

Small businesses fail for many reasons (see Table 2.5). A poor business concept—such as insecticides for garbage cans (research found that consumers are not concerned with insects in their garbage)—will produce disaster nearly every time. Expanding a hobby into a business may work if a genuine market niche exists, but all too often people start such a business without identifying a real need for the goods or services. Other notable causes of small-business failure include the burdens imposed by government regulation, insufficient funds to withstand slow sales, and vulnerability to competition from larger companies. However, three major causes of small-business failure deserve a close look: undercapitalization, managerial inexperience or incompetence, and inability to cope with growth.

Entrepreneurs experience a great deal of independence but also a great deal of stress. Many fail.

TABLE 2.5
Challenges in Starting a New Business

1. Underfunded (not providing adequate startup capital)
2. Not understanding your competitive niche
3. Lack of effective utilization of websites and social media
4. Lack of a marketing and business plan
5. If operating a retail store, poor site selection
6. Pricing mistakes—too high or too low
7. Underestimating the time commitment for success
8. Not finding complementary partners to bring in additional experience
9. Not hiring the right employees and/or not training them properly
10. Not understanding legal and ethical responsibilities

资本不足
undercapitalization
the lack of funds to operate a business normally

资本不足
Undercapitalization. The shortest path to failure in business is **undercapitalization,** the lack of funds to operate a business normally. Too many entrepreneurs think that all they need is enough money to get started, that the business can survive on cash generated from sales soon thereafter. But almost all businesses suffer from seasonal variations in sales, which make cash tight, and few businesses make money from the start. Many small rural operations cannot obtain financing within their own communities because small rural banks often lack the necessary financing expertise or assets sizable enough to counter the risks involved with small-business loans. Without sufficient funds, the best small-business idea in the world will fail.

缺乏管理经验与能力
Managerial Inexperience or Incompetence. Poor management is the cause of many business failures. Just because an entrepreneur has a brilliant vision for a small business does not mean he or she has the knowledge or experience to manage a growing business effectively. A person who is good at creating great product ideas and marketing them may lack the skills and experience to make good management decisions in hiring, negotiating, finance, and control. Moreover, entrepreneurs may neglect those areas of management they know little about or find tedious, at the expense of the business's success.

没有能力应对增长
Inability to Cope with Growth. Sometimes, the very factors that are advantages for a small business turn into serious disadvantages when the time comes to grow. Growth often requires the owner to give up a certain amount of direct authority, and it is frequently hard for someone who has called all the shots to give up control. It has often been said that the greatest impediment to the success of a business is the entrepreneur. Similarly, growth requires specialized management skills in areas such as credit analysis and promotion—skills that the founder may lack or not have time to apply. The founders of many small businesses, including Dell Computers, found that they needed to bring in more experienced managers to help manage their companies through growing pains.

Poorly managed growth probably affects a company's reputation more than anything else, at least initially. And products that do not arrive on time or goods that are poorly made can quickly reverse a success. The principal immediate threats to small and mid-sized businesses include rising inflation, energy and other supply shortages or cost escalations, and excessive household and/or corporate debt.

Consider Ethics and Social Responsibility

The Differences between Successful Entrepreneurs and Fraudsters

What do Steve Jobs and Bernie Madoff have in common? One is a highly admired entrepreneur responsible for creating one of the most valuable brands in the world. The other is a criminal guilty of operating the largest Ponzi scheme in the United States. The outcomes of the two men could not be more different. However, there are surprising similarities in the characteristics of famous entrepreneurs and fraudsters.

For instance, fraudsters tend to be intelligent, creative, persuasive, and seemingly confident—all characteristics of many successful entrepreneurs. Bernie Madoff built his enterprise from the ground-up, much like Oprah Winfrey, Bill Gates, and Steve Jobs. Successful entrepreneurs and fraudsters often display what has been termed "fearless dominance." Those that display fearless dominance demonstrate boldness, grace under pressure, charisma, and intelligence.

If fraudsters and entrepreneurs share so many characteristics, then what keeps entrepreneurs from becoming fraudsters? One trait is empathy. Being able to sympathize and care about others' well-being is lacking among fraudsters. Al Dunlap, former CEO of Sunbeam, was known for firing people and taking an aggressive approach to business. He was later implicated in accounting fraud. Another major characteristic is the ability to bounce back from failure. When Steve Jobs was ousted from Apple, he went on to found Pixar and later returned to save Apple from bankruptcy. When Bernie Madoff encountered financial difficulties, he covered them up through fraud.[23]

Discussion Questions

1. What characteristics do fraudsters and successful entrepreneurs share?
2. What are some major differences in the personalities of fraudsters and successful entrepreneurs?
3. Why is a lack of empathy fairly common among fraudsters?

LO 2-5

小型企业的创办
Starting a Small Business

We've told you how important small businesses are, and why they succeed and fail, but *how do you go about* starting your own business in the first place? To start any business, large or small, you must have some kind of general idea. Sam Walton, founder of Walmart stores, had a vision of a discount retailing enterprise that spawned the world's largest retailing empire and changed the way companies look at business. Next, you need to devise a strategy to guide planning and development in the business. Finally, you must make decisions about form of ownership, the financial resources needed, and whether to acquire an existing business, start a new one, or buy a franchise.

商业计划
The Business Plan

商业计划
business plan
a precise statement of the rationale for a business and a step-by-step explanation of how it will achieve its goals

A key element of business success is a **business plan**—a precise statement of the rationale for the business and a step-by-step explanation of how it will achieve its goals. The business plan should include an explanation of the business, an analysis of the competition, estimates of income and expenses, and other information. It should also establish a strategy for acquiring sufficient funds to keep the business going. Many financial institutions decide whether to loan a small business money based on its business plan. A good business plan should act as a guide and reference document—not a shackle that limits the business's flexibility and decision-making ability. The business plan must be revised periodically to ensure that the firm's goals and strategies adapt to changes in the environment. Business plans allow companies to assess market potential, determine price and manufacturing requirements, identify optimal distribution channels, and refine product selection. Two college students had an innovative idea that prompted them to create a business plan. They recognized a need for people to get a hold of their personal medical information. The two developed the concept for a medical management company that helps clients locate their records and pitched it in the Rutgers Business Plan Competition. After winning the first prize of $20,000, the students launched Opcura.com, started hiring employees, and began promoting their business.[24] The SBA website provides an overview of a plan for small businesses to use to gain financing. Appendix A presents a comprehensive business plan.

企业所有权形式

Forms of Business Ownership

After developing a business plan, the entrepreneur has to decide on an appropriate legal form of business ownership—whether it is best to operate as a sole proprietorship, partnership, or corporation—and to examine the many factors that affect that decision, which we explored in Chapter 1.

connect

Need help understanding How an Entrepreneur Can Secure Financing for a Small Business? Visit your Connect ebook video tab for a brief animated explanation.

融资来源

Financial Resources

The expression "it takes money to make money" holds especially true in developing a business enterprise. To make money from a small business, the owner must first provide or obtain money (capital) to get started and to keep it running smoothly. Even a small retail store will probably need at least $50,000 in initial financing to rent space, purchase or lease necessary equipment and furnishings, buy the initial inventory, and provide working capital. Often, the small-business owner has to put up a significant percentage of the necessary capital. Few new business owners have a large amount of their own capital and must look to other sources for additional financing.

股权融资

Equity Financing. The most important source of funds for any new business is the owner. Many owners include among their personal resources ownership of a home, the accumulated value in a life-insurance policy, or a savings account. A new business owner may sell or borrow against the value of such assets to obtain funds to operate a business. Additionally, the owner may bring useful personal assets—such as a computer, desks and other furniture, a car or truck—as part of his or her ownership interest in the firm. Such financing is referred to as *equity financing* because the owner uses real personal assets rather than borrowing funds from outside sources to get started in a new business. The owner can also provide working capital by reinvesting profits into the business or simply by not drawing a full salary.

Small-business owners often use debt financing from banks or the Small Business Administration to start their own organization.

Small businesses can also obtain equity financing by finding investors for their operations. They may sell stock in the business to family members, friends, employees, or other investors. For example, Harvard alumnus Katrina Lake created a website called Stitch Fix that uses algorithms and personal stylists

Some of the advantages of small businesses include flexibility, lower startup costs, and perhaps most desirable, the ability to be your own boss.

风险投资家
venture capitalists
persons or organizations that agree to provide some funds for a new business in exchange for an ownership interest or stock

to develop sets, or "fixes," of clothes based upon the consumer's individual tastes. The fixes are mailed to the consumer, who pays for what she wants to keep and mails the rest back. Stich Fix is meant to appeal to consumers who want to keep shopping simple and are turned off by the large number of choices on websites such as Amazon.com. Despite high shipping costs, Stich Fix received $12 million from a venture-capital firm. These investors believe Stitch Fix has significant potential to expand and be successful.[25] **Venture capitalists** are persons or organizations that agree to provide some funds for a new business in exchange for an ownership interest or stock. Venture capitalists hope to purchase the stock of a small business at a low price and then sell the stock for a profit after the business has grown successful. Although these forms of equity financing have helped many small businesses, they require that the small-business owner share the profits of the business—and sometimes control, as well—with the investors.

债务融资

Debt Financing. New businesses sometimes borrow more than half of their financial resources. Banks are the main suppliers of external financing to small businesses. On the federal level, the SBA offers financial assistance to qualifying businesses. They can also look to family and friends as sources for long-term loans or other assets, such as computers or an automobile, that are exchanged for an ownership interest in a business. In such cases, the business owner can usually structure a favorable repayment schedule and sometimes negotiate an interest rate below current bank rates. If the business goes bad, however, the emotional losses for all concerned may greatly exceed the money involved. Anyone lending a friend or family member money for a venture should state the agreement clearly in writing before any money changes hands.

The amount a bank or other institution is willing to loan depends on its assessment of the venture's likelihood of success and of the entrepreneur's ability to repay the loan. The bank will often require the entrepreneur to put up *collateral,* a financial interest in the property or fixtures of the business, to guarantee payment of the debt. Additionally, the small-business owner may have to provide personal property as collateral, such as his or her home, in which case the loan is called a *mortgage.* If the small business fails to repay the loan, the lending institution may eventually claim and sell the collateral or mortgage to recover its loss.

Banks and other financial institutions can also grant a small business a *line of credit*—an agreement by which a financial institution promises to lend a business a predetermined sum on demand. A line of credit permits an entrepreneur to take quick advantage of opportunities that require external funding. Small businesses may obtain funding from their suppliers in the form of a *trade credit*—that is, suppliers allow the business to take possession of the needed goods and services and pay for them at a later date or in installments. Occasionally, small businesses engage in *bartering*—trading their own products for the goods and services offered by other businesses. For example, an accountant may offer accounting services to an office supply firm in exchange for office supplies and equipment.

Going Green

ReFleece: A Simple but Sustainable Product

Sam Palmer and Jennifer Feller took a risk with their idea for a sustainable iPad case. They refinanced their home and took out a home equity loan for $150,000 to found ReFleece in 2012, a business that uses up-cycled fleece as material for tablet cases. *Up-cycling* refers to reusing material without compromising its quality. Equipped with design experience and a concern for sustainability, Palmer and Feller partnered with Patagonia's Common Threads Initiative that brings in old consumer fleece to be recycled. ReFleece gets most of its raw materials from this program. The only new materials on these tablet cases are thread, snaps, and elastic. These sustainable tablet cases are manufactured in the United States, which helps the company save on costs. ReFleece is sold on Amazon, in Patagonia stores, and on refleece.com for $25 to $32, depending on the size of the case.

The entrepreneurs have been praised for their ability to create a useful product from old materials as well as for their commitment toward social responsibility. The company is a member of 1 percent for the Planet, donating 1 percent of its profits toward environmental nonprofits. ReFleece expects to earn $150,000 in sales of sustainable tablet cases.[26]

Discussion Questions

1. Why do you think a simple concept such as a tablet case made from up-cycled material became successful?
2. How were the ReFleece founders able to fund their startup company? What risks did they accept to make their idea into a reality?
3. How has the partnership with Patagonia likely affected ReFleece's sales?

Additionally, some community groups sponsor loan funds to encourage the development of particular types of businesses. State and local agencies may guarantee loans, especially to minority business people or for development in certain areas.

创办小型企业的方法
Approaches to Starting a Small Business

从头做起还是收购已有企业

Starting from Scratch versus Buying an Existing Business. Although entrepreneurs often start new small businesses from scratch much the way we have discussed in this section, they may elect instead to buy an existing business. This has the advantage of providing a built-in network of customers, suppliers, and distributors and reducing some of the guesswork inherent in starting a new business from the ground up. However, an entrepreneur who buys an existing business also takes on any problems the business already has.

特许经营

Franchising. Many small-business owners find entry into the business world through franchising. A license to sell another's products or to use another's name in business, or both, is a **franchise.** The company that sells a franchise is the **franchiser.** Dunkin' Donuts, Subway, and Jiffy Lube are well-known franchisers with national visibility. The purchaser of a franchise is called a **franchisee.**

特许经营权
franchise
a license to sell another's products or to use another's name in business, or both

特许经营权出售者
franchiser
the company that sells a franchise

特许经营权购买者
franchisee
the purchaser of a franchise

The franchisee acquires the rights to a name, logo, methods of operation, national advertising, products, and other elements associated with the franchiser's business in return for a financial commitment and the agreement to conduct business in accordance with the franchiser's standard of operations. The initial fee to join a franchise varies greatly. In addition, franchisees buy equipment, pay for training, and obtain a mortgage or lease. The franchisee also pays the franchiser a monthly or annual fee based on a percentage of sales or profits. In return, the franchisee often receives building specifications and designs, site recommendations, management and accounting support, and perhaps most importantly, immediate name recognition. Visit the website of the International Franchise Association to learn more on this topic.

TABLE 2.6
Fastest Growing and Hottest New Franchises

Top 10 Fastest Growing Franchises	Top 10 Hottest New Franchises
Subway	Kona Ice
Jan-Pro Franchising Int'l. Inc.	Menchie's
7-Eleven Inc.	Orange Leaf Frozen Yogurt
Vanguard Cleaning Systems	ShelfGenie Franchise Systems LLC
Liberty Tax Service	Bricks 4 Kidz
Chester's	Smashburger Franchising LLC
Jazzercise Inc.	Game Truck Licensing LLC
Jimmy John's Gourmet Sandwiches	Paul Davis Emergency Services
Dunkin' Donuts	Signal 88 Security
Anago Cleaning Systems	Mac Tools

Sources: "2013 Fastest-Growing Franchise Rankings," Entrepreneur; *"2013 New Franchise Rankings,"* Entrepreneur.

The practice of franchising first began in the United States in the 19th century when Singer used it to sell sewing machines. The method of goods distribution soon became commonplace in the automobile, gasoline, soft drink, and hotel industries. The concept of franchising grew especially rapidly during the 1960s, when it expanded to diverse industries. Table 2.6 shows the 10 fastest growing franchises and the top 10 new franchises.

The entrepreneur will find that franchising has both advantages and disadvantages. Franchising allows a franchisee the opportunity to set up a small business relatively quickly, and because of its association with an established brand, a franchise outlet often reaches the break-even point faster than an independent business would. Franchisees commonly report the following advantages:

- Management training and support.
- Brand-name appeal.
- Standardized quality of goods and services.
- National and local advertising programs.
- Financial assistance.
- Proven products and business formats.
- Centralized buying power.
- Site selection and territorial protection.
- Greater chance for success.[27]

However, the franchisee must sacrifice some freedom to the franchiser. Some shortcomings experienced by franchisees include:

- Franchise fees and profit sharing with the franchiser.
- Strict adherence to standardized operations.
- Restrictions on purchasing.

- Limited product line.
- Possible market saturation.
- Less freedom in business decisions.[28]

Strict uniformity is the rule rather than the exception. Entrepreneurs who want to be their own bosses are often frustrated with the restrictions of a franchise.

小型企业管理者可获得的帮助
Help for Small-Business Managers

Because of the crucial role that small business and entrepreneurs play in the U.S. economy, a number of organizations offer programs to improve the small-business owner's ability to compete. These include entrepreneurial training programs and programs sponsored by the SBA. Such programs provide small-business owners with invaluable assistance in managing their businesses, often at little or no cost to the owner.

Entrepreneurs can learn critical marketing, management, and finance skills in seminars and college courses. In addition, knowledge, experience, and judgment are necessary for success in a new business. While knowledge can be communicated and some experiences can be simulated in the classroom, good judgment must be developed by the entrepreneur. Local chambers of commerce and the U.S. Department of Commerce offer information and assistance helpful in operating a small business. National publications such as *Inc.* and *Entrepreneur* share statistics, advice, tips, and success/failure stories. Additionally, most urban areas have weekly business journals/newspapers that provide stories on local businesses as well as on business techniques that a manager or small business can use.

The SBA offers many types of management assistance to small businesses, including counseling for firms in difficulty, consulting on improving operations, and training for owner/managers and their employees. Among its many programs, the SBA funds Small Business Development Centers (SBDCs). These are business clinics, usually located on college campuses, that provide counseling at no charge and training at only a nominal charge. SBDCs are often the SBA's principal means of providing direct management assistance.

The Service Corps of Retired Executives (SCORE) and the Active Corps of Executives (ACE) are volunteer agencies funded by the SBA to provide advice for owners of small firms. Both are staffed by experienced managers whose talents and experience the small firms could not ordinarily afford. SCORE has more than 13,000 volunteers at 354 locations in the United States and has served more than 8.5 million small businesses.[29] The SBA also has organized Small Business Institutes (SBIs) on almost 500 university and college campuses in the United States. Seniors, graduate students, and faculty at each SBI provide onsite management counseling.

Finally, the small-business owner can obtain advice from other small-business owners, suppliers, and even customers. A customer may approach a small business it frequents with a request for a new product, for example, or a supplier may offer suggestions for improving a manufacturing process. Networking—building relationships and sharing information with colleagues—is vital for any businessperson, whether you work for a huge corporation or run your own small business. Communicating with other business owners is a great way to find ideas for dealing with employees and government regulation, improving processes, or solving problems. New technology is making it easier to network. For example, some states are establishing social networking sites for the use of their businesses to network and share ideas.

LO 2-6

小型企业的未来
The Future for Small Business[30]

Although small businesses are crucial to the economy, their size and limited resources can make them more vulnerable to turbulence and change in the marketplace than large businesses. Next, we take a brief look at the demographic, technological, and economic trends that will have the most impact on small business in the future.

人口发展趋势
Demographic Trends

America's baby boom started in 1946 and ended in 1964. Many boomers are over 50, and in the next few years, millions more will pass that mark. The baby boomer generation represents 26 percent of Americans.[31] This segment of the population is wealthy, but many small businesses do not actively pursue it. Some exceptions, however, include Gold Violin, which sells designer canes and other products online and through a catalog, and LifeSpring, which delivers nutritional meals and snacks directly to the customer. Industries such as travel, financial planning, and health care will continue to grow as boomers age. Many experts believe that the boomer demographic is the market of the future.

Another market with huge potential for small business is the echo boomers, also called millennials or Generation Y. Millennials number around 75 million and possess a number of unique characteristics. Born between the early 1980s and the early 2000s, this cohort is not solely concerned about money. Those that fall into this group are also concerned with advancement, recognition, and improved capabilities. They need direct, timely feedback and frequent encouragement and recognition. Millennials do well when training sessions combine entertainment with learning. Working remotely is more acceptable to this group than previous generations, and virtual communication may become as important as face-to-face meetings.[32]

The Latino population is the biggest and fastest growing minority segment in the United States—and a lucrative market for businesses looking for ways to meet the segment's many needs.

TABLE 2.7
Most Business-Friendly Cities

1. Austin, Texas
2. Virginia Beach, Virginia
3. Houston, Texas
4. Colorado Springs, Colorado
5. San Antonio, Texas
6. Nashville, Tennessee
7. Dallas-Fort Worth, Texas
8. Raleigh-Durham, North Carolina

Source: "8 most business-friendly cities," CNN Money, *2013.*

Yet another trend is the growing number of immigrants living in the United States, who now represent about 16 percent of the population. If this trend continues, by 2050 nearly one in five Americans will be classified as immigrants. The Latino population, the nation's largest minority group, is expected to triple in size by 2050.[33]

This vast group provides still another greatly untapped market for small businesses. Retailers who specialize in ethnic products, and service providers who offer bi- or multilingual employees, will find a large amount of business potential in this market. Table 2.7 ranks top cities in the United States for small businesses and startups.

科技与经济趋势
Technological and Economic Trends

Advances in technology have opened up many new markets to small businesses. Undoubtedly, the Internet will continue to provide new opportunities for small businesses. Imgur is a photo-sharing hub filled with trivial and humorous photos. It has become popular as a meme site. The company generates income by posting display advertisements from movie studios and videogame publishers. It charges users of the site $24 a year if they want features like unlimited data storage. Users do not have to register to show approval or disapproval of a photo. The company's users upload 1.5 million images every day and is becoming one of the most traveled to sites in the world—despite the fact that it only has 11 employees.[34]

Technological advances and an increase in service exports have created new opportunities for small companies to expand their operations abroad. Changes in communications and technology can allow small companies to customize their services quickly for international customers. Also, free trade agreements and trade alliances are helping to create an environment in which small businesses have fewer regulatory and legal barriers.

In recent years, economic turbulence has provided both opportunities and threats for small businesses. As large information technology companies such as Cisco, Oracle, and Sun Microsystems had to recover from an economic slowdown and an oversupply of Internet infrastructure products, some smaller firms found new niche markets. Smaller companies can react quickly to change and can stay close to their customers. While well-funded dot-coms were failing, many small businesses were learning how to use the Internet to promote themselves and sell products online. For example, arts and crafts dealers and makers of specialty products found they could sell their wares on existing websites, such as eBay. Service providers related to tourism, real estate, and construction also found they could reach customers through their own or existing websites.

Deregulation of the energy market and interest in alternative fuels and in fuel conservation have spawned many small businesses. Southwest Windpower Inc. manufactures and markets small wind turbines for producing electric power for homes, sailboats, and telecommunications. Solar Attic Inc. has developed a process to recover heat from home attics to use in heating water or swimming pools. As entrepreneurs begin to realize that worldwide energy markets are valued in the hundreds of billions of dollars, the number of innovative companies entering this market will increase. In addition, many small businesses have the desire and employee commitment to purchase such environmentally friendly products. New Belgium Brewing Company received the U.S. Environmental Protection Agency and Department of Energy Award for leadership in conservation for making a 10-year commitment to purchase wind energy. The company's employees unanimously agreed to cover the increased costs of wind-generated electricity from the employee profit-sharing program.

The future for small business remains promising. The opportunities to apply creativity and entrepreneurship to serve customers are unlimited. While large organizations such as Walmart, which has more than 2.1 million employees, typically must adapt to change slowly, a small business can adapt immediately to customer and community needs and changing trends. This flexibility provides small businesses with a definite advantage over large companies.

LO 2-7

大公司如何像小型企业那样行动
Making Big Businesses Act "Small"

The continuing success and competitiveness of small businesses through rapidly changing conditions in the business world have led many large corporations to take a closer look at what makes their smaller rivals tick. More and more firms are emulating small businesses in an effort to improve their own bottom line. Beginning in the 1980s and continuing through the present, the buzzword in business has been to *downsize* or *right-size* to reduce management layers, corporate staff, and work tasks in order to make the firm more flexible, resourceful, and innovative. Many well-known U.S. companies, including IBM, Ford, Apple Computer, General Electric, Xerox, and 3M, have downsized to improve their competitiveness, as have German, British, and Japanese firms. Other firms have sought to make their businesses "smaller" by making their operating units function more like independent small businesses, each responsible for its profits, losses, and resources. Of course, some large corporations, such as Southwest Airlines, have acted like small businesses from their inception, with great success.

企业开拓者
intrapreneurs
individuals in large firms who take responsibility for the development of innovations within the organizations

Trying to capitalize on small-business success in introducing innovative new products, more and more companies are attempting to instill a spirit of entrepreneurship into even the largest firms. In major corporations, **intrapreneurs,** like entrepreneurs, take responsibility for, or "champion," the development of innovations of any kind *within* the larger organization.[35] Often, they use company resources and time to develop a new product for the company.

So You Want to Be an Entrepreneur or Small-Business Owner

In times when jobs are scarce, many people turn to entrepreneurship as a way to find employment. As long as there are unfulfilled needs from consumers, there will be a demand for entrepreneurs and small businesses. Entrepreneurs and small-business owners have been, and will continue to be, a vital part of the U.S. economy, whether in retailing, wholesaling, manufacturing, technology, or services. Creating a business around your idea has a lot of advantages. For many people, independence is the biggest advantage of forming their own small business, especially for those who do not work well in a corporate setting and like to call their own shots. Smaller businesses are also cheaper to start up than large ones in terms of salaries, infrastructure, and equipment. Smallness also provides a lot of flexibility to change with the times. If consumers suddenly start demanding new and different products, a small business is more likely to deliver quickly.

Starting your own business is not easy, especially in slow economic times. Even in a good economy, taking an idea and turning it into a business has a very high failure rate. The possibility of failure can increase even more when money is tight. Reduced revenues and expensive materials can hurt a small business more than a large one because small businesses have fewer resources. When people are feeling the pinch from rising food and fuel prices, they tend to cut back on other expenditures—which could potentially harm your small business. The increased cost of materials will also affect your bottom line. However, several techniques can help your company survive:

- Set clear payment schedules for all clients. Small businesses tend to be worse about collecting payments than large ones, especially if the clients are acquaintances. However, you need to keep cash flowing into the company in order to keep business going.
- Take the time to learn about tax breaks. A lot of people do not realize all of the deductions they can claim on items such as equipment and health insurance.
- Focus on your current customers, and don't spend a lot of time looking for new ones. It is far less expensive for a company to keep its existing customers happy.
- Although entrepreneurs and small-business owners are more likely to be friends with their customers, do not let this be a temptation to give things away for free. Make it clear to your customers what the basic price is for what you are selling and charge for extra features, extra services, etc.
- Make sure the office has the conveniences employees need—like a good coffee maker and other drinks and snacks. This will not only make your employees happy, but it will also help maintain productivity by keeping employees closer to their desks.
- Use your actions to set an example. If money is tight, show your commitment to cutting costs and making the business work by doing simple things like taking the bus to work or bringing a sack lunch every day.
- Don't forget to increase productivity in addition to cutting costs. Try not to focus so much attention on cost cutting that you don't try to increase sales.

In unsure economic times, these measures should help new entrepreneurs and small-business owners sustain their businesses. Learning how to run a business on a shoestring is a great opportunity to cut the fat and to establish lean, efficient operations.[36]

Review Your Understanding

Define entrepreneurship and small business.

An entrepreneur is a person who creates a business or product and manages his or her resources and takes risks to gain a profit; entrepreneurship is the process of creating and managing a business to achieve desired objectives. A small business is one that is not dominant in its competitive area and does not employ more than 500 people.

Investigate the importance of small business in the U.S. economy and why certain fields attract small business.

Small businesses are vital to the American economy because they provide products, jobs, innovation, and opportunities. Retailing, wholesaling, services, manufacturing, and high technology attract small businesses because these industries are relatively easy to enter, require relatively low initial financing, and may experience less heavy competition.

Specify the advantages of small-business ownership.

Small-business ownership offers some personal advantages, including independence, freedom of choice, and the option of working at home. Business advantages include flexibility, the ability to focus on a few key customers, and the chance to develop a reputation for quality and service.

Summarize the disadvantages of small-business ownership, and analyze why many small businesses fail.

Small businesses have many disadvantages for their owners such as expense, physical and psychological stress, and a high failure rate. Small businesses fail for many reasons: undercapitalization, management inexperience or incompetence, neglect, disproportionate burdens imposed by government regulation, and vulnerability to competition from larger companies.

Describe how you go about starting a small business and what resources are needed.

First, you must have an idea for developing a small business. Next, you need to devise a business plan to guide planning and development of the business. Then you must decide what form of business ownership to use: sole proprietorship, partnership, or corporation. Small-business owners are expected to provide some of the funds required to start their businesses, but funds also can be obtained from friends and family, financial institutions, other businesses in the form of trade credit, investors (venture capitalists), state and local organizations, and the Small Business Administration. In addition to loans, the Small Business Administration and other organizations offer counseling, consulting, and training services. Finally, you must decide whether to start a new business from scratch, buy an existing one, or buy a franchise operation.

Evaluate the demographic, technological, and economic trends that are affecting the future of small business.

Changing demographic trends that represent areas of opportunity for small businesses include more elderly people as baby boomers age, a large group in the 11 to 28 age range known as echo boomers, millennials, or Generation Y, and an increasing number of immigrants to the United States. Technological advances and an increase in service exports have created new opportunities for small companies to expand their operations abroad, while trade agreements and alliances have created an environment in which small business has fewer regulatory and legal barriers. Economic turbulence presents both opportunities and threats to the survival of small businesses.

Explain why many large businesses are trying to "think small."

More large companies are copying small businesses in an effort to make their firms more flexible, resourceful, and innovative, and generally to improve their bottom line. This effort often involves downsizing (reducing management layers, laying off employees, and reducing work tasks) and intrapreneurship, when an employee takes responsibility for (champions) developing innovations of any kind within the larger organization.

Assess two entrepreneurs' plans for starting a small business.

Based on the facts given in "Solve the Dilemma" on page 168 and the material presented in this chapter, you should be able to assess the feasibility and potential success of Gray and McVay's idea for starting a small business.

Revisit the World of Business

1. What are some likely reasons that Chobani Yogurt has become such a success?
2. Describe some of the challenges that Chobani is facing.
3. Why is it such an issue when a major retailer drops a product from its shelves?

Learn the Terms

business plan
entrepreneurship
franchise
franchisee
franchiser
intrapreneurs
small business
Small Business Administration (SBA)
undercapitalization
venture capitalists

Check Your Progress

1. Why are small businesses so important to the U.S. economy?
2. Which fields tend to attract entrepreneurs the most? Why?
3. What are the advantages of starting a small business? The disadvantages?
4. What are the principal reasons for the high failure rate among small businesses?
5. What decisions must an entrepreneur make when starting a small business?
6. What types of financing do small entrepreneurs typically use? What are some of the pros and cons of each?
7. List the types of management and financial assistance that the Small Business Administration offers.
8. Describe the franchising relationship.
9. What demographic, technological, and economic trends are influencing the future of small business?
10. Why do large corporations want to become more like small businesses?

Get Involved

1. Interview a local small-business owner. Why did he or she start the business? What factors have led to the business's success? What problems has the owner experienced? What advice would he or she offer a potential entrepreneur?
2. Using business journals, find an example of a company that is trying to emulate the factors that make small businesses flexible and more responsive. Describe and evaluate the company's activities. Have they been successful? Why or why not?
3. Using the business plan outline in Appendix A, create a business plan for a business idea that you have. (A man named Fred Smith once did a similar project for a business class at Yale. His paper became the basis for the business he later founded: Federal Express!)

Build Your Skills

Creativity

Background

The entrepreneurial success stories in this chapter are about people who used their creative abilities to develop innovative products or ways of doing something that became the basis of a new business. Of course, being creative is not just for entrepreneurs or inventors; creativity is an important tool to help you find the optimal solutions to the problems you face on a daily basis. Employees rely heavily on their creativity skills to help them solve daily workplace problems.

According to brain experts, the right-brain hemisphere is the source of creative thinking; and the creative part of the brain can "atrophy" from lack of use. Let's see how much "exercise" you're giving your right-brain hemisphere.

Task

1. Take the following self-test to check your Creativity Quotient.[37]
2. Write the appropriate number in the box next to each statement according to whether the statement describes your behavior always (3), sometimes (2), once in a while (1), or never (0).

	Always 3	Sometimes 2	Once in a While 1	Never 0
1. I am a curious person who is interested in other people's opinions.				
2. I look for opportunities to solve problems.				
3. I respond to changes in my life creatively by using them to redefine my goals and revising plans to reach them.				
4. I am willing to develop and experiment with ideas of my own.				
5. I rely on my hunches and insights.				
6. I can reduce complex decisions to a few simple questions by seeing the "big picture."				
7. I am good at promoting and gathering support for my ideas.				
8. I think further ahead than most people I associate with by thinking long term and sharing my vision with others.				
9. I dig out research and information to support my ideas.				
10. I am supportive of the creative ideas from my peers and subordinates and welcome "better ideas" from others.				
11. I read books and magazine articles to stay on the "cutting edge" in my areas of interest. I am fascinated by the future.				
12. I believe I am creative and have faith in my good ideas.				
Subtotal for each column				
	Grand Total			

3. Check your score using the following scale:

30–36 High creativity. You are giving your right-brain hemisphere a regular workout.

20–29 Average creativity. You could use your creativity capacity more regularly to ensure against "creativity atrophy."

10–19 Low creativity. You could benefit by reviewing the questions you answered "never" in the above assessment and selecting one or two of the behaviors that you could start practicing.

0–9 Undiscovered creativity. You have yet to uncover your creative potential.

Solve the Dilemma

The Small-Business Challenge

Jack Gray and his best friend, Bruce McVay, decided to start their own small business. Jack had developed recipes for fat-free and low-fat cookies and muffins in an effort to satisfy his personal health needs. Bruce had extensive experience in managing food-service establishments. They knew that a startup company needs a quality product, adequate funds, a written business plan, some outside financial support, and a good promotion program. Jack and Bruce felt they had all of this and more and were ready to embark on their new low-fat cookie/muffin store. Each had $35,000 to invest and with their homes and other resources, they had borrowing power of an additional $125,000.

However, they still have many decisions to make, including what form or organization to use, how to market their product, and how to determine exactly what products to sell—whether just cookies and muffins or additional products.

Discussion Questions

1. Evaluate the idea of a low-fat cookie and muffin retail store.
2. Are there any concerns in connection with starting a small business that Jack and Bruce have not considered?
3. What advice would you give Jack and Bruce as they start up their business?

Build Your Business Plan

Small Business, Entrepreneurship, and Franchising

Now you can get started writing your business plan! As you are developing your business plan, keep in mind that potential investors might be reviewing it. Or you might have plans to go to Your local Small Buiness Development Center for an SBA loan.

At this point in the process, you should think about collecting information from a variety of (free) resources. For example, if you are developing a business plan for a local business, product good, or service, you might want to check out any of the following sources for demographic information: your local Chamber of Commerce, Economic Development office, census bureau, or City Planning office.

Go on the Internet and see if there have been any recent studies done or articles on your specific type of business, especially in your area. Remember, you always want to explore any secondary data before trying to conduct your own research.

See for Yourself Videocase

Sonic—A Successful Franchise with an Old-Fashioned Drive-In Experience

For those who are nostalgic for the classic drive-in diner experience, the Sonic fast-food chain helps fill that need. Sonic offers customers a dose of nostalgia with its 1950s-style curbside speakers and carhop service. As the United States' largest drive-in fast-food chain, Sonic offers a unique and diverse menu selection that helps set it apart from a highly competitive fast-food franchise market. Founder Troy Smith launched the first Sonic Drive-In (known then as Top Hat Drive-In) in Shawnee, Oklahoma, in 1953 as a sole proprietorship. He later added a partner, Charlie Pappe, and eventually turned the business into a franchise.

Despite its traditional feel, the company has seized upon new trends and opportunities to secure more business. Customers at Sonic frequently eat in their cars or at tables outside the restaurant. However, Sonic has begun building indoor dining prototypes in colder areas to test whether this will entice more customers to eat at its locations. The prototype still makes use of the restaurant's traditional patio but encloses it to protect customers from the elements. So far, prototypes have been set up in 10 locations. Each of these restaurants maintains its carhop and drive-thru features in order to retain the "Sonic experience."

Today, Sonic is a publicly traded company and ranks as the 10th largest fast-food franchise in terms of sales revenue. Franchising is an appealing option for entrepreneurs looking to begin businesses without creating them from scratch. In the case of Sonic, when a franchisee purchases a franchise, he or she is getting a business that already has a national reputation and a national advertising campaign. The company also offers its franchisees tremendous support and training. As a pioneer, Troy Smith was required to innovate; as a Sonic franchisee, one steps into an already proven system.

That being said, successfully running a franchise is not easy. One entrepreneur who owns 22 Sonic franchises says the franchisee's job is to ensure that each customer has the best experience possible, thereby making repeat visits more likely. To accomplish this, a franchisee must build his or her locations, purchase equipment, hire excellent employees, make certain the products live up to Sonic's reputation, maintain a clean, inviting facility, and much more. In order to run 22 franchises, the entrepreneur runs his locations as limited partnerships, ensuring that a managing partner is on site at each location to keep day-to-day operations running smoothly.

Some of Sonic's success may be attributed to its stringent requirements for selecting franchisees. Although franchisees must have excellent financial credentials and prior restaurant/entrepreneurial experience, the most important factor is that each franchisee fit into the Sonic culture. Sonic offers two types of franchises. The traditional franchise, which includes the full restaurant set-up, requires a total investment of between $1.1 million and $3 million. Franchisees are required to pay 2 to 5 percent in ongoing royalty fees and a franchise fee of $45,000. A Sonic in a travel plaza, a mall food court, or a college campus are all examples of the nontraditional model. Because these set-ups do not include the drive-in and carhop features, initial investment is less. However, royalty and advertising fees still apply.

For entrepreneurs looking for limited risk, franchises like Sonic are great options. The advantages are abundant, as discussed earlier. There is a high failure rate among small businesses. Entering into a successful franchise significantly cuts down on the risk of failure, although a franchisee does have to watch for market saturation, poor location choice, and other determining factors. However, there are also disadvantages; chiefly, franchisees are often required to follow a strict model set by the franchiser. For instance, in addition to prior restaurant experience, Sonic requires its franchisees to be financially and operationally able to open two or more drive-ins. These types of requirements may make it difficult for entrepreneurs who want to set their own terms. However, with Sonic's successful business model and brand equity, there is no shortage of individuals who would like to operate a Sonic franchise.[38]

Discussion Questions

1. What is Sonic's competitive advantage over other fast-food franchises?
2. What are the advantages of becoming a Sonic franchisee?
3. What are the disadvantages of buying into the Sonic franchise?

You can find the related video in the Video Library in Connect. Ask your instructor how you can access Connect.

Team Exercise

Explore successful global franchises. Go to the companies' websites and find the requirements for applying for three franchises. The chapter provides examples of successful franchises. What do the companies provide, and what is expected to be provided by the franchiser? Compare and contrast each group's findings for the franchises researched. For example, at Subway, the franchisee is responsible for the initial franchise fee, finding locations, leasehold improvements and equipment, hiring employees and operating restaurants, and paying an 8 percent royalty to the company and a fee into the advertising fund. The company provides access to formulas and operational systems, store design and equipment ordering guidance, a training program, an operations manual, a representative on-site during opening, periodic evaluations and ongoing support, and informative publications.

3 The Nature of Management
管理的本质

Learning Objectives

After reading this chapter, you will be able to:

LO 3-1 Define *management*, and explain its role in the achievement of organizational objectives.

LO 3-2 Describe the major functions of management.

LO 3-3 Distinguish among three levels of management and the concerns of managers at each level.

LO 3-4 Specify the skills managers need in order to be successful.

LO 3-5 Summarize the systematic approach to decision making used by many business managers.

LO 3-6 Recommend a new strategy to revive a struggling business.

Chapter Outline

进入商业世界

Enter the World of Business

中层管理者的重要性

The Importance of Middle Managers

Middle managers are responsible for tactical planning and implementing top management's guidelines. Middle managers are expected to work across departments, put in long hours, and often remain available outside of work. Unfortunately, many middle managers feel that while they have much responsibility, they have very little authority. When cutbacks occur within an organization, middle managers are often the ones who are eliminated. Today there are 10.8 million middle managers in the United States, or 7.6 percent of the workforce.

As the major contact person between front-line employees and top managers, middle managers are required to have strong people skills and good communication. Middle managers have the responsibility of managing their teams while creating a positive influence on the company. Despite their often hectic work schedules, 44 percent of middle managers in one study reported that they were satisfied with their work/life balance, compared with 70 percent of nonmanagers.

There are different steps middle managers can take to improve their careers and move into top leadership positions. Suggestions include thinking big, asking for input, being flexible to new situations, clearly communicating between front-line employees and managers, and showing empathy for employees. Companies are also beginning to realize the benefit of middle managers when it comes to leadership. Half of mid-level executives receive leadership training. Although it is possible to eliminate the middle manager position, it is impossible to eliminate their functions—including communication, team building, and tactical planning—which are essential to leading the firm to success.[1]

引言
Introduction

For any organization—small or large, for profit or nonprofit—to achieve its objectives, it must have equipment and raw materials to turn into products to market, employees to make and sell the products, and financial resources to purchase additional goods and services, pay employees, and generally operate the business. To accomplish this, it must also have one or more managers to plan, organize, staff, direct, and control the work that goes on.

This chapter introduces the field of management. It examines and surveys the various functions, levels, and areas of management in business. The skills that managers need for success and the steps that lead to effective decision making are also discussed.

LO 3-1

管理的重要性
The Importance of Management

管理
management
a process designed to achieve an organization's objectives by using its resources effectively and efficiently in a changing environment

管理者
managers
those individuals in organizations who make decisions about the use of resources and who are concerned with planning, organizing, staffing, directing, and controlling the organization's activities to reach its objectives

Management is a process designed to achieve an organization's objectives by using its resources effectively and efficiently in a changing environment. *Effectively* means having the intended result; *efficiently* means accomplishing the objectives with a minimum of resources. **Managers** make decisions about the use of the organization's resources and are concerned with planning, organizing, staffing, directing, and controlling the organization's activities so as to reach its objectives. The decision to introduce new products in order to reach objectives is often a key management duty. For instance, Samsung managers were involved in the decision to introduce their new line of curved televisions with Ultra High Definition to rejuvenate sales. The curved screen increases the clarity of viewing from all angles and has proportions similar to movie theater screens, making this an attractive alternative to going to movie theaters.[2] Management is universal. It takes place not only in business, but also in government, the military, labor unions, hospitals, schools, and religious groups—any organization requiring the coordination of resources.

Every organization must acquire resources (people, raw materials and equipment, money, and information) to effectively pursue its objectives and coordinate their use to turn out a final good or service. Employees are one of the most important resources in helping a business attain its objectives. Successful companies recruit, train, compensate, and provide benefits (such as shares of stock and health insurance) to foster employee loyalty. Acquiring suppliers is another important part of managing resources and ensuring that products are made available to customers. As firms reach global markets, companies such as Walmart, Corning, and Charles Schwab enlist hundreds of diverse suppliers that provide goods and services to support operations. A good supplier maximizes efficiencies and provides creative solutions to help the company reduce expenses and reach its objectives. Finally, the manager needs adequate financial resources to pay for essential activities. Primary funding comes from owners and shareholders, as well as banks and other financial institutions. All these resources and activities must be coordinated and controlled if the company is to earn a profit. Organizations must also have adequate supplies of resources of all types, and managers must carefully coordinate their use if they are to achieve the organization's objectives.

Mary Barra, the CEO of General Motors, must lead the company through a recall crisis involving faulty ignition switches.

管理的职能
Management Functions

LO 3-2

To harmonize the use of resources so that the business can develop, produce, and sell products, managers engage in a series of activities: planning, organizing, staffing, directing, and controlling (Figure 3.1). Although this book discusses each of the five functions separately, they are interrelated; managers may perform two or more of them at the same time.

规划
Planning

Planning, the process of determining the organization's objectives and deciding how to accomplish them, is the first function of management. Planning is a crucial activity, for it designs the map that lays the groundwork for the other functions. It involves forecasting events and determining the best course of action from a set of options or choices. The plan itself specifies what should be done, by whom, where, when, and how. For example, Toys "R" Us implemented a plan to refresh operations, strengthen customer experience, and improve its image. The plan—called "Tru Transformation"—is based on consumer research and vendor feedback. It aims to simplify stores and bring them back to profitability. The three major components of the plan are customers, inventory management, and cost management tactics. Stores will be redesigned with self-checkout lanes, wider aisles, and knowledgeable salespeople; product life-cycle management initiatives have begun allowing inventory to move more quickly; and pricing, discount, and promotional activities are being simplified and more targeted.[3] All businesses—from the smallest restaurant to the largest multinational corporation—need to develop plans for achieving success. But before an organization can plan a course of action, it must first determine what it wants to achieve.

规划
planning
the process of determining the organization's objectives and deciding how to accomplish them; the first function of management

使命
Mission. A **mission,** or mission statement, is a declaration of an organization's fundamental purpose and basic philosophy. It seeks to answer the question: "What business are we in?" Good mission statements are clear and concise statements that explain the organization's reason for existence. A well-developed mission statement, no matter what the industry or size of business, will answer five basic questions:

1. Who are we?
2. Who are our customers?
3. What is our operating philosophy (basic beliefs, values, ethics, etc.)?
4. What are our core competencies and competitive advantages?
5. What are our responsibilities with respect to being a good steward of environmental, financial, and human resources?

使命
mission
the statement of an organization's fundamental purpose and basic philosophy

FIGURE 3.1
The Functions of Management

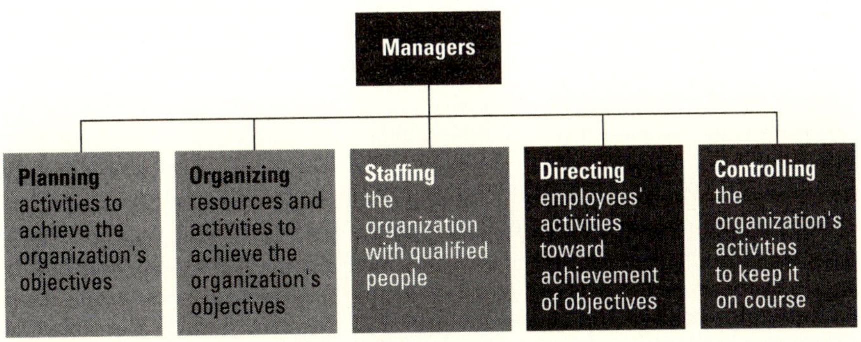

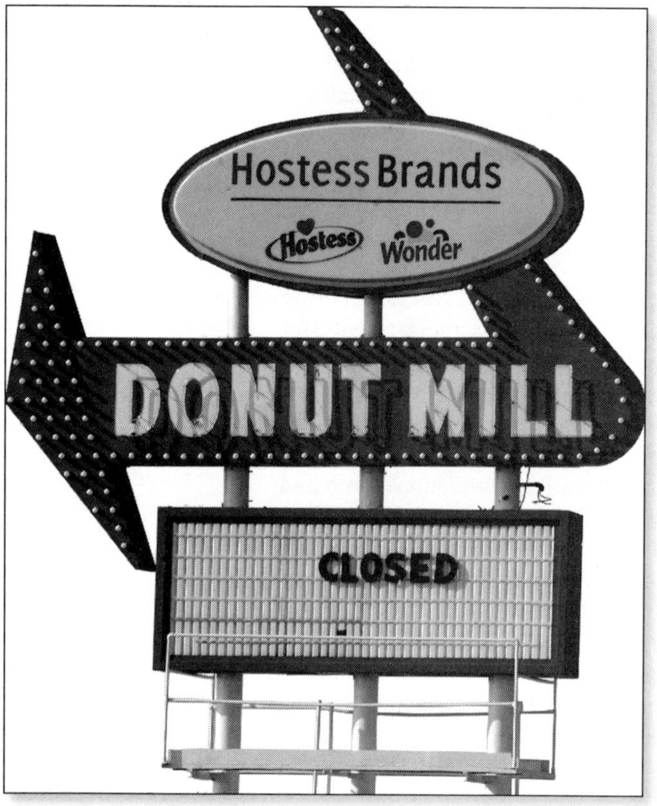

Private-equity firms Apollo Global Management and Metropoulos made the strategic plan to purchase the Hostess snack business after the firm declared bankruptcy.

A mission statement that delivers a clear answer to these questions provides the foundation for the development of a strong organizational culture, a good marketing plan, and a coherent business strategy. Sustainable cleaning products company Seventh Generation states that its mission is to "inspire a revolution that nurtures the health of the next seven generations."[4]

目的

Goals. A goal is the result that a firm wishes to achieve. A company almost always has multiple goals, which illustrates the complex nature of business. A goal has three key components: an attribute sought, such as profits, customer satisfaction, or product quality; a target to be achieved, such as the volume of sales or extent of management training to be achieved; and a time frame, which is the time period in which the goal is to be achieved. CVS Caremark, under CEO Larry J. Merlo, set the goal of becoming a health care provider. As a result, the organization announced it would no longer sell cigarettes because it fundamentally conflicts with the company's goal. Electronic cigarettes are also not sold at CVS because the harm they may cause consumers is still to be determined. To be successful, company goals should be specific. This allows for better decision making in organizations.[5] To be successful at achieving goals, it is necessary to know what is to be achieved, how much, when, and how succeeding at a goal is to be determined.

目标

Objectives. Objectives, the ends or results desired by an organization, derive from the organization's mission. A business's objectives may be elaborate or simple. Common objectives relate to profit, competitive advantage, efficiency, and growth. The principal difference between goals and objectives is that objectives are generally stated in such a way that they are measurable. Organizations with profit as an objective want to have money and assets left over after paying off business expenses. Objectives regarding competitive advantage are generally stated in terms of percentage of sales increase and market share, with the goal of increasing those figures. Efficiency objectives involve making the best use of the organization's resources. Dalhousie University has developed energy calculators for small and medium-sized businesses to help them become more aware of their energy usage and to reduce their energy expenditure. Growth objectives relate to an organization's ability to adapt and to get new products to the marketplace in a timely fashion. One of the most important objectives for businesses is sales. Nike, for example, has set its sales objectives for 2017 to reach $36 billion. In order to do this, it is putting effort into direct-to-consumer sales channels and using brick-and-mortar locations for testing new products.[6] Objectives provide direction for all managerial decisions; additionally, they establish criteria by which performance can be evaluated.

Herbalife does businesses in 90 countries, and contingency plans must often be made for fluctuating exchange rates.

计划

Plans. There are three general types of plans for meeting objectives—strategic, tactical, and operational. A firm's highest managers develop its **strategic plans,** which establish the long-range objectives and overall strategy or course of action by which the firm fulfills its mission. Strategic plans generally cover periods ranging from one year or longer. They include plans to add products, purchase companies, sell unprofitable segments of the business, issue stock, and move into international markets. For example, Sony decided to sell its unprofitable personal computer unit in order to mitigate against projected losses of up to $1.1 billion. Companies have been known to close U.S. plants and move manufacturing activities overseas when faced with stiff competition, rising costs, and slowing sales. However, many companies, including General Electric, Ford, and Whirlpool, are moving these activities back to the United States (an activity known as re-shoring) as transportation costs and wages in Asian countries rise.[7] Strategic plans must take into account the organization's capabilities and resources, the changing business environment, and organizational objectives. Plans should be market-driven, matching customers' desire for value with operational capabilities, processes, and human resources.[8]

战略计划
strategic plans
those plans that establish the long-range objectives and overall strategy or course of action by which a firm fulfills its mission

Tactical plans are short range and designed to implement the activities and objectives specified in the strategic plan. These plans, which usually cover a period of one year or less, help keep the organization on the course established in the strategic plan. Because tactical plans allow the organization to react to changes in the environment while continuing to focus on the company's overall strategy, management must periodically review and update them. Declining performance or failure to meet objectives set out in tactical plans may be one reason for revising them. The Michigan Department of Natural Resources Fisheries division developed a strategic plan to run through 2017. To implement this strategic plan, the department constructed a tactical plan with about 100 tasks to complete. For instance, a major goal of the tactical plan is to prevent the introduction of aquatic invasive species.[9] The differences between the two types of planning result in different activities in the short term versus the

战术计划
tactical plans
short-range plans designed to implement the activities and objectives specified in the strategic plan

long term. For instance, a strategic plan might include the use of social media to reach consumers. A tactical plan could involve finding ways to increase traffic to the site or promoting premium content to those who visit the site. A fast-paced and ever-changing market requires companies to develop short-run or tactical plans to deal with the changing environment.

A retailing organization with a five-year strategic plan to invest $5 billion in 500 new retail stores may develop five tactical plans (each covering one year) specifying how much to spend to set up each new store, where to locate, and when to open each new store. Tactical plans are designed to execute the overall strategic plan. Because of their short-term nature, they are easier to adjust or abandon if changes in the environment or the company's performance so warrant.

工作计划
operational plans very short-term plans that specify what actions individuals, work groups, or departments need to accomplish in order to achieve the tactical plan and ultimately the strategic plan

Operational plans are very short term and specify what actions specific individuals, work groups, or departments need to accomplish in order to achieve the tactical plan and ultimately the strategic plan. They apply to details in executing activities in one month, week, or even day. For example, a work group may be assigned a weekly production quota to ensure there are sufficient products available to elevate market share (tactical goal) and ultimately help the firm be number one in its product category (strategic goal). Returning to our retail store example, operational plans may specify the schedule for opening one new store, hiring and training new employees, obtaining merchandise, and opening for actual business.

危机管理（应急计划）
crisis management (contingency planning) an element in planning that deals with potential disasters such as product tampering, oil spills, fire, earthquake, computer virus, or airplane crash

Another element of planning is **crisis management** or **contingency planning,** which deals with potential disasters such as product tampering, oil spills, fire, earthquake, computer viruses, or even a reputation crisis due to unethical or illegal conduct by one or more employees. Unfortunately, many businesses do not have updated contingency plans to handle the types of crises that their companies might encounter. Approximately 51 percent of companies have outdated disaster recovery and business continuity plans.[10] Businesses that have correct and well-thought-out contingency plans tend to respond more effectively when problems occur than do businesses who lack such planning.

Many companies, including Ashland Oil, H. J. Heinz, and Johnson & Johnson, have crisis management teams to deal specifically with problems, permitting other managers to continue to focus on their regular duties. Some companies even hold periodic disaster drills to ensure that their employees know how to respond when a crisis does occur. After the horrific earthquake in Japan, many companies in U.S. earthquake zones reevaluated their crisis management plans. Crisis management plans generally cover maintaining business operations throughout a crisis and communicating with the public, employees, and officials about the nature of and the company's response to the problem. Communication is especially important to minimize panic and damaging rumors; it also demonstrates that the company is aware of the problem and plans to respond.

Sometimes disasters occur that no one can anticipate, but companies can still plan for how to react to the disaster. The investment company Fred Alger Management Inc. was one company that displayed exemplary disaster recovery planning. When the company's core investment team—including its president—was killed during the September 11 attacks (the office was located in the World Trade Center), the firm relied upon its employee assistance programs and a recovery office located in New Jersey to help weather the emergency. Ten years later, the successful company continues to maintain disaster recovery plans, such as an unoccupied office for emergencies and the use of vendors to back up essential data in case the company's own data are destroyed.[11] Incidents such as this highlight the importance of planning for crises and the need to respond publicly and quickly when a disaster occurs.

组织
Organizing

Rarely are individuals in an organization able to achieve common goals without some form of structure. **Organizing** is the structuring of resources and activities to accomplish objectives in an efficient and effective manner. Managers organize by reviewing plans and determining what activities are necessary to implement them; then, they divide the work into small units and assign it to specific individuals, groups, or departments. As companies reorganize for greater efficiency, more often than not, they are organizing work into teams to handle core processes such as new product development instead of organizing around traditional departments such as marketing and production. Organizing occurs continuously because change is inevitable.

组织
organizing
the structuring of resources and activities to accomplish objectives in an efficient and effective manner

Organizing is important for several reasons. It helps create synergy, whereby the effect of a whole system equals more than that of its parts. It also establishes lines of authority, improves communication, helps avoid duplication of resources, and can improve competitiveness by speeding up decision making. When Japanese consumer electronics firm Panasonic decided to reorganize its business, it reduced its workforce, formed overseas alliances to expand into new product areas such as industrial-use solar systems, and stopped investing in less profitable areas. Although eliminating jobs was a difficult move, Panasonic believed that it must reduce redundancies and streamline operations to create a more efficient business.[12] Because organizing is so important, we'll take a closer look at it in Chapter 4.

人员配置
Staffing

Once managers have determined what work is to be done and how it is to be organized, they must ensure that the organization has enough employees with appropriate skills to do the work. Hiring people to carry out the work of the organization is known as **staffing.** Beyond recruiting people for positions within the firm, managers must determine what skills are needed for specific jobs, how to motivate and train employees, how much to pay, what benefits to provide, and how to prepare employees for higher-level jobs in the firm at a later date.

人员配置
staffing
the hiring of people to carry out the work of the organization

裁员
downsizing
the elimination of a significant number of employees from an organization

Another aspect of staffing is **downsizing,** the elimination of significant numbers of employees from an organization, which has been a pervasive and much-talked-about trend. Staffing can be outsourced to companies that focus on hiring and managing employees. For instance, Collabera provides IT staffing and a range of services to both *Fortune* 500 companies and mid-sized companies across the globe. The company has also been named "Best Staffing Firm to Work For" for three consecutive years, citing excellence in teamwork, trust, effectiveness, and compensation and benefits.[13] Many firms downsize by outsourcing production, sales, and technical positions to companies in other countries with lower labor costs. Downsizing has helped numerous firms reduce costs quickly and become more profitable (or become profitable after lengthy losses) in a short period of time. Whether it is called downsizing, rightsizing, trimming the fat, or the new reality in business, the implications of downsizing have been dramatic. During the recent economic recession, many companies laid off workers to cut costs. The nationwide unemployment rate climbed above 10 percent, but after the recovery, unemployment dropped significantly.[14]

Downsizing and outsourcing, however, have painful consequences. Obviously, the biggest casualty is those who lose their jobs, along with their incomes, insurance, and pensions. Some find new jobs quickly; others do not. Another victim is the morale of the remaining employees at downsized firms. Those left behind often feel insecure,

Some companies choose to recruit people to hire through online job websites such as Monster.com. Monster.com is one of the world's largest employment websites. Using websites like Monster.com falls under the staffing function of management.

angry, and sad, and their productivity may decline as a result, the opposite of the effect sought. Studies have found that firms that lay off more than 10 percent of their surviving workforce can expect to see turnover increase to 15.5 percent versus 10.4 percent at firms that do not have layoffs.[15]

After a downsizing situation, an effective manager will promote optimism and positive thinking and minimize criticism and fault-finding. Management should also build teamwork and encourage positive group discussions. Honest communication is important during a time of change and will lead to trust. In reality, when departments are downsized, the remaining employees end up working harder to fill the gaps left by layoffs. Truthfulness about what has happened and about future expectations is essential.

指导
Directing

指导
directing
motivating and leading employees to achieve organizational objectives

Once the organization has been staffed, management must direct the employees. **Directing** is motivating and leading employees to achieve organizational objectives. Good directing involves telling employees what to do and when to do it through the implementation of deadlines, and then encouraging them to do their work. For example, as a sales manager, you would need to learn how to motivate salespersons; provide leadership; teach sales teams to be responsive to customer needs; and manage organizational issues as well as evaluate sales results. Finally, directing also involves determining and administering appropriate rewards and recognition. All managers are involved in directing, but it is especially important for lower-level managers who interact daily with the employees operating the organization. For example, an assembly-line supervisor for Frito-Lay must ensure that her workers know how to use their equipment properly and have the resources needed to carry out their jobs safely and efficiently, and she must motivate her workers to achieve their expected output of packaged snacks.

Managers may motivate employees by providing incentives—such as the promise of a raise or promotion—for them to do a good job. But most workers want more than money from their jobs: They need to know that their employer values their ideas and input. Managers should give younger employees some decision-making authority as soon as possible. Smart managers, therefore, ask workers to contribute ideas for reducing costs, making equipment more efficient, improving customer service, or even developing new products. For example, Rackspace, an IT hosting company, has made employee engagement a top priority to bring customer service to the highest level.[16] This participation makes workers feel important, and

Going Green

Ken Grossman's Management of Sierra Nevada's Growth

Ken Grossman, founder and CEO of Sierra Nevada Brewing Co., is familiar with the management challenges that accompany growth. Founded in 1980 in Chico, California, Sierra Nevada is now building another brewery in Mills River, North Carolina. This is a challenge to Grossman's management style because he is very involved in the day-to-day operations of the brewery. Walking around, talking to the company's 650 employees every day, and ensuring the quality of the brews are just a few of his managerial responsibilities.

Grossman also had to make the managerial decision to expand operations. The decision to expand was not merely driven by economic impetus, but also by environmental concerns. The new brewery will reduce the emissions the company creates in distribution. In addition, Grossman has installed 10,000 solar panels on the brewery in Chico, the largest private installation in the country, which accounts for 80 percent of its energy usage.

It is not all business for Grossman, however. He encourages employees to think like owners and takes a group of employees out to lunch with him every other week. This allows him to know people in the company on a personal level and establishes a mutual loyalty. Employees also receive subsidized meals at the brewery restaurant and day care, as well as a free health clinic for employees and their families.[17]

Questions for Discussion

1. Describe some of the managerial skills that Ken Grossman possesses in successfully leading Sierra Nevada.
2. How are the breweries increasing the firm's sustainability?
3. How does Ken Grossman motivate his employees?

the company benefits. Recognition and appreciation are often the best motivators. Employees who understand more about their effect on the financial success of the company may be induced to work harder for that success, and managers who understand the needs and desires of workers can encourage their employees to work harder and more productively.

控制
Controlling

Planning, organizing, staffing, and directing are all important to the success of an organization, whether its objective is earning a profit or something else. But what happens when a firm fails to reach its goals despite a strong planning effort? **Controlling** is the process of evaluating and correcting activities to keep the organization on course. Control involves five activities: (1) measuring performance, (2) comparing present performance with standards or objectives, (3) identifying deviations from the standards, (4) investigating the causes of deviations, and (5) taking corrective action when necessary.

控制
controlling
the process of evaluating and correcting activities to keep the organization on course

Controlling and planning are closely linked. Planning establishes goals and standards. By monitoring performance and comparing it with standards, managers can determine whether performance is on target. When performance is substandard, management must determine why and take appropriate actions to get the firm back on course. In short, the control function helps managers assess the success of their plans. You might relate this to your performance in this class. If you did not perform as well on early projects or exams, you must take corrective action such as increasing studying or using website resources to achieve your overall objective of getting an A or B in the course. When the outcomes of plans do not meet expectations, the control process facilitates revision of the plans. Control can take many forms such as visual inspections, testing, and statistical modeling processes. The basic idea is to ensure that operations meet requirements and are satisfactory to reach objectives.

The control process also helps managers deal with problems arising outside the firm. For example, if a firm is the subject of negative publicity, management should use the control process to determine why and to guide the firm's response.

管理的类型
Types of Management

LO 3-3

高层管理者
top managers
the president and other top executives of a business, such as the chief executive officer (CEO), chief financial officer (CFO), and chief operations officer (COO), who have overall responsibility for the organization

All managers—whether the sole proprietor of a jewelry store or the hundreds of managers of a large company such as Paramount Pictures—perform the five functions just discussed. In the case of the jewelry store, the owner handles all the functions, but in a large company with more than one manager, responsibilities must be divided and delegated. This division of responsibility is generally achieved by establishing levels of management and areas of specialization—finance, marketing, and so on.

管理层级
Levels of Management

As we have hinted, many organizations have multiple levels of management—top management, middle management, and first-line, or supervisory management. These levels form a pyramid, as shown in Figure 3.2. As the pyramid shape implies, there are generally more middle managers than top managers, and still more first-line managers. Very small organizations may have only one manager (typically, the owner), who assumes the responsibilities of all three levels. Large businesses have many managers at each level to coordinate the use of the organization's resources. Managers at all three levels perform all five management functions, but the amount of time they spend on each function varies, as we shall see (Figure 3.3).

John Hammergren, CEO of McKesson, is the highest paid CEO at $131.2 million.

高层管理

Top Management. In businesses, **top managers** include the president and other top executives, such as the chief executive officer (CEO), chief financial officer (CFO), and chief operations officer (COO), who have overall responsibility for the organization. For example, Mark Zuckerberg, CEO and founder of Facebook, manages the overall strategic direction of the company and plays a key role in representing the company to stakeholders. Sheryl Sandberg, Facebook's chief operating officer, is responsible for the daily operation of the company. The COO reports to the CEO and is often considered to be number two in command. In public corporations, even chief executive officers have a boss—the firm's board of directors. With technological advances accelerating and privacy concerns increasing, some companies are adding a new top management position—chief privacy officer (CPO). The position of privacy officer has grown so widespread that the International Association of Privacy Professionals boasts 14,000 members in 83 countries.[18] In government, top management refers to the president, a governor, or a mayor or city manager; in education, a chancellor of a university or a superintendent of education.

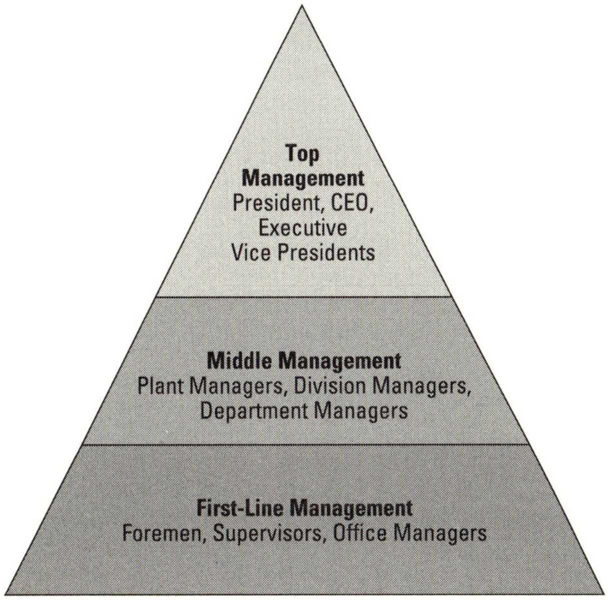

FIGURE 3.2
Levels of Management

Top-level managers spend most of their time planning. They make the organization's strategic decisions, decisions that focus on an overall scheme or key idea for using resources to take advantage of opportunities. They decide whether to add products, acquire companies, sell unprofitable business segments, and move into foreign markets. Top managers also represent their company to the public and to government regulators.

DID YOU KNOW? Only 4.6 percent of *Fortune* 500 CEOs are women.[19]

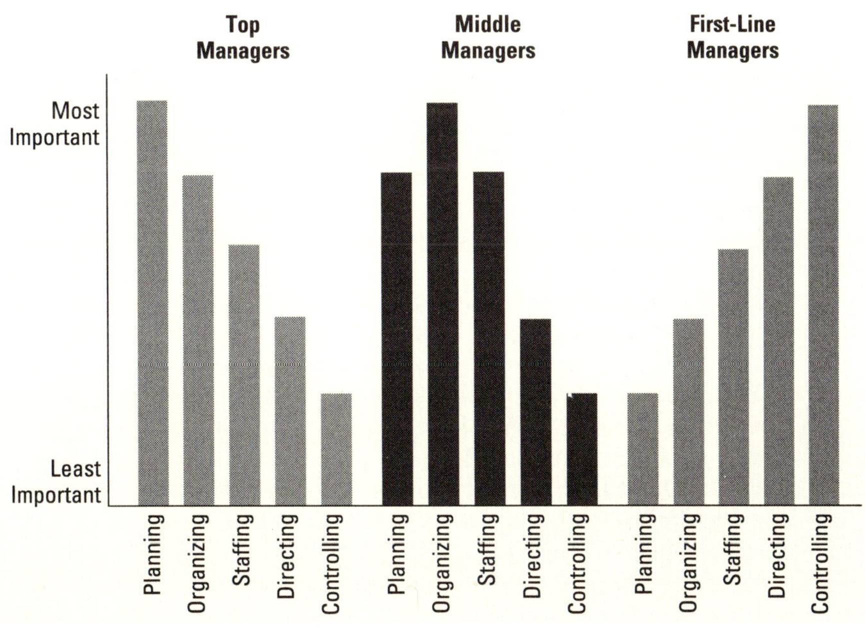

FIGURE 3.3
Importance of Management Functions to Managers in Each Level

TABLE 3.1
The Highest Paid CEOs

CEO	Company	Compensation*
Larry Ellison	Oracle	$78.4 million
Robert Iger	Walt Disney Productions	$34.3 million
Kenneth I. Chenault	American Express	$24.4 million
Randall L. Stephenson	Apple	$20.6 million
Muhtar Kent	Coca-Cola	$20.4 million
James P. Gorman	Morgan Stanley	$18 million
Meg Whitman	Hewlett-Packard	$17.6 million
Virginia Rometty	IBM	$13.97 million
Jeff Bezos	Amazon	$1.68 million
Warren Buffett	Berkshire Hathaway	$485,606

**2013 compensation results compiled from publicly available data.*

Given the importance and range of top managements' decisions, top managers generally have many years of varied experience and command top salaries. In addition to salaries, top managers' compensation packages typically include bonuses, long-term incentive awards, stock, and stock options. Table 3.1 lists the compensation packages of different CEOs. Top management may also get perks and special treatment that is criticized by stakeholders.

Compensation committees are increasingly working with boards of directors and CEOs to attempt to keep pay in line with performance in order to benefit stockholders and key stakeholders. The majority of major companies cite their concern about attracting capable leadership for the CEO and other top executive positions in their organizations. However, many firms are trying to curb criticism of excessive executive compensation by trying to align CEO compensation with performance. In other words, if the company performs poorly, the CEO will not be paid as well. This type of compensation method is making a difference. An analysis of CEO compensation of 46 companies in the Standard & Poor's 500 Index showed that the median increase in pay for 2013 amounted to 1 percent. This is compared to the year before when the increase was calculated at 15 percent.[20] Successful management translates into happy stockholders who are willing to compensate their top executives fairly and in line with performance.

Workforce diversity is an important issue in today's corporations. Effective managers at enlightened corporations have found that diversity is good for workers and for the bottom line. Putting together different kinds of people to solve problems often results in better solutions. Sodexo Inc. topped DiversityInc's list as the most diverse company of 2014. It has consistently been ranked on the list due to its corporate culture of inclusion and diversity and their priority as a part of the company's overall strategy.[21] A diverse workforce is better at making decisions regarding issues related to consumer diversity. Public relations agencies are working toward making their workforces more diverse with the help of special interest groups such as the Public Relations Society of America, PRSA Foundation, and the Council of Public Relations Firms. Reaching fast-growing demographic groups such as Hispanics, African

Rule	Action
1. Get everyone involved.	Educate all employees on the tangible benefits of diversity recruiting to garner support and enthusiasm for those initiatives.
2. Showcase your diversity.	Prospective employees are not likely to become excited about joining your company just because you say that your company is diversity-friendly; they need to see it.
3. Work with diversity groups within your community.	By supporting community-based diversity organizations, your company will generate the priceless word-of-mouth publicity that will lead qualified diversity candidates to your company.
4. Spend money.	If you are serious about diversity recruiting, you will need to spend some money getting your message out to the right places.
5. Sell, sell, sell—and measure your return on investment.	Employers need to sell their company to prospective diversity employees and present them with a convincing case as to why their company is a good fit for the diversity candidate.

Source: Adapted from Juan Rodriguez, "The Five Rules of Successful Diversity Recruiting," Diversityjobs.com.

TABLE 3.2
Five Rules of Successful Diversity Recruiting

Americans, Asian Americans, and others will be beneficial to large companies as they begin to target these markets.[22] Managers from companies devoted to workforce diversity devised five rules that make diversity recruiting work (see Table 3.2).

中层管理

Middle Management. Rather than making strategic decisions about the whole organization, **middle managers** are responsible for tactical planning that will implement the general guidelines established by top management. Thus, their responsibility is more narrowly focused than that of top managers. Middle managers are involved in the specific operations of the organization and spend more time organizing than other managers. In business, plant managers, division managers, and department managers make up middle management. The product manager for laundry detergent at a consumer products manufacturer, the department chairperson in a university, and the head of a state public health department are all middle managers. The ranks of middle managers have been shrinking as more and more companies downsize to be more productive.

一线管理

First-Line Management. Most people get their first managerial experience as **first-line managers,** those who supervise workers and the daily operations of the organization. They are responsible for implementing the plans established by middle management and directing workers' daily performance on the job. They spend most of their time directing and controlling. Common titles for first-line managers are foreman, supervisor, and office service manager.

管理的领域

Areas of Management

At each level, there are managers who specialize in the basic functional areas of business: finance, production and operations, human resources (personnel), marketing, and administration.

中层管理者
middle managers
those members of an organization responsible for the tactical planning that implements the general guidelines established by top management

一线管理者
first-line managers
those who supervise both workers and the daily operations of an organization

财务管理者
financial managers
those who focus on obtaining needed funds for the successful operation of an organization and using those funds to further organizational goals

生产运营管理者
production and operations managers
those who develop and administer the activities involved in transforming resources into goods, services, and ideas ready for the marketplace

人力资源管理者
human resources managers
those who handle the staffing function and deal with employees in a formalized manner

市场营销管理者
marketing managers
those who are responsible for planning, pricing, and promoting products and making them available to customers through distribution

信息技术（IT）管理者
information technology (IT) managers
those who are responsible for implementing, maintaining, and controlling technology applications in business, such as computer networks

Entrepreneurship in Action

Philip Pillsbury: The Entrepreneur behind the Billion-Dollar Brand

Pillsbury Company
Founder: Charles A. Pillsbury and John S. Pillsbury
Founded: 1872, in Minneapolis, Minnesota
Success: In its transition from commodities to consumer products, the Pillsbury Company became so successful that it was purchased by General Mills in 2001 for $10.5 billion.

Although Charles Pillsbury co-founded the successful Pillsbury Company, it was his grandson who led the company toward its status as a billion-dollar brand. In 1940, Philip Pillsbury became president of his grandfather's flour milling company. He had worked as a miller early in life and knew the industry. As the markets changed, Pillsbury's entrepreneurial instinct and management skills allowed him to transform the company's direction from commodities to consumer products.

Pillsbury was a visionary with strong conceptual skills who recognized growing opportunities in the consumer market. He targeted this market by investing in product research and development, resulting in product lines such as cake mixes and refrigerated rolls, biscuits, and cookies. He also infused the company's marketing with the Grand National Recipe & Baking Contest, which later became known as the annual Pillsbury Bake-Off. Influential judges—including Eleanor Roosevelt—drew the attention of 700,000 new customers. International expansion was also part of Pillsbury's strategy, and he implemented it with global acquisitions. By 1974, Pillsbury had increased the company's sales by seven times the 1940 level to $315 million.[23]

行政管理者
administrative managers those who manage an entire business or a major segment of a business; they are not specialists but coordinate the activities of specialized managers

Each of these management areas is important to a business's success. For instance, a firm cannot survive without someone obtaining needed financial resources (financial managers) or staff (human resources managers). While larger firms will most likely have all of these managers, and even more depending upon that particular firm's needs, in smaller firms these important tasks may fall onto the owner or a few employees. Yet whether or not companies have managers for specific areas, every company must have someone responsible for obtaining financial resources, transforming resources into finished products for the marketplace, hiring and/or dealing with staff, marketing products, handling the firm's information technology resources, and managing a business segment or the overall business. These different types of managers are discussed in more detail in Table 3.3.

TABLE 3.3 Areas of Management

Manager	Function
Financial manager	Focus on obtaining the money needed for the successful operation of the organization and using that money in accordance with organizational goals.
Production and operations manager	Develop and administer the activities involved in transforming resources into goods, services, and ideas ready for the marketplace.
Human resources manager	Handle the staffing function and deals with employees in a formalized manner.
Marketing manager	Responsible for planning, pricing, and promoting products and making them available to customers through distribution.
Information technology (IT) manager	Responsible for implementing, maintaining, and controlling technology applications in business, such as computer networks.
Administrative manager	Manage an entire business or a major segment of a business; do not specialize in a particular function.

TABLE 3.4 Managerial Roles

Type of Role	Specific Role	Examples of Role Activities
Decisional	Entrepreneur	Commit organizational resources to develop innovative goods and services; decide to expand internationally to obtain new customers for the organization's products.
	Disturbance handler	Move quickly to take corrective action to deal with unexpected problems facing the organization from the external environment, such as a crisis like an oil spill, or from the internal environment, such as producing faulty goods or services.
	Resource allocator	Allocate organizational resources among different functions and departments of the organization; set budgets and salaries of middle and first-level managers.
	Negotiator	Work with suppliers, distributors, and labor unions to reach agreements about the quality and price of input, technical, and human resources; work with other organizations to establish agreements to pool resources to work on joint projects.
Informational	Monitor	Evaluate the performance of managers in different functions and take corrective action to improve their performance; watch for changes occurring in the external and internal environment that may affect the organization in the future.
	Disseminator	Inform employees about changes taking place in the external and internal environment that will affect them and the organization; communicate to employees the organization's vision and purpose.
	Spokesperson	Launch a national advertising campaign to promote new goods and services; give a speech to inform the local community about the organization's future intentions.
Interpersonal	Figurehead	Outline future organizational goals to employees at company meetings; open a new corporate headquarters building; state the organization's ethical guidelines and the principles of behavior employees are to follow in their dealings with customers and suppliers.
	Leader	Provide an example for employees to follow; give direct commands and orders to subordinates; make decisions concerning the use of human and technical resources; mobilize employee support for specific organizational goals.
	Liaison	Coordinate the work of managers in different departments; establish alliances between different organizations to share resources to produce new goods and services.

Source: Gareth R. Jones and Jennifer M. George, Essentials of Contemporary Management *(Burr Ridge, IL: McGraw-Hill/Irwin, 2007, 3rd edition), p. 14.*

管理者需要的技能
Skills Needed by Managers

LO 3-4

Managers are typically evaluated using the metrics of how effective and efficient they are. Managing effectively and efficiently requires certain skills—technical expertise, conceptual skills, analytical skills, human relations skills and leadership. Table 3.4 describes some of the roles managers may fulfill.

专业技能
Technical Expertise

Managers need **technical expertise,** the specialized knowledge and training required to perform jobs related to their area of management. Accounting managers need to be able to perform accounting jobs, and production managers need to be able to perform production jobs. Although a production manager may not actually perform a job, he or she needs technical expertise to train employees, answer questions, provide guidance, and solve problems. Technical skills are most needed by first-line managers and are least critical to top-level managers.

专业技能
technical expertise the specialized knowledge and training needed to perform jobs that are related to particular areas of management

This financial manager of a city hedge fund analyzes data from financial charts. Financial managers are responsible for obtaining the necessary funding for organizations to succeed, both in the short term and in the long term.

概念化技能
Conceptual Skills

Conceptual skills, the ability to think in abstract terms, and to see how parts fit together to form the whole, are needed by all managers, but particularly top-level managers. Top management must be able to evaluate continually where the company will be in the future. Conceptual skills also involve the ability to think creatively. Recent scientific research has revealed that creative thinking, which is behind the development of many innovative products and ideas, including fiber optics and compact disks, can be learned. As a result, IBM, AT&T, GE, Hewlett-Packard, Intel, and other top U.S. firms hire creative consultants to teach their managers how to think creatively.

概念化技能
conceptual skills
the ability to think in abstract terms and to see how parts fit together to form the whole

分析技能
Analytical Skills

Analytical skills refer to the ability to identify relevant issues and recognize their importance, understand the relationships between them, and perceive the underlying causes of a situation. When managers have identified critical factors and causes, they can take appropriate action. All managers need to think logically, but this skill is probably most important to the success of top-level managers. To be analytical, it is necessary to think about a broad range of issues and to weigh different options before taking action. Because analytical skills are so important, questions that require analytical skills are often a part of job interviews. Questions such as "Tell me how you would resolve a problem at work if you had access to a large amount of data?" may be part of the interview process. The answer would require the interviewee to try to explain how to sort data to find relevant facts that could resolve the issue. Analytical thinking is required in complex or difficult situations where the solution is often not clear. Resolving ethical issues often requires analytical skills.

分析技能
analytical skills
the ability to identify relevant issues, recognize their importance, understand the relationships between them, and perceive the underlying causes of a situation

人际交往技能
Human Relations Skills

People skills, or **human relations skills,** are the ability to deal with people, both inside and outside the organization. Those who can relate to others, communicate well with others, understand the needs of others, and show a true appreciation for others are generally more successful than managers who lack such skills. People skills are especially important in hospitals, airline companies, banks, and other organizations that provide services. For example, Southwest Airlines places great value on its employees. New hires go through extensive training to teach employees about the airline and its reputation for impeccable customer service. All employees in management positions at Southwest take mandatory leadership classes that address skills related to listening, staying in touch with employees, and handling change without compromising values.

人际交往技能
human relations skills
the ability to deal with people, both inside and outside the organization

领导力
Leadership

Leadership is the ability to influence employees to work toward organizational goals. Strong leaders manage and pay attention to the culture of their organizations and the needs of their customers. Table 3.5 offers some tips for successful leadership.

领导力
leadership
the ability to influence employees to work toward organizational goals

Howard Schultz, CEO of Starbucks, has great human relations skills and leadership abilities, as demonstrated by his ability to relate to others. Under his leadership, Starbucks decided to offer health insurance to its part-time workers.

Managers often can be classified into three types based on their leadership style. *Autocratic leaders* make all the decisions and then tell employees what must be done and how to do it. They generally use their authority and economic rewards to get employees to comply with their directions. Martha Stewart is an example of an autocratic leader. She built up her media empire by paying close attention to every detail.[24] *Democratic leaders* involve their employees in decisions. The manager presents a

TABLE 3.5
Seven Tips for Successful Leadership

• Build effective and responsive interpersonal relationships.
• Communicate effectively—in person, print, e-mail, etc.
• Build the team and enable employees to collaborate effectively.
• Understand the financial aspects of the business.
• Know how to create an environment in which people experience positive morale and recognition.
• Lead by example.
• Help people grow and develop.

Source: Susan M. Heathfield, "Seven Tips About Successful Management," About.com.

connect

Need help understanding Leaders vs. Managers? Visit your Connect ebook video tab for a brief animated explanation.

situation and encourages his or her subordinates to express opinions and contribute ideas. The manager then considers the employees' points of view and makes the decision. Herb Kelleher, co-founder of Southwest Airlines, had a democratic leadership style. Under his leadership, employees were encouraged to discuss concerns and provide input.[25] *Free-rein leaders* let their employees work without much interference. The manager sets performance standards and allows employees to find their own ways to meet them. For this style to be effective, employees must know what the standards are, and they must be motivated to attain them. The free-rein style of leadership can be a powerful motivator because it demonstrates a great deal of trust and confidence in the employee. Warren Buffett, CEO of Berkshire Hathaway, exhibits free-rein leadership among the managers who run the company's various businesses.

The effectiveness of the autocratic, democratic, and free-rein styles depends on several factors. One consideration is the type of employees. An autocratic style of leadership is generally best for stimulating unskilled, unmotivated employees; highly skilled, trained, and motivated employees may respond better to democratic or free-rein leadership styles. Employees who have been involved in decision making generally require less supervision than those not similarly involved. Other considerations are the manager's abilities and the situation itself. When a situation requires quick decisions, an autocratic style of leadership may be best because the manager does not have to consider input from a lot of people. If a special task force must be set up to solve a quality-control problem, a normally democratic manager may give free rein to the task force.

Many managers, however, are unable to use more than one style of leadership. Some are incapable of allowing their subordinates to participate in decision making, let alone make any decisions. Thus, what leadership style is "best" depends on specific circumstances, and effective managers will strive to adapt their leadership style as circumstances warrant. Many organizations offer programs to develop goal leadership skills. When plans fail, very often leaders are held responsible for what goes wrong. For example, JCPenney Co.'s CEO Ron Johnson was booted out of the position after an unsuccessful attempt at turning the struggling company around. This came only 17 months after the company hired him to lead the company after a successful run at Apple.[26]

Another type of leadership style that has been gaining in popularity is authentic leadership. Authentic leadership is a bit different from the other three leadership styles because it is not exclusive. Both democratic and free-rein leaders could qualify as authentic leaders depending upon how they conduct themselves among stakeholders. Authentic leaders are passionate about the goals and mission of the company, display corporate values in the workplace, and form long-term relationships with stakeholders.[27] Kim Jordan of New Belgium Brewing is an authentic leader. As co-founder of the company, she helped develop the firm's core values and has ensured that everything New Belgium does aligns with these values.

While leaders might incorporate different leadership styles depending on the business and the situation, all leaders must be able to align employees behind a common vision to be effective.[28] Strong leaders also realize the value that employees can provide by participating in the firm's corporate culture. It is important that companies develop leadership training programs for employees. Because managers cannot oversee everything that goes on in the company, empowering employees to take more responsibility for their decisions can aid in organizational growth and productivity. Leadership training also enables a smooth transition when an executive or manager leaves the organization. For instance, when CEO Jim Skinner of McDonald's retired, he made sure the current chief operating officer had enough leadership experience to take over the position of CEO. While it is common for stock prices to drop whenever an effective leader leaves the organization, in this case investors seemed so reassured that the new leader was up to the task that stock prices hardly dropped when Skinner's resignation was announced.[29]

员工授权
Employee Empowerment

Businesses are increasingly realizing the benefits of participative corporate cultures characterized by employee empowerment. **Employee empowerment** occurs when employees are provided with the ability to take on responsibilities and make decisions about their jobs. Employee empowerment does not mean that managers are not needed. Managers are important for guiding employees, setting goals, making major decisions, and other responsibilities emphasized throughout this chapter. However, companies that have a participative corporate culture have been found to be beneficial because employees feel like they are taking an active role in the firm's success.

员工授权
employee empowerment when employees are provided with the ability to take on responsibilities and make decisions about their jobs

Leaders who wish to empower employees must adopt systems that support an employee's ability to provide input and feedback on company decisions. Employees must be encouraged to actively participate in decision making. While this might be simpler for some employees, other employees might find it difficult if they come from more of an autocratic or authoritarian background, where lower-level employees were discouraged from speaking up. Managers also might find it difficult to support a participative culture if they come from similar backgrounds. One of the best ways to overcome these challenges is through employee and managerial training. As mentioned earlier, employees should be trained in leadership skills, including teamwork, conflict resolution, and decision making. Managers should also be trained in ways to empower employees to make decisions while also guiding employees to challenging situations in which the right decision might not be so clear.[30]

A section on leadership would not be complete without a discussion of leadership in teams. In today's business world, decisions made by teams are becoming the norm. Employees at Zappos, for instance, often work in teams and are encouraged to make decisions that they believe will reinforce the company's mission and values. Teamwork has often been an effective way for encouraging employee empowerment. Although decision making in teams is collective, the most effective teams are those in which all employees are encouraged to contribute their ideas and recommendations. Because each employee can bring in his or her own unique insights, teams often result in innovative ideas or decisions that would not have been reached by only one or two people. However, truly empowering employees in team decision making can be difficult. It is quite common for more outspoken employees to dominate the team and engage in groupthink, in which team members go with the majority rather than what they think is the right decision. Training employees how to listen to one another and provide relevant feedback can help to prevent these common challenges. Another way is to rotate the team leader so that no one person can assume dominancy.[31]

决策制定
Decision Making

LO 3-5

Managers make many different kinds of decisions, such as the hours in a workday, which employees to hire, what products to introduce, and what price to charge for a product. Decision making is important in all management functions and at all levels, whether the decisions are on a strategic, tactical, or operational level.

Responding to Business Challenges

Managers Discover Benefits of Feminine Traits for Leadership

The collective idea of what it means to be a great leader is changing. In the past, successful leadership has often been associated with authoritative traits such as decisiveness, resilience, and confidence. These leaders tend to exude confidence and charisma, resulting in admiration and a desire to follow. However, over the past several years, the leadership landscape has been changing. Recurring scandals involving leaders and the widespread use of technology has increased the need for leadership traits such as integrity. Employees as well as consumers are placing a major emphasis on the values of leaders.

One study showed that traits increasingly desired in leaders include patience, flexibility, empathy, vulnerability, inclusiveness, generosity, and balance. Interestingly, all of these characteristics are generally considered to be feminine. While assertiveness and ambition—considered more masculine traits—remain important, leaders who have an emotional connection to their work, good listening skills, and generosity are now thought to be important for a successful firm. For instance, Oprah Winfrey, who has been described as a demanding but caring boss, and Whole Foods CEO John Mackey, who donates $100,000 every year toward a fund to help employees with personal struggles, have come to be highly admired. Leaders who exhibit these traits have been found to make more thoughtful decisions and have better relationships with their employees and customers, often resulting in successful company operations and profits.[32]

Discussion Questions

1. Why are some characteristics traditionally associated as feminine considered important for leadership?
2. Why might a lack of empathy create a significant disadvantage in leadership?
3. Describe ways in which Oprah Winfrey and John Mackey of Whole Foods demonstrate strong leadership characteristics.

A systematic approach using the following six steps usually leads to more effective decision making: (1) recognizing and defining the decision situation, (2) developing options to resolve the situation, (3) analyzing the options, (4) selecting the best option, (5) implementing the decision, and (6) monitoring the consequences of the decision (Figure 3.4).

识别和界定决策情形

Recognizing and Defining the Decision Situation

The first step in decision making is recognizing and defining the situation. The situation may be negative—for example, huge losses on a particular product—or positive—for example, an opportunity to increase sales.

Situations calling for small-scale decisions often occur without warning. Situations requiring large-scale decisions, however, generally occur after some warning signs.

FIGURE 3.4
Steps in the Decision-Making Process

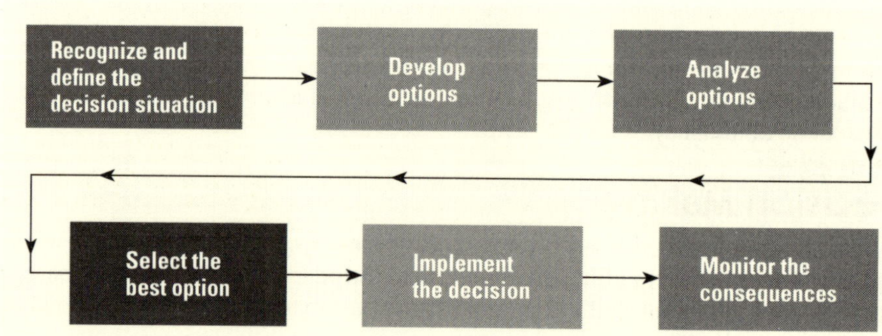

Effective managers pay attention to such signals. Declining profits, small-scale losses in previous years, inventory buildup, and retailers' unwillingness to stock a product are signals that may foreshadow huge losses to come. If managers pay attention to such signals, problems can be contained.

Once a situation has been recognized, management must define it. Losses reveal a problem—for example, a failing product. One manager may define the situation as a product quality problem; another may define it as a change in consumer preference. These two viewpoints may lead to vastly different solutions. The first manager, for example, may seek new sources of raw materials of better quality. The second manager may believe that the product has reached the end of its lifespan and decide to discontinue it. This example emphasizes the importance of carefully defining the problem rather than jumping to conclusions.

制订可选方案
Developing Options

Once the decision situation has been recognized and defined, the next step is to develop a list of possible courses of action. The best lists include both standard and creative plans. As a general rule, more time and expertise are devoted to the development stage of decision making when the decision is of major importance. When the decision is of less importance, less time and expertise will be spent on this stage. Options may be developed individually, by teams, or through analysis of similar situations in comparable organizations. Creativity is a very important part of selecting the most viable option. Creativity depends on new and useful ideas, regardless of where they originate or the method used to create them. The best option can range from a required solution to an identified problem or a volunteered solution, to an observed problem by an outside work group member.[33]

分析可选方案
Analyzing Options

After developing a list of possible courses of action, management should analyze the practicality and appropriateness of each option. An option may be deemed impractical because of a lack of financial resources, legal restrictions, ethical and social responsibility considerations, authority constraints, technological constraints, economic limitations, or simply a lack of information and expertise. For example, a small computer manufacturer may recognize an opportunity to introduce a new type of computer but lack the financial resources to do so. Other options may be more practical for the computer company: It may consider selling its technology to another computer company that has adequate resources, or it may allow itself to be purchased by a larger company that can introduce the new technology.

When assessing appropriateness, the decision maker should consider whether the proposed option adequately addresses the situation. When analyzing the consequences of an option, managers should consider its impact on the situation and on the organization as a whole. For example, when considering a price cut to boost sales, management must think about the consequences of the action on the organization's cash flow and consumers' reaction to the price change.

Technology can help managers maintain an agenda, analyze options, and make decisions.

选择最佳方案
Selecting the Best Option

When all courses of action have been analyzed, management must select the best one. Selection is often a subjective procedure because many situations do not lend themselves to quantitative analysis. Of course, it is not always necessary to select only one option and reject all others; it may be possible to select and use a combination of several options. William Wrigley Jr. made a decision to sell his firm to Mars for $23 billion. The firm was founded by his great-grandfather in 1891, but hard times forced Wrigley to take what was considered to be the best option. This option was to create the Mars-Wrigley firm, currently the world's largest confectionary company with a distribution network in 180 countries.[34] A different set of choices would have been available to the company had it been able to purchase Hershey for $12 billion a few years earlier.

执行决策
Implementing the Decision

To deal with the situation at hand, the selected option or options must be put into action. Implementation can be fairly simple or very complex, depending on the nature of the decision. Effective implementation of a decision to abandon a product, close a plant, purchase a new business, or something similar requires planning. For example, when a product is dropped, managers must decide how to handle distributors and customers and what to do with the idle production facility. Additionally, they should anticipate resistance from people within the organization. (People tend to resist change because they fear the unknown.) Finally, management should be ready to deal with the unexpected consequences. No matter how well planned implementation is, unforseen problems will arise. Management must be ready to address these situations when they occur.

监测效果
Monitoring the Consequences

After managers have implemented the decision, they must determine whether it has accomplished the desired result. Without proper monitoring, the consequences of decisions may not be known quickly enough to make efficient changes. If the desired result is achieved, management can reasonably conclude that it made a good choice. If the desired result is not achieved, further analysis is warranted. Was the decision simply wrong, or did the situation change? Should some other option have been implemented?

If the desired result is not achieved, management may discover that the situation was incorrectly defined from the beginning. That may require starting the decision-making process all over again. Finally, management may determine that the decision was good even though the desired results have not yet shown up, or it may determine a flaw in the decision's implementation. In the latter case, management would not change the decision but would change the way in which it is implemented.

实践中的管理
Management in Practice

Management is not a cut-and-dried process. There is no mathematical formula for managing an organization and achieving organizational goals, although many managers passionately wish for one! Managers plan, organize, staff, direct, and control, but management expert John P. Kotter says even these functions can be boiled down to two basic activities:

1. Figuring out what to do despite uncertainty, great diversity, and an enormous amount of potentially relevant information, and

2. Getting things done through a large and diverse set of people despite having little direct control over most of them.[35]

Managers spend as much as 75 percent of their time working with others—not only with subordinates but with bosses, people outside their hierarchy at work, and people outside the organization itself. In these interactions, they discuss anything and everything remotely connected with their business.

Managers spend a lot of time establishing and updating an agenda of goals and plans for carrying out their responsibilities. An **agenda** contains both specific and vague items, covering short-term goals and long-term objectives. Like a calendar, an agenda helps the manager figure out what must be done and how to get it done to meet the objectives set by the organization. Technology tools such as smartphones can help managers manage their agendas, contacts, communications, and time.

日程表
agenda
a calendar, containing both specific and vague items, that covers short-term goals and long-term objectives

建立关系网
networking
the building of relationships and sharing of information with colleagues who can help managers achieve the items on their agendas

Managers also spend a lot of time **networking**—building relationships and sharing information with colleagues who can help them achieve the items on their agendas. Managers spend much of their time communicating with a variety of people and participating in activities that on the surface do not seem to have much to do with the goals of their organization. Nevertheless, these activities are crucial to getting the job done. Networks are not limited to immediate subordinates and bosses; they include other people in the company as well as customers, suppliers, and friends. These contacts provide managers with information and advice on diverse topics. Managers ask, persuade, and even intimidate members of their network in order to get information and to get things done. Networking helps managers carry out their responsibilities. Social media sites have increased the ability of both managers and subordinates to network. Internal social networks such as Yammer allow employees to connect with one another, while social networks such as Facebook or Twitter enable managers to connect with customers. Sales managers are even using social networks to communicate with their distributors. LinkedIn has been used for job networking and is gaining in popularity among the younger generation as an alternative to traditional job hunting. Some speculate that social networks might eventually replace traditional résumés and job boards.[36]

Finally, managers spend a great deal of time confronting the complex and difficult challenges of the business world today. Some of these challenges relate to rapidly changing technology (especially in production and information processing), increased scrutiny of individual and corporate ethics and social responsibility, the impact of social media, the changing nature of the workforce, new laws and regulations, increased global competition and more challenging foreign markets, declining educational standards (which may limit the skills and knowledge of the future labor and customer pool), and time itself—that is, making the best use of it. But such diverse issues cannot simply be plugged into a computer program that supplies correct, easy-to-apply solutions. It is only through creativity and imagination that managers can make effective decisions that benefit their organizations.

Websites like LinkedIn are helping managers and employees network with one another to achieve their professional goals.

So You Want to Be a Manager

What Kind of Manager Do You Want to Be?

Managers are needed in a wide variety of organizations. Experts suggest that employment will increase by millions of jobs by 2016. But the requirements for the jobs become more demanding with every passing year—with the speed of technology and communication increasing by the day, and the stress of global commerce increasing pressures to perform. However, if you like a challenge and if you have the right kind of personality, management remains a viable field. Even as companies are forced to restructure, management remains a vital role in business. In fact, the Bureau of Labor Statistics predicts that management positions in public relations, marketing, and advertising are set to increase around 12 percent overall between 2006 and 2016. Financial managers will be in even more demand, with jobs increasing 13 percent in the same time period. Computer and IT managers will continue to be in strong demand, with the number of jobs increasing 16 percent between 2006 and 2016.[37]

Salaries for managerial positions remain strong overall. While pay can vary significantly depending on your level of experience, the firm where you work, and the region of the country where you live, below is a list of the nationwide average incomes for a variety of different managers:

Chief executive: $178,400
Computer and IT manager: $132,570
Marketing manager: $133,700
Financial manager: $126,660
General and operations manager: $116,090
Medical/health services manager: $101,340
Administrative services manager: $90,190
Human resources manager: $111,180
Sales manager: $123,150[38]

In short, if you want to be a manager, there are opportunities in almost every field. There may be fewer middle management positions available in firms, but managers remain a vital part of most industries and will continue to be long into the future—especially as navigating global business becomes ever more complex.

Review Your Understanding

Define management, and explain its role in the achievement of organizational objectives.

Management is a process designed to achieve an organization's objectives by using its resources effectively and efficiently in a changing environment. Managers make decisions about the use of the organization's resources and are concerned with planning, organizing, staffing, directing, and controlling the organization's activities so as to reach its objectives.

Describe the major functions of management.

Planning is the process of determining the organization's objectives and deciding how to accomplish them. Organizing is the structuring of resources and activities to accomplish those objectives efficiently and effectively. Staffing obtains people with the necessary skills to carry out the work of the company. Directing is motivating and leading employees to achieve organizational objectives. Controlling is the process of evaluating and correcting activities to keep the organization on course.

Distinguish among three levels of management and the concerns of managers at each level.

Top management is responsible for the whole organization and focuses primarily on strategic planning. Middle management develops plans for specific operating areas and carries out the general guidelines set by top management. First-line, or supervisory, management supervises the workers and day-to-day operations. Managers can also be categorized as to their area of responsibility: finance, production and operations, human resources, marketing, or administration.

Specify the skills managers need in order to be successful.

To be successful, managers need leadership skills (the ability to influence employees to work toward organizational goals), technical expertise (the specialized knowledge and training needed to perform a job), conceptual skills (the ability to think in abstract terms and see how parts fit together to form the whole), analytical skills (the ability to identify relevant issues and recognize their importance, understand the relationships between issues, and perceive the underlying causes of a situation), and human relations (people) skills.

Summarize the systematic approach to decision making used by many business managers.

A systematic approach to decision making follows these steps: recognizing and defining the situation, developing options, analyzing options, selecting the best option, implementing the decision, and monitoring the consequences.

Recommend a new strategy to revive a struggling business.

Using the decision-making process described in this chapter, analyze the struggling company's problems described in "Solve the Dilemma" on page 199 and formulate a strategy to turn the company around and aim it toward future success.

Revisit the World of Business

1. What are the challenges middle managers commonly face?
2. What are some good characteristics for effective middle managers to have?
3. Why are the job functions of middle management important to organizational success?

Learn the Terms

administrative managers
agenda
analytical skills
conceptual skills
controlling
crisis management or contingency planning
directing
downsizing
employee empowerment
financial managers
first-line managers
human relations skills
human resources managers
information technology (IT) managers
leadership
management
managers
marketing managers
middle managers
mission
networking
operational plans
organizing
planning
production and operations managers
staffing
strategic plans
tactical plans
technical expertise
top managers

Check Your Progress

1. Why is management so important, and what is its purpose?
2. Explain why the American Heart Association would need management, even though its goal is not profit related.
3. Why must a company have financial resources before it can use human and physical resources?
4. Name the five functions of management, and briefly describe each function.
5. Identify the three levels of management. What is the focus of managers at each level?
6. In what areas can managers specialize? From what area do top managers typically come?
7. What skills do managers need? Give examples of how managers use these skills to do their jobs.
8. What are three styles of leadership? Describe situations in which each style would be appropriate.
9. Explain the steps in the decision-making process.
10. What is the mathematical formula for perfect management? What do managers spend most of their time doing?

Get Involved

1. Give examples of the activities that each of the following managers might be involved in if he or she worked for the Coca-Cola Company:

   Financial manager
   Production and operations manager
   Personnel manager
   Marketing manager
   Administrative manager
   Information technology manager
   Foreman

2. Interview a small sample of managers, attempting to include representatives from all three levels and all areas of management. Discuss their daily activities and relate these activities to the management functions of planning, organizing, staffing, directing, and controlling. What skills do the managers say they need to carry out their tasks?

3. You are a manager of a firm that manufactures conventional ovens. Over the past several years, sales of many of your products have declined; this year, your losses may be quite large. Using the steps of the decision-making process, briefly describe how you arrive at a strategy for correcting the situation.

Build Your Skills

Functions of Management

Background

Although the text describes each of the five management functions separately, you learned that these five functions are interrelated, and managers sometimes perform two or more of them at the same time. Here you will broaden your perspective of how these functions occur simultaneously in management activities.

Task

1. Imagine that you are the manager in each scenario described in the following table and you have to decide which management function(s) to use in each.
2. Mark your answers using the following codes:

Codes	Management Functions
P	Planning
O	Organizing
S	Staffing
D	Directing
C	Controlling

No.	Scenario	Answer(s)
1	Your group's work is centered on a project that is due in two months. Although everyone is working on the project, you have observed your employees involved in what you believe is excessive socializing and other time-filling behaviors. You decide to meet with the group to have them help you break down the project into smaller subprojects with mini-deadlines. You believe this will help keep the group members focused on the project and that the quality of the finished project will then reflect the true capabilities of your group.	
2	Your first impression of the new group you'll be managing is not too great. You tell your friend at dinner after your first day on the job: "Looks like I got a baby sitting job instead of a management job."	
3	You call a meeting of your work group and begin it by letting them know that a major procedure used by the work group for the past two years is being significantly revamped, and your department will have to phase in the change during the next six weeks. You proceed by explaining to them the reasoning your boss gave you for this change. You then say, "Let's take the next 5 to 10 minutes to let you voice your reactions to this change." After 10 minutes elapse with the majority of comments being critical of the change, you say: "I appreciate each of you sharing your reactions; and I, too, recognize that *all* change creates problems. The way I see it, however, is that we can spend the remaining 45 minutes of our meeting focusing on why we don't want the change and why we don't think it's necessary; or we can work together to come up with viable solutions to solve the problems that implementing this change will most likely create." After about five more minutes of comments being exchanged, the consensus of the group is that the remainder of the meeting needs to be focused on how to deal with the potential problems the group anticipates having to deal with as the new procedure is implemented.	
4	You are preparing for the annual budget allocation meetings to be held in the plant manager's office next week. You are determined to present a strong case to support your department getting money for some high-tech equipment that will help your employees do their jobs better. You will stand firm against any suggestions of budget cuts in your area.	

5	Early in your career, you learned an important lesson about employee selection. One of the nurses on your floor unexpectedly quit. The other nurses were putting pressure on you to fill the position quickly because they were overworked even before the nurse left, and then things were really bad. After a hasty recruitment effort, you made a decision based on insufficient information. You ended up regretting your quick decision during the three months of problems that followed until you finally had to discharge the new hire. Since then, you have never let anybody pressure you into making a quick hiring decision.	

Solve the Dilemma LO 3-6

Making Infinity Computers Competitive

Infinity Computers Inc. produces notebook computers, which it sells through direct mail catalog companies under the Infinity name and in some retail computer stores under their private brand names. Infinity's products are not significantly different from competitors', nor do they have extra product-enhancing features, although they are very price competitive. The strength of the company has been its CEO and president, George Anderson, and a highly motivated, loyal workforce. The firm's weakness is having too many employees and too great a reliance on one product. The firm switched to computers with the Intel Core i5 processors after it saw a decline in its netbook computer sales.

Recognizing that the strategies that initially made the firm successful are no longer working effectively, Anderson wants to reorganize the company to make it more responsive and competitive and to cut costs. The threat of new technological developments and current competitive conditions could eliminate Infinity.

Discussion Questions

1. Evaluate Infinity's current situation and analyze its strengths and weaknesses.
2. Evaluate the opportunities for Infinity, including using its current strategy, and propose alternative strategies.
3. Suggest a plan for Infinity to compete successfully over the next 10 years.

Build Your Business Plan

The Nature of Management

The first thing you need to be thinking about is "What is the mission of your business? What is the shared vision your team members have for this business? How do you know if there is demand for this particular business?" Remember, you need to think about the customer's *ability and willingness* to try this particular product.

Think about the various processes or stages of your business in the creation and selling of your good, or service. What functions need to be performed for these processes to be completed? These functions might include buying, receiving, selling, customer service, and/or merchandising.

Operationally, if you are opening up a retail establishment, how do you plan to provide your customers with superior customer service? What hours will your customers expect you to be open? At this point in time, how many employees are you thinking you will need to run your business? Do you (or one of your partners) need to be there all the time to supervise?

See for Yourself Videocase

Planning Drives the Success of Ford Fusion

The release of the Ford Fusion was the culmination of six years of planning, implementation, and monitoring. Before the process began, top managers established the mission for the new vehicle as "the most talked about car of 2012." This guided the strategic plan during various levels of the project. The three goals for driving this strategy were to (1) become the company's highest volume car in order to gain market share, (2) offer customers unparalleled levels of choice, and (3) have green offerings.

When Alan Mulally became CEO, he instituted the One Ford Strategy. The One Ford Strategy unites the operations of the company through four clear objectives. The first objective involves having the ability to adapt to the current status of demand and change the model mix to achieve operational profitability. The second focuses on the rate of new product development while keeping customers' wants and values in mind. The third objective aims toward the improvement of financial planning. The final objective is focused on teamwork. This plan has helped the company focus their efforts and work together through a single approach toward the same goals. The plan also encourages measuring activities based on customer satisfaction and the happiness of employees and business partners. This allows the company to create high-quality, environmentally friendly, safe, and smart vehicles; create a durable and stable business; and contribute to the improvement of the world through sustainability efforts.

The One Ford Plan facilitated the collaboration between marketing and product development for the Ford Fusion project. This ensured the final product was cohesive both in design and market positioning. This collaboration was especially important to the execution of tactical plans for this project. The tactical plans focused on suppliers, design, parts needed, and marketing plans (channels that would be used, which audience would be targeted, and the determination of communication objectives). Furthermore, the team developed plans for potential capacity issues such as shutdowns or ramp-ups, as well as for scenarios in which there would be an over- or undersupply.

It is not enough to simply create plans—measuring the effects of a plan is imperative to successful execution. Ford uses a system called Launch Readiness, which began about two years before the launch with phase 1 or LR1. For example, Ford's marketing department measured consumer interest months before the Fusion was introduced onto the market by holding events and using "Build and Price" on Ford.com. This allowed customers to log on to the website and choose features, colors, and prices of the new vehicle. The company measured customer interest by determining how many people logged onto to the website and used Build and Price. The Fusion generated 1.6 million interactions, which was significantly more interest than any other vehicle generated. This phase also measured the various aspects of quality present in suppliers, design, and parts.

The operational part of planning is encompassed by LR2, the next phase in Launch Readiness. This phase focuses on execution and is informed by the previous phase. Details on the specifics of plans are established and refined, such as what events the company will attend and how they will use Facebook. This phase precedes the Final Status Review. Each of these phases serves as an overall control process for the entire project, and all phases are considered to be milestones that determine the project's progress.

The results of the Ford Fusion launch exceeded the company's aggressive expectations, and these significant results can be attributed to the level of planning the company engaged in. The Ford Fusion became one of the company's best-selling vehicles, second only to the popular F-150 pickup truck. The company also achieved another one of its goals by gaining two points in market share as a result of its new product launch. This is especially significant as a successful gain in market share in the automobile industry is one-tenth of a percentage point.

The Ford Fusion became one of the most popular vehicles in the mid-sized sedan segment because it offered consumers more luxury and choices than were previously available. They were able to choose from four different types of engines and two types of transmissions (6-speed automatic or manual). The Fusion also propelled the company toward one of its long-term strategic goals to offer economically friendly vehicles, which Ford has continued to introduce to the market.[39]

Discussion Questions

1. How did Ford use strategic and tactical planning in its launch of the Ford Fusion?
2. How did the companywide One Ford Plan contribute to the project-specific Launch Readiness plan?
3. What was the role of implementation in the success of the Ford Fusion?

You can find the related video in the Video Library in Connect. Ask your instructor how you can access Connect.

Team Exercise

Form groups and assign the responsibility of locating examples of crisis management implementation for companies dealing with natural disasters (explosions, fires, earthquakes, etc.), technology disasters (viruses, plane crashes, compromised customer data, etc.), or ethical or legal disasters. How did these companies communicate with key stakeholders? What measures did the company take to provide support to those involved in the crisis? Report your findings to the class.

4 Organization, Teamwork, and Communication

组织、团队和沟通

Learning Objectives

After reading this chapter, you will be able to:

- **LO 4-1** Define organizational structure, and relate how organizational structures develop.
- **LO 4-2** Describe how specialization and departmentalization help an organization achieve its goals.
- **LO 4-3** Determine how organizations assign responsibility for tasks and delegate authority.
- **LO 4-4** Compare and contrast some common forms of organizational structure.
- **LO 4-5** Distinguish between groups and teams, and identify the types of groups that exist in organizations.
- **LO 4-6** Describe how communication occurs in organizations.
- **LO 4-7** Analyze a business's use of teams.

Chapter Outline

Introduction
Organizational Culture
Developing Organizational Structure
Assigning Tasks
Specialization
Departmentalization
Assigning Responsibility
Delegation of Authority
Degree of Centralization
Span of Management
Organizational Layers
Forms of Organizational Structure
Line Structure
Line-and-Staff Structure
Multidivisional Structure
Matrix Structure
The Role of Groups and Teams in Organizations
Committees
Task Forces
Teams
Communicating in Organizations
Formal Communication
Informal Communication Channels
Monitoring Communications
Improving Communication Effectiveness

进入商业世界
Enter the World of Business

车美仕采用分权式组织结构加强团队合作
CarMax Uses Decentralized Structure to Support Teamwork

In 1991, some executives from Circuit City decided to test-launch a new business idea for a used car company termed Project X. Two years later, CarMax was officially launched. CarMax makes it a priority to develop satisfied employees. The company has a decentralized structure where employees are encouraged to submit recommendations and develop leadership skills. Over the past 20 years, CarMax has grown to 119 stores with 18,000 employees. In 2013, CarMax was listed as one of *Fortune's* Best Companies to Work For.

CarMax uses RFID technology to track how long cars sit in the lot, extensive sales data to determine inventory needs accurately, and a flat commission compensation system so salespeople will promote the cars that best meet customer needs rather than trying to sell the most expensive car.

Tom Folliard, the CEO of CarMax, learned that developing a decentralized corporate culture focusing on teamwork and employee empowerment generates positive results. CarMax prides itself on being founded on fundamental principles that every store must abide by. Values include respect, communication, customer focus, and teamwork. CarMax believes that employees who work together are able to place the customer first and serve their best interests. Folliard stays accessible for employees through town hall meetings and steak cookouts.

With this type of company culture, employees are able to feel a sense of ownership and high levels of contribution to the company. This allows for employees to hold themselves to higher standards, resulting in higher work performance. In an industry that has a certain stigma about car salespeople, CarMax's focus of empowering employees to provide quality customer service and take ownership of the company has revolutionized the used car industry.[1]

引言
Introduction

An organization's structure determines how well it makes decisions and responds to problems, and it influences employees' attitudes toward their work. A suitable structure can minimize a business's costs and maximize its efficiency. Even companies that operate within the same industry may utilize different organizational structures. For example, in the consumer electronics industry, Samsung is organized as a conglomerate with separate business units or divisions. Samsung is largely decentralized. Apple, under CEO Tim Cook, has moved from a hierarchical structure to a more collaborative approach between divisions.[2]

Because a business's structure can so profoundly affect its success, this chapter will examine organizational structure in detail. First, we discuss how an organization's culture affects its operations. Then we consider the development of structure, including how tasks and responsibilities are organized through specialization and departmentalization. Next, we explore some of the forms organizational structure may take. Finally, we consider communications within business.

企业文化
Organizational Culture

企业文化
organizational culture
a firm's shared values, beliefs, traditions, philosophies, rules, and role models for behavior

One of the most important aspects of organizing a business is determining its **organizational culture,** a firm's shared values, beliefs, traditions, philosophies, rules, and role models for behavior. Also called corporate culture, an organizational culture exists in every organization, regardless of size, organizational type, product, or profit objective. Sometimes behaviors, programs, and policies enhance and support the organizational culture. Netflix, for example, established a "freedom and responsibility culture," which has become a culture code many Silicon Valley companies have used as a template for establishing their organizational cultures. One way Netflix expresses this culture is by not having a vacation policy. Employees are expected to be responsible and disciplined while working, and in exchange, they are allowed the freedom to take vacation when they like and for as long as they like.[3] A firm's culture may be expressed formally through its mission statement, codes of ethics, memos, manuals, and ceremonies, but it is more commonly expressed informally. Examples of informal expressions of culture include dress codes (or the lack thereof), work habits, extracurricular activities, and stories. Employees often learn the accepted standards through discussions with co-workers.

TOMS Shoes' organizational culture is determined by the founder's desire to provide as many shoes as possible to children in developing countries (where shoeless children walk for miles to get water, food, and medical care). Blake Mycoskie gives hundreds of thousands of shoes to children around the world each year, creating a strong organizational culture of giving back and corporate social responsibility. His company operates with a program that for every pair of shoes purchased, a pair will be donated to children in need.[4] Disneyland/DisneyWorld and McDonald's have organizational cultures focused on cleanliness, value, and service. The company Zappos.com created a culture of "fun and a little weirdness." The company has a flexible work environment with very few rules, and employees are encouraged to socialize and engage in unique activities (such as ringing cowbells when visitors arrive). Zappos' goal is to make both employees and customers feel good. Customer service is such a must at Zappos that new hires must work for one month at a call center, even if the new employees are not going to be interacting with customers normally.[5] When such values

Responding to Business Challenges

Companies Embracing Greater Employee Interaction

Getting rid of cubicles, creating inconvenient work spaces, and eliminating work-from-home programs are some of the methods being used by companies to increase collaboration, communication, and teamwork. Yahoo! and Best Buy, for example, have eliminated their work-from-home programs to increase face-to-face interaction among employees. Studies have shown that employee interaction leads to more innovative ideas.

Google and Zappos are among those companies taking the lead in using their space to encourage collaboration and innovation. Both are designing new buildings with smaller workspaces and break rooms and narrower hallways so employees will see each other more often and have more opportunity for chance discussions. Zappos CEO Tony Hsieh is purposefully designing inconvenience into the new Zappos headquarters so that employees will have to interact with one another. Campbell's Soup is removing cubicles and installing more common spaces to increase employee teamwork and problem-solving.

Other companies are installing interactive devices in elevators where silence is usually the norm. Salesforce.com is installing a lunch button kiosk. Employees can push a button on the kiosk, and the kiosk matches a fellow co-worker that shares a common interest with the employee. The employee can then invite that person to lunch—and a new relationship is formed. This increase in interaction is anticipated to improve communication and relationships in companies.[6]

Discussion Questions

1. Describe methods some companies are using to increase employee interaction.
2. Why is it important that employees interact with one another?
3. Do you feel that the disadvantages of work-from-home programs are higher than their benefits?

and philosophies are shared by all members of an organization, they will be expressed in its relationships with stakeholders. However, organizational cultures that lack such positive values may result in employees who are unproductive and indifferent and have poor attitudes, which will be reflected externally to customers. The corporate culture may have contributed to the misconduct at a number of well-known companies. A survey found that executives in financial and technology companies are mostly cut-throat in collecting intelligence about competition, creating a corporate culture in which unethical acts might be tolerated if it means beating the competition.[7]

Organizational culture helps ensure that all members of a company share values and suggests rules for how to behave and deal with problems within the organization. Table 4.1 confirms that executives in this study believe that corporate culture has a significant impact on organizational performance and the ability to retain good employees. The key to success in any organization is satisfying stakeholders, especially customers. Establishing a positive organizational culture sets the tone for all other decisions, including building an efficient organizational structure.

The organizational structure at TOMS Shoes consists of two parts. The for-profit component of the company manages overall operations. Its nonprofit component, Friends of TOMS, is responsible for volunteer activities and shoe donations.

TABLE 4.1
Attitudes and Behaviors Associated with Corporate Cultures

	Employees Who View Their Culture Negatively	Employees Who View Their Culture Positively
Committed toward organization	17%	86%
Satisfied with organization	13	87
Likely to recommend their organization to others	13	88
Intend to leave the organizations	63	10
Alignment with leadership	8	59

N = 236 management and human resources professionals from U.S. companies with more than 100 employees.

Source: Survey conducted by Critical Metrics LLC, CR Magazine *3, June 2012.*

LO 4-1

制定组织结构
Developing Organizational Structure

结构
structure
the arrangement or relationship of positions within an organization

Structure is the arrangement or relationship of positions within an organization. Rarely is an organization, or any group of individuals working together, able to achieve common objectives without some form of structure, whether that structure is explicitly defined or only implied. A professional baseball team such as the Colorado Rockies is a business organization with an explicit formal structure that guides the team's activities so that it can increase game attendance, win games, and sell souvenirs such as T-shirts. But even an informal group playing softball for fun has an organization that specifies who will pitch, catch, bat, coach, and so on. Governments and nonprofit organizations also have formal organizational structures to facilitate the achievement of their objectives. Getting people to work together efficiently and coordinating the skills of diverse individuals require careful planning. Developing appropriate organizational structures is therefore a major challenge for managers in both large and small organizations.

An organization's structure develops when managers assign work tasks and activities to specific individuals or work groups and coordinate the diverse activities required to reach the firm's objectives. When Macy's, for example, has a sale, the store manager must work with the advertising department to make the public aware of the sale, with department managers to ensure that extra salespeople are scheduled to handle the increased customer traffic, and with merchandise buyers to ensure that enough sale merchandise is available to meet expected consumer demand. All the people occupying these positions must work together to achieve the store's objectives.

The best way to begin to understand how organizational structure develops is to consider the evolution of a new business such as a clothing store. At first, the business is a sole proprietorship in which the owner does everything—buys, prices, and displays the merchandise; does the accounting and tax records; and assists customers. As the business grows, the owner hires a salesperson and perhaps a merchandise buyer to help run the store. As the business continues to grow, the owner hires more salespeople. The growth and success of the business now require the owner to be away from the store frequently, meeting with suppliers, engaging in public relations, and attending trade shows. Thus, the owner must designate someone to manage the salespeople and maintain the accounting, payroll, and tax functions. If the owner decides to expand by opening more stores, still more managers will be needed. Figure 4.1 shows these stages of growth with three **organizational charts** (visual displays of organizational structure, chain of command, and other relationships).

组织结构图
organizational chart
a visual display of the organizational structure, lines of authority (chain of command), staff relationships, permanent committee arrangements, and lines of communication

FIGURE 4.1 The Evolution of a Clothing Store, Phases 1, 2, and 3

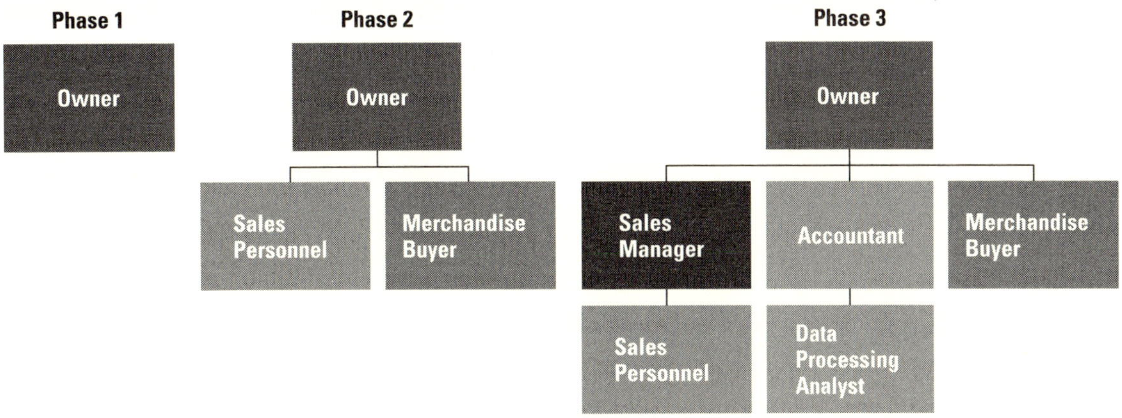

Growth requires organizing—the structuring of human, physical, and financial resources to achieve objectives in an effective and efficient manner. Growth necessitates hiring people who have specialized skills. With more people and greater specialization, the organization needs to develop a formal structure to function efficiently. Imagine the various organizational changes that Nokia has undergone. It was founded in 1865 as a paper mill in Finland and has become a global telecommunications company serving more than 1 billion customers. During its history, the company has transformed itself various times—including as a rubber company, television maker, and a cable company—each time changing the organizational structure to accommodate its business.[8] As we shall see, structuring an organization requires that management assign work tasks to specific individuals and departments and assign responsibility for the achievement of specific organizational objectives.

任务的分配
Assigning Tasks

LO 4-2

For a business to earn profits from the sale of its products, its managers must first determine what activities are required to achieve its objectives. At Celestial Seasonings, for example, employees must purchase herbs from suppliers, dry the herbs and place them in tea bags, package and label the tea, and then ship the packages to grocery stores around the country. Other necessary activities include negotiating with supermarkets and other retailers for display space, developing new products, planning advertising, managing finances, and managing employees. All these activities must be coordinated, assigned to work groups, and controlled. Two important aspects of assigning these work activities are specialization and departmentalization.

专业化
Specialization

After identifying all activities that must be accomplished, managers then break these activities down into specific tasks that can be handled by individual employees. This division of labor into small, specific tasks and the assignment of employees to do a single task is called **specialization.**

专业化
specialization
the division of labor into small, specific tasks and the assignment of employees to do a single task

Job specialization is common in automobile manufacturing. By dividing work into smaller specialized tasks, employees can perform their work more quickly and efficiently.

The rationale for specialization is efficiency. People can perform more efficiently if they master just one task rather than all tasks. In *The Wealth of Nations,* 18th-century economist Adam Smith discussed specialization, using the manufacture of straight pins as an example. Individually, workers could produce 20 pins a day when each employee produced complete pins. Thus, 10 employees working independently of each other could produce 200 pins a day. However, when one worker drew the wire, another straightened it, a third cut it, and a fourth ground the point, 10 workers could produce 48,000 pins per day.[9] To save money and achieve the benefits of specialization, some companies outsource and hire temporary workers to provide key skills. Many highly skilled, diverse, experienced workers are available through temp agencies.

Specialization means workers do not waste time shifting from one job to another, and training is easier. However, efficiency is not the only motivation for specialization. Specialization also occurs when the activities that must be performed within an organization are too numerous for one person to handle. Recall the example of the clothing store. When the business was young and small, the owner could do everything; but when the business grew, the owner needed help waiting on customers, keeping the books, and managing other business activities.

Overspecialization can have negative consequences. Employees may become bored and dissatisfied with their jobs, and the result of their unhappiness is likely to be poor quality work, more injuries, and high employee turnover. In extreme cases, employees in crowded specialized electronic plants are unable to form working relationships with one another. At Foxconn, a multinational electronics manufacturing firm and one of the suppliers of Apple iPhones and iPads, lack of working relationships, long work hours, low pay, and other conditions resulted in employee dissatisfaction and, tragically, depression and even suicide.[10] This is why some manufacturing firms allow job rotation so that employees do not become dissatisfied and leave. Although some degree of specialization is necessary for efficiency, because of differences in skills, abilities, and interests, all people are not equally suited for all jobs.

部门化
Departmentalization

部门化
departmentalization
the grouping of jobs into working units usually called departments, units, groups, or divisions

After assigning specialized tasks to individuals, managers next organize workers doing similar jobs into groups to make them easier to manage. **Departmentalization** is the grouping of jobs into working units usually called departments, units, groups, or divisions. As we shall see, departments are commonly organized by function, product, geographic region, or customer (Figure 4.2). Most companies use more than one departmentalization plan to enhance productivity. For instance, many consumer

FIGURE 4.2 **Departmentalization**

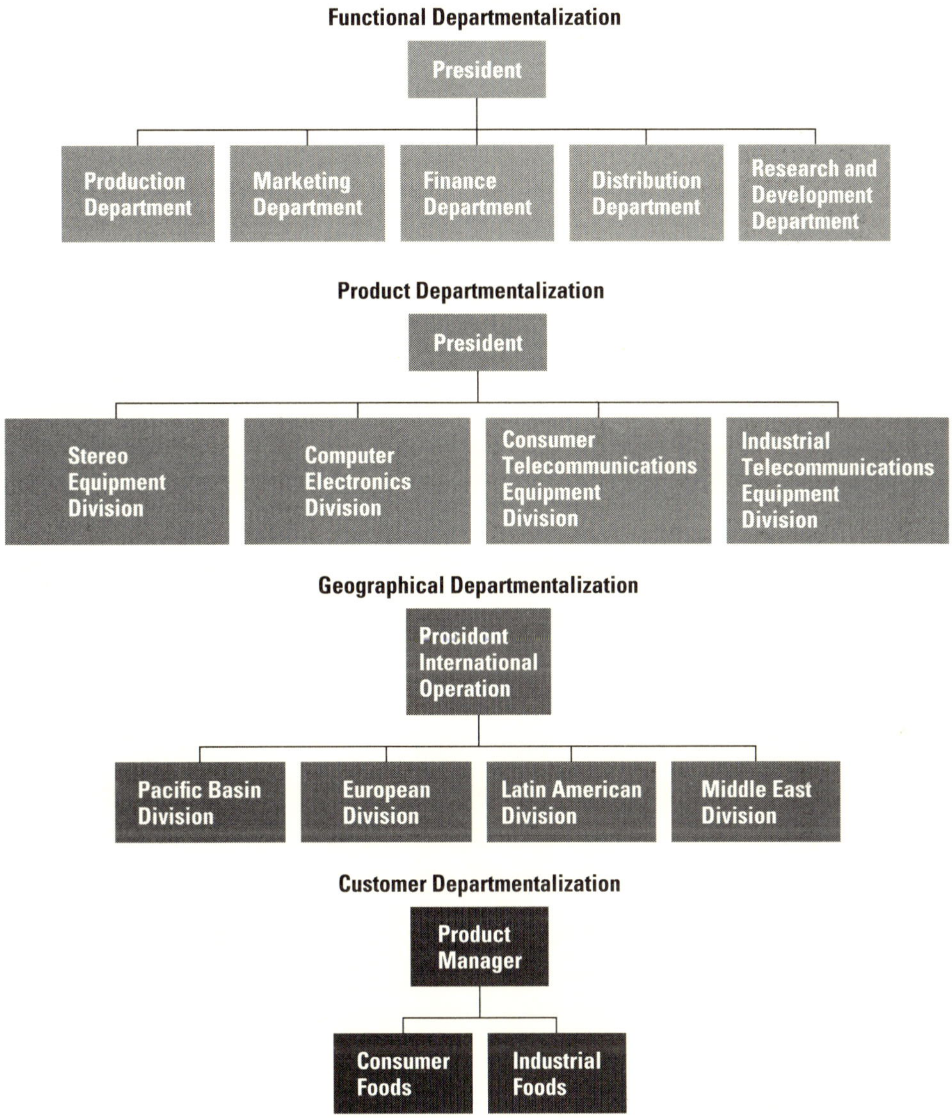

goods manufacturers have departments for specific product lines (beverages, frozen dinners, canned goods, and so on) as well as departments dealing with legal, purchasing, finance, human resources, and other business functions. For smaller companies, accounting can be set up online, almost as an automated department. Accounting software can handle electronic transfers so you never have to worry about a late bill. Many city governments also have departments for specific services (e.g., police, fire, waste disposal) as well as departments for legal, human resources, and other business functions. Figure 4.3 depicts the organizational chart for the city of Corpus Christi, Texas, showing these departments.

FIGURE 4.3 An Organizational Chart for the City of Corpus Christi

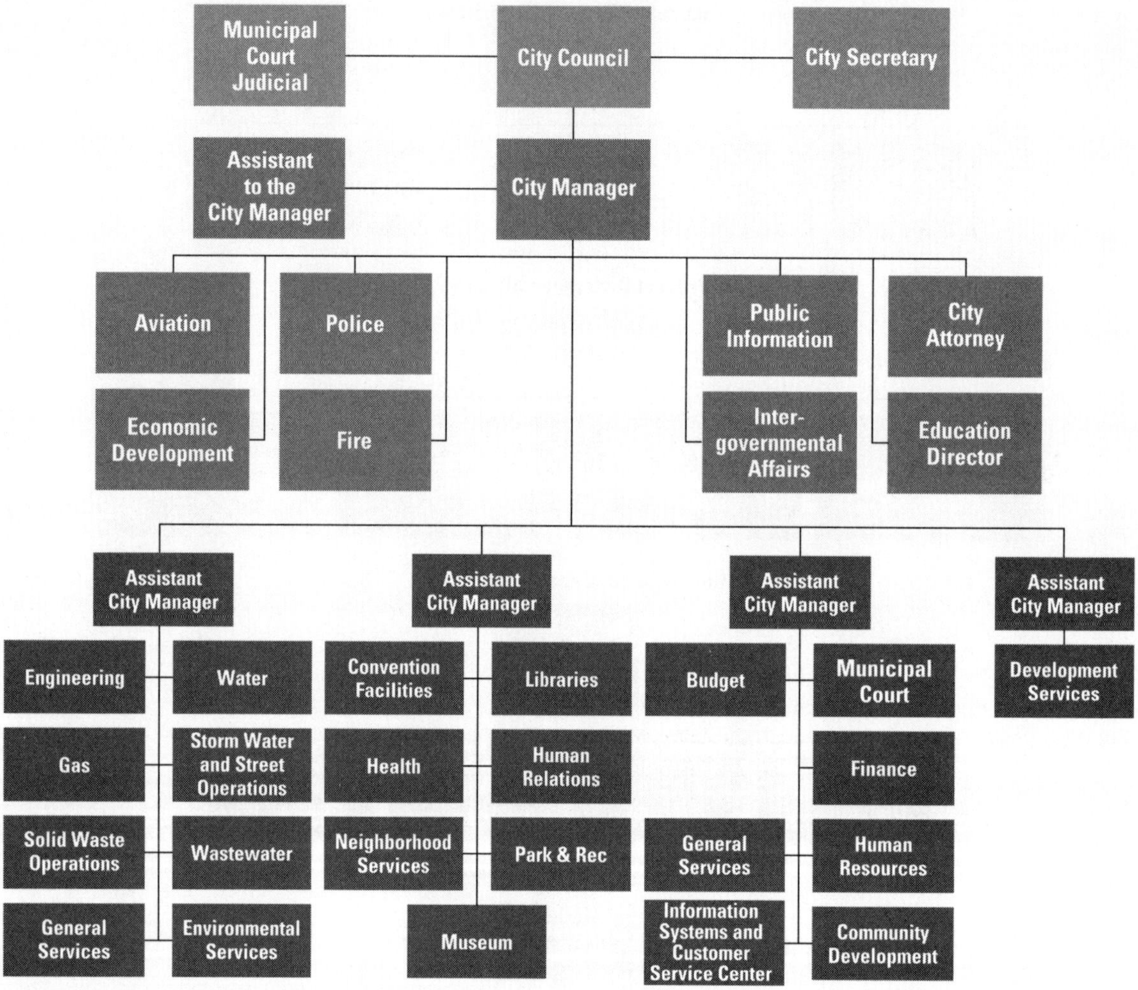

Source: "City of Corpus Christi Organizational Chart," City of Corpus Christi.

按职能划分部门
functional departmentalization the grouping of jobs that perform similar functional activities, such as finance, manufacturing, marketing, and human resources

按职能划分部门

Functional Departmentalization. **Functional departmentalization** groups jobs that perform similar functional activities, such as finance, manufacturing, marketing, and human resources. Each of these functions is managed by an expert in the work done by the department—an engineer supervises the production department; a financial executive supervises the finance department. This approach is common in small organizations. Green Mountain Coffee is departmentalized into six functions: sales and marketing, operations, human resources, finance, information systems, and social responsibility. A weakness of functional departmentalization is that, because it tends to emphasize departmental units rather than the organization as a whole, decision making that involves more than one department may be slow, and it requires greater coordination. Thus, as businesses grow, they tend to adopt other approaches to organizing jobs.

按产品划分部门

Product Departmentalization. **Product departmentalization,** as you might guess, organizes jobs around the products of the firm. Unilever has global units, including personal care, foods, refreshment, and home care.[11] Each division develops and implements its own product plans, monitors the results, and takes corrective action as necessary. Functional activities—production, finance, marketing, and others—are located within each product division. Consequently, organizing by products duplicates functions and resources and emphasizes the product rather than achievement of the organization's overall objectives. However, it simplifies decision making and helps coordinate all activities related to a product or product group. PepsiCo Inc. is organized into four business units: (1) PepsiCo Americas Foods, which includes brands such as Frito-Lay North America, Quaker Foods North America, and all of its Latin American food and snack businesses; (2) PepsiCo Americas Beverages, which includes the Mountain Dew, Lipton, and Tropicana brands; (3) PepsiCo Europe, which includes regional brands like Wimm-Bill-Dann and Marbo as well as all beverage, food, and snack businesses in Europe and South Africa; and (4) PepsiCo Asia, Middle East and Africa, which includes all beverage, food, and snack businesses in these regions. PepsiCo has actually adopted a combination of two types of departmentalization. While it clearly separates foods from beverages in the Americas, the company chooses to divide its segments into geographic regions—a type of geographic departmentalization.[12]

按产品划分部门
product departmentalization
the organization of jobs in relation to the products of the firm

按地理区域划分部门

Geographical Departmentalization. **Geographical departmentalization** groups jobs according to geographic location, such as a state, region, country, or continent. Diageo, the premium beverage company known for brands such as Johnny Walker and Tanqueray, is organized into five geographic regions, allowing the company to get closer to its customers and respond more quickly and efficiently to regional competitors.[13] Multinational corporations often use a geographical approach because of vast differences between different regions. Coca-Cola, General Motors, and Caterpillar are organized by region. However, organizing by region requires a large administrative staff and control system to coordinate operations, and tasks are duplicated among the different regions.

按地理区域划分部门
geographical departmentalization
the grouping of jobs according to geographic location, such as state, region, country, or continent

按客户划分部门

Customer Departmentalization. **Customer departmentalization** arranges jobs around the needs of various types of customers. Proctor & Gamble, for example, recently restructured their business divisions according to types of customers: global baby, feminine and family care; global beauty; global health and grooming; and global fabric and home care. This allows the company to address the unique requirements of each group.[14] Airlines, such as British Airways and Delta, provide prices and services customized for either business/frequent travelers or infrequent/vacationing customers. Customer departmentalization, like geographical departmentalization, does not focus on the organization as a whole and therefore requires a large administrative staff to coordinate the operations of the various groups.

按客户划分部门
customer departmentalization
the arrangement of jobs around the needs of various types of customers

责任的分配
Assigning Responsibility

LO 4-3

After all workers and work groups have been assigned their tasks, they must be given the responsibility to carry them out. Management must determine to what extent it will delegate responsibility throughout the organization and how many employees will report to each manager.

授权
Delegation of Authority

授权
delegation of authority giving employees not only tasks, but also the power to make commitments, use resources, and take whatever actions are necessary to carry out those tasks

Delegation of authority means not only giving tasks to employees but also empowering them to make commitments, use resources, and take whatever actions are necessary to carry out those tasks. Let's say a marketing manager at Nestlé has assigned an employee to design a new package that is less wasteful (more environmentally responsible) than the current package for one of the company's frozen dinner lines. To carry out the assignment, the employee needs access to information and the authority to make certain decisions on packaging materials, costs, and so on. Without the authority to carry out the assigned task, the employee would have to get the approval of others for every decision and every request for materials.

As a business grows, so do the number and complexity of decisions that must be made; no one manager can handle them all. Nordstrom delegates authority to its customer service personnel by telling them to use their best judgment when dealing with customers. This allows employees to offer the best tailored service to each individual customer and is one reason the retailer is known for its superior customer service.[15] Delegation of authority frees a manager to concentrate on larger issues, such as planning or dealing with problems and opportunities.

责任
responsibility the obligation, placed on employees through delegation, to perform assigned tasks satisfactorily and be held accountable for the proper execution of work

问责制
accountability the principle that employees who accept an assignment and the authority to carry it out are answerable to a superior for the outcome

Delegation also gives a **responsibility,** or obligation, to employees to carry out assigned tasks satisfactorily and holds them accountable for the proper execution of their assigned work. The principle of **accountability** means that employees who accept an assignment and the authority to carry it out are answerable to a superior for the outcome. Returning to the Nestlé example, if the packaging design prepared by the employee is unacceptable or late, the employee must accept the blame. If the new design is innovative, attractive, and cost-efficient, as well as environmentally responsible, or is completed ahead of schedule, the employee will accept the credit.

The process of delegating authority establishes a pattern of relationships and accountability between a superior and his or her subordinates. The president of a firm delegates responsibility for all marketing activities to the vice president of marketing. The vice president accepts this responsibility and has the authority to obtain all relevant information, make certain decisions, and delegate any or all activities to his or her subordinates. The vice president, in turn, delegates all advertising activities to the advertising manager, all sales activities to the sales manager, and so on. These managers then delegate specific tasks to their subordinates. However, the act of delegating authority to a subordinate does not relieve the superior of accountability for the delegated job. Even though the vice president of marketing delegates work to subordinates, he or she is still ultimately accountable to the president for all marketing activities.

集权程度
Degree of Centralization

The extent to which authority is delegated throughout an organization determines its degree of centralization.

集权制组织
centralized organization a structure in which authority is concentrated at the top, and very little decision-making authority is delegated to lower levels

集权制组织
Centralized Organizations. In a **centralized organization,** authority is concentrated at the top, and very little decision-making authority is delegated to lower levels. Although decision-making authority in centralized organizations rests with top levels of management, a vast amount of responsibility for carrying out daily and routine procedures is delegated to even the lowest levels of the organization. Many government organizations, including the U.S. Army, the Postal Service, and the IRS, are centralized.

Businesses tend to be more centralized when the decisions to be made are risky and when low-level managers are not highly skilled in decision making. In the banking

Entrepreneurship in Action

Forming a Successful New Business: Group Collaboration

Nota Bene
Founders: Amy Bass and Evvy Diamond
Founded: 2007, in Aspinwall, Pennsylvania
Success: Through intense teamwork and collaboration, Nota Bene has become a successful stationery business with $500,000 in annual revenues.

The stationery shop Nota Bene was founded through the collaboration between the skills and interests of two friends, Amy Bass and Evvy Diamond. Diamond, who had had a lifelong attraction to stationery, started designing note cards when her children left for college. After an unsuccessful effort to sell her craft at a stationery show, she realized she needed a different outlet and a significant investment in order to properly sell her designs. Diamond sparked the interest of her friend Amy, who had business experience, and together they invested their money and started the business full-time in 2007. They formed a group with complementary skills in business and design and differentiated themselves from their competition by offering original designs, customization, and in-depth personal interaction with their customers. For instance, the entrepreneurs frequently meet with brides after-hours to go over their needs for wedding announcements. Five years after its creation, the company is generating $500,000 in annual revenues despite intense online competition.[16]

industry, for example, authority to make routine car loans is given to all loan managers, while the authority to make high-risk loans, such as for a large residential development, may be restricted to upper-level loan officers.

Overcentralization can cause serious problems for a company, in part because it may take longer for the organization as a whole to implement decisions and to respond to changes and problems on a regional scale. McDonald's, for example, was one of the last chains to introduce a chicken sandwich because of the amount of research, development, test marketing, and layers of approval the product had to go through.

分权制组织

Decentralized Organizations. A **decentralized organization** is one in which decision-making authority is delegated as far down the chain of command as possible. Decentralization is characteristic of organizations that operate in complex, unpredictable environments. Businesses that face intense competition often decentralize to improve responsiveness and enhance creativity. Lower-level managers who interact with the external environment often develop a good understanding of it and thus are able to react quickly to changes. Johnson & Johnson has a very decentralized, flat organizational structure.

分权制组织
decentralized organization
an organization in which decision-making authority is delegated as far down the chain of command as possible

Delegating authority to lower levels of managers may increase the organization's productivity. Decentralization requires that lower-level managers have strong decision-making skills. In recent years, the trend has been toward more decentralized organizations, and some of the largest and most successful companies, including GE, IBM, Google, and Nike, have decentralized decision-making authority. McDonald's, Taco Bell, and Pizza Hut have established themselves in the growing Indian market by decentralizing operations by varying products in specific markets to better meet customer demands. McDonald's, for example, has implemented spicy and vegetarian menu options in India to appeal to the native tastes. Becoming decentralized can be difficult for a fast-food restaurant that relies on standardized processes and core products. Burger King's core offering, the Whopper, will not likely be well accepted in India because beef is rarely eaten. Some suggest the chain should offer vegetarian pizza since it is popular in India. Diversity and decentralization are the keys to being better, not just bigger.[17] Nonprofit organizations benefit from decentralization as well.

管理幅度
Span of Management

How many subordinates should a manager manage? There is no simple answer. Experts generally agree, however, that top managers should not directly supervise more than four to eight people, while lower-level managers who supervise routine tasks are capable of managing a much larger number of subordinates. For example, the manager of the finance department may supervise 25 employees, whereas the vice president of finance may supervise only five managers. **Span of management** refers to the number of subordinates who report to a particular manager. A *wide span of management* exists when a manager directly supervises a very large number of employees. A *narrow span of management* exists when a manager directly supervises only a few subordinates (Figure 4.4). At Whole Foods, the best employees are recruited and placed in small teams. Employees are empowered to discount, give away, and sample products, as well as to assist in creating a respectful workplace where goals are achieved, individual employees succeed, and customers are core in business decisions. Whole Foods teams get to vote on new employee hires as well. This approach allows Whole Foods to offer unique and "local market" experiences in each of its stores. This level of customization is in contrast to more centralized national supermarket chains such as Kroger, Safeway, and Publix.[18]

管理幅度
span of management the number of subordinates who report to a particular manager

Should the span of management be wide or narrow? To answer this question, several factors need to be considered. A narrow span of management is appropriate when superiors and subordinates are not in close proximity, the manager has many responsibilities in addition to the supervision, the interaction between superiors and subordinates is frequent, and problems are common. However, when superiors and subordinates are located close to one another, the manager has few responsibilities other than supervision, the level of interaction between superiors and subordinates is low, few problems arise, subordinates are highly competent, and a set of specific operating procedures governs the activities of managers and their subordinates, a wide span of management will be more appropriate. Narrow spans of management are typical in centralized organizations, while wide spans of management are more common in decentralized firms.

组织层级
Organizational Layers

组织层级
organizational layers the levels of management in an organization

Complementing the concept of span of management is **organizational layers,** the levels of management in an organization. A company with many layers of managers is considered tall; in a tall organization, the span of management is narrow (see Figure 4.4). Because each manager supervises only a few subordinates, many

FIGURE 4.4
Span of Management: Wide Span and Narrow Span

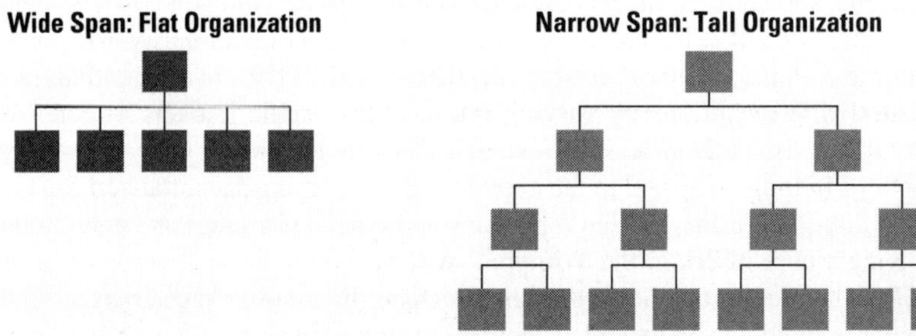

layers of management are necessary to carry out the operations of the business. McDonald's, for example, has a tall organization with many layers, including store managers, district managers, regional managers, and functional managers (finance, marketing, and so on), as well as a chief executive officer and many vice presidents. Because there are more managers in tall organizations than in flat organizations, administrative costs are usually higher. Communication is slower because information must pass through many layers.

Organizations with few layers are flat and have wide spans of management. When managers supervise a large number of employees, fewer management layers are needed to conduct the organization's activities. Managers in flat organizations typically perform more administrative duties than managers in tall organizations because there are fewer of them. They also spend more time supervising and working with subordinates.

Many of the companies that have decentralized also flattened their structures and widened their spans of management, often by eliminating layers of middle management. As mentioned earlier in this chapter, Johnson & Johnson has both a decentralized and flat organizational structure. Other corporations, including Avon, AT&T, and Ford Motor Company, embraced a more decentralized structure to reduce costs, speed up decision making, and boost overall productivity.

组织结构的形式
Forms of Organizational Structure

LO 4-4

Along with assigning tasks and the responsibility for carrying them out, managers must consider how to structure their authority relationships—that is, what structure the organization itself will have and how it will appear on the organizational chart. Common forms of organization include line structure, line-and-staff structure, multidivisional structure, and matrix structure.

直线式结构
Line Structure

The simplest organizational structure, **line structure,** has direct lines of authority that extend from the top manager to employees at the lowest level of the organization. For example, a convenience store employee at 7-Eleven may report to an assistant manager, who reports to the store manager, who reports to a regional manager, or, in an independent store, directly to the owner (Figure 4.5). This structure has a clear chain of command, which enables managers to make decisions quickly. A mid-level manager facing a decision must consult only one person, his or her immediate supervisor. However, this structure requires that managers possess a wide range of knowledge and skills. They are responsible for a variety of activities and must be knowledgeable about them all. Line structures are most common in small businesses.

直线式结构
line structure
the simplest organizational structure, in which direct lines of authority extend from the top manager to the lowest level of the organization

FIGURE 4.5 Line Structure

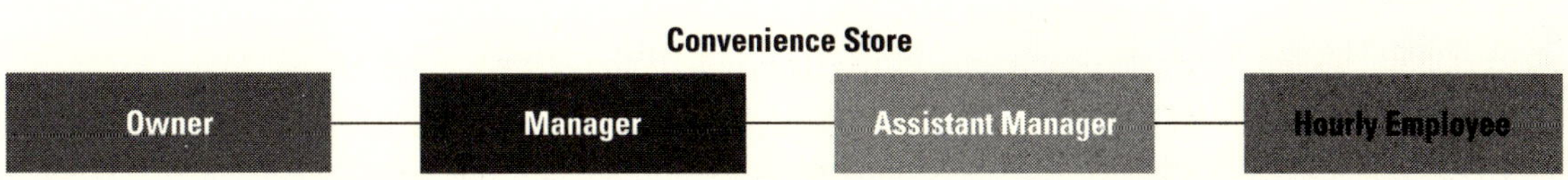

FIGURE 4.6
Line-and-Staff Structure

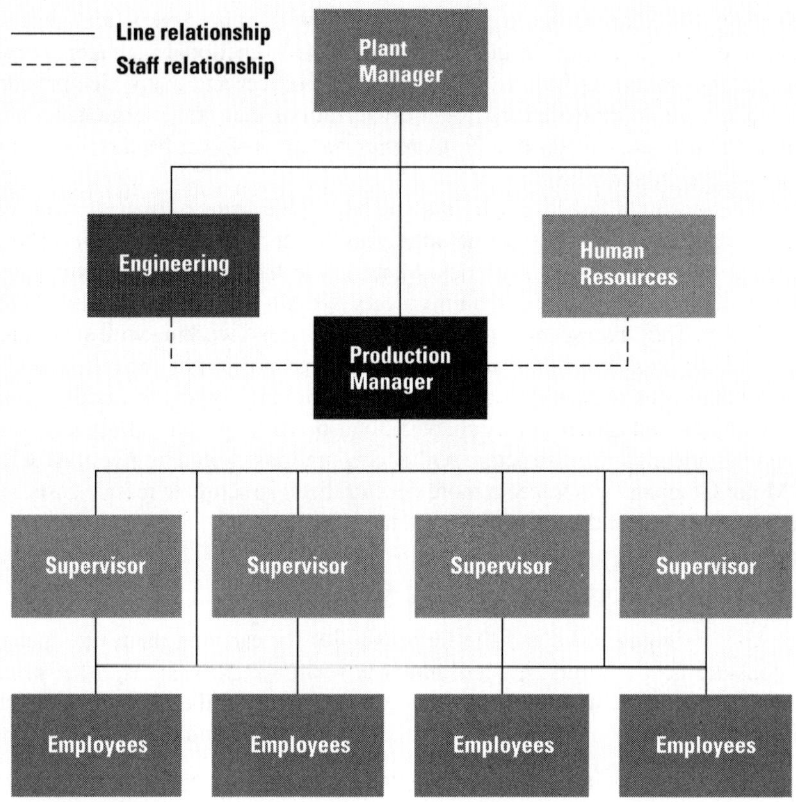

直线参谋式结构
line-and-staff structure
a structure having a traditional line relationship between superiors and subordinates and also specialized managers—called staff managers—who are available to assist line managers

直线参谋式结构
Line-and-Staff Structure

The **line-and-staff structure** has a traditional line relationship between superiors and subordinates, and specialized managers—called staff managers—are available to assist line managers (Figure 4.6). Line managers can focus on their area of expertise in the operation of the business, while staff managers provide advice and support to line departments on specialized matters such as finance, engineering, human resources, and the law. In the city of Corpus Christi (refer back for Figure 4.3), for example, assistant city managers are line managers who oversee groups of related departments. However, the city attorney, police chief, and fire chief are effectively staff managers who report directly to the city manager (the city equivalent of a business chief executive officer). Staff managers do not have direct authority over line managers or over the line manager's subordinates, but they do have direct authority over subordinates in their own departments. However, line-and-staff organizations may experience problems with overstaffing and ambiguous lines of communication. Additionally, employees may become frustrated because they lack the authority to carry out certain decisions.

connect

Need help understanding Line vs. Staff Employees? Visit your Connect ebook video tab for a brief animated explanation.

多事业部制结构
Multidivisional Structure

As companies grow and diversify, traditional line structures become difficult to coordinate, making communication difficult and decision making slow. When the weaknesses of the structure—the "turf wars," miscommunication, and working at cross-purposes—exceed the benefits, growing firms tend to restructure, often into the divisionalized form. A **multidivisional structure** organizes departments into larger groups called divisions. Just as departments might be formed on the basis of geography, customer, product, or a combination of these, so too divisions can be formed based on any of these methods of organizing. Within each of these divisions, departments may be organized by product, geographic region, function, or some combination of all three. Indra Nooyi, CEO of PepsiCo, rearranged the company's organizational structure. Prior to her tenure, PepsiCo was organized geographically. She created new units—PepsiCo Americas Foods (PAF), PepsiCo Americas Beverages (PAB), PepsiCo Europe, and PepsiCo Asia, Middle East & Africa—that span international boundaries and make it easier for employees in different geographic regions to share business practices.[19]

多事业部制结构
multidivisional structure
a structure that organizes departments into larger groups called divisions

Multidivisional structures permit delegation of decision-making authority, allowing divisional and department managers to specialize. They allow those closest to the action to make the decisions that will affect them. Delegation of authority and divisionalized work also mean that better decisions are made faster, and they tend to be more innovative. Most importantly, by focusing each division on a common region, product, or customer, each is more likely to provide products that meet the needs of its particular customers. However, the divisional structure inevitably creates work duplication, which makes it more difficult to realize the economies of scale that result from grouping functions together.

矩阵式结构
Matrix Structure

矩阵式结构
matrix structure
a structure that sets up teams from different departments, thereby creating two or more intersecting lines of authority; also called a project-management structure

Another structure that attempts to address issues that arise with growth, diversification, productivity, and competitiveness, is the matrix. A **matrix structure,** also called a project management structure, sets up teams from different departments, thereby creating two or more intersecting lines of authority (Figure 4.7). One of the first

FIGURE 4.7
Matrix Structure

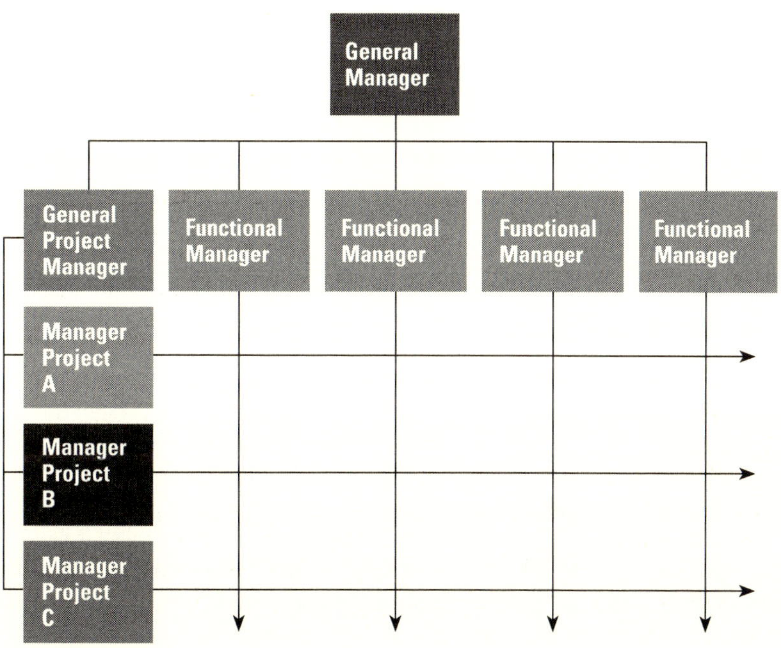

organizations to design and implement a matrix structure was the National Aeronautics and Space Administration (NASA) for the space program because it needed to coordinate different projects at the same time. The matrix structure superimposes project-based departments on the more traditional, function-based departments. Project teams bring together specialists from a variety of areas to work together on a single project, such as developing a new fighter jet. In this arrangement, employees are responsible to two managers—functional managers and project managers. Matrix structures are usually temporary: Team members typically go back to their functional or line department after a project is finished. However, more firms are becoming permanent matrix structures, creating and dissolving project teams as needed to meet customer needs. The aerospace industry was one of the first to apply the matrix structure, but today it is used by universities and schools, accounting firms, banks, and organizations in other industries.

Matrix structures provide flexibility, enhanced cooperation, and creativity, and they enable the company to respond quickly to changes in the environment by giving special attention to specific projects or problems. However, they are generally expensive and quite complex, and employees may be confused as to whose authority has priority—the project manager's or the immediate supervisor's.

LO 4-5

小组与团队在组织中的角色
The Role of Groups and Teams in Organizations

Regardless of how they are organized, most of the essential work of business occurs in individual work groups and teams, so we'll take a closer look at them now. Although some experts do not make a distinction between groups and teams, in recent years there has been a gradual shift toward an emphasis on teams and managing them to enhance individual and organizational success. Some experts now believe that highest productivity results only when groups become teams.[20]

小组
group
two or more individuals who communicate with one another, share a common identity, and have a common goal

团队
team
a small group whose members have complementary skills; have a common purpose, goals, and approach; and hold themselves mutually accountable

Traditionally, a **group** has been defined as two or more individuals who communicate with one another, share a common identity, and have a common goal. A **team** is a small group whose members have complementary skills; have a common purpose, goals, and approach; and hold themselves mutually accountable.[21] All teams are groups, but not all groups are teams. Table 4.2 points out some important differences between them. Work groups emphasize individual work products, individual accountability, and even individual leadership. Salespeople working independently for the same company could be a work group. In contrast, work teams share leadership roles, have both individual and mutual accountability, and create collective work products. In other words, a work group's performance depends on what its members do as individuals, while a team's performance is based on creating a knowledge center and a competency to work together to accomplish a goal. On the other hand, it is also important for team members to retain their individuality and avoid becoming just "another face in the crowd." According to former corporate lawyer and negotiations consultant Susan Cain, the purpose of teams should be toward collaboration versus collectivism. Although the team is working toward a common goal, it is important that all team members actively contribute their ideas and work together to achieve this common goal.[22]

The type of groups an organization establishes depends on the tasks it needs to accomplish and the situation it faces. Some specific kinds of groups and teams include committees, task forces, project teams, product-development teams, quality-assurance teams, and self-directed work teams. All of these can be *virtual teams*—employees in

TABLE 4.2
Differences between Groups and Teams

Working Group	Team
Has strong, clearly focused leader	Has shared leadership roles
Has individual accountability	Has individual and group accountability
Has the same purpose as the broader organizational mission	Has a specific purpose that the team itself delivers
Creates individual work products	Creates collective work products
Runs efficient meetings	Encourages open-ended discussion and active problem-solving meetings
Measures its effectiveness indirectly by its effects on others (e.g., financial performance of the business)	Measures performance directly by assessing collective work products
Discusses, decides, and delegates	Discusses, decides, and does real work together

Source: Robert Gatewood, Robert Taylor, and O. C. Ferrell, Management: Comprehension Analysis and Application, *1995, p. 427.*

different locations who rely on e-mail, audio conferencing, fax, Internet, videoconferencing, or other technological tools to accomplish their goals. Virtual teams are becoming a part of everyday business, with the number of employees working remotely from their employer increasing more than 80 percent in the last several years.[23] Virtual teams have also opened up opportunities for different companies. Not only does Cisco Systems Inc. work in virtual teams, but the company makes networking technology to support video conferencing. At Cisco Europe, 10,000 employees across 21 countries developed a set of team operating principles to aid team collaboration.[24]

委员会
Committees

A **committee** is usually a permanent, formal group that does some specific task. For example, many firms have a compensation or finance committee to examine the effectiveness of these areas of operation as well as the need for possible changes. Ethics committees are formed to develop and revise codes of ethics, suggest methods for implementing ethical standards, and review specific issues and concerns.

委员会
committee
a permanent, formal group that performs a specific task

特别工作组
Task Forces

A **task force** is a temporary group of employees responsible for bringing about a particular change. They typically come from across all departments and levels of an organization. Task force membership is usually based on expertise rather than organizational position. Occasionally, a task force may be formed from individuals outside a company. Coca-Cola has often used task forces to address problems and provide recommendations for improving company practices or products. While some task forces might last a few months, others last for years. When Coca-Cola faced lawsuits alleging discrimination practices in hiring and promotion, it developed a five-year task force to examine pay and promotion practices among minority employees. Its experiences helped Coca-Cola realize the advantages of having a cross-functional task force made up of employees from different departments, and it continued to use task forces to

特别工作组
task force
a temporary group of employees responsible for bringing about a particular change

At Google, small teams work on research and engineering projects that often last 6–12 months.

tackle major company issues. Other companies that have also recognized the benefits of task forces include IBM, Prudential, and General Electric.[25]

团队
Teams

Teams are becoming far more common in the U.S. workplace as businesses strive to enhance productivity and global competitiveness. In general, teams have the benefit of being able to pool members' knowledge and skills and make greater use of them than can individuals working alone. Team building is becoming increasingly popular in organizations, with around half of executives indicating their companies had team-building training. Teams require harmony, cooperation, synchronized effort, and flexibility to maximize their contribution.[26] Teams can also create more solutions to problems than can individuals. Furthermore, team participation enhances employee acceptance of, understanding of, and commitment to team goals. Teams motivate workers by providing internal rewards in the form of an enhanced sense of accomplishment for employees as they achieve more, and external rewards in the form of praise and certain perks. Consequently, they can help get workers more involved. They can help companies be more innovative, and they can boost productivity and cut costs.

According to psychologist Ivan Steiner, team productivity peaks at about five team members. People become less motivated and group coordination becomes more difficult after this size. Jeff Bezos, Amazon.com CEO, says that he has a "two-pizza rule": If a team cannot be fed by two pizzas, it is too large. Keep teams small enough where everyone gets a piece of the action.[27]

项目团队
project teams
groups similar to task forces that normally run their operation and have total control of a specific work project

产品开发团队
product-development teams
a specific type of project team formed to devise, design, and implement a new product

质量保证团队
quality-assurance teams (or quality circles)
small groups of workers brought together from throughout the organization to solve specific quality, productivity, or service problems

项目团队
Project Teams. **Project teams** are similar to task forces, but normally they run their operation and have total control of a specific work project. Like task forces, their membership is likely to cut across the firm's hierarchy and be composed of people from different functional areas. They are almost always temporary, although a large project, such as designing and building a new airplane at Boeing Corporation, may last for years.

Product-development teams are a special type of project team formed to devise, design, and implement a new product. Sometimes product-development teams exist within a functional area—research and development—but now they more frequently include people from numerous functional areas and may even include customers to help ensure that the end product meets the customers' needs. Intel informs their product development process through indirect input from customers. They have a social scientist on staff who leads a research team on how customers actually use products. This is done mainly by observation and asking questions. Once enough information is gathered, it is relayed to the product-development team and incorporated into their designs.[28]

质量保证团队
Quality-Assurance Teams. **Quality-assurance teams,** sometimes called **quality circles,** are fairly small groups of workers brought together from throughout the organization to solve specific quality, productivity, or service problems. Although the *quality circle* term is not as popular as it once was, the concern about quality is stronger than ever. Companies such as IBM and Xerox as well as companies in the

Going Green

Numi Organic Tea Utilizes Teamwork to Increase Sustainability Initiatives

Numi Organic Tea was organized as a Benefit (B) corporation in 1999 in Oakland, California. This benefit status is a certification that implies the company adheres to strict environmental and socially responsible standards. Numi, a dried lime that can be brewed as tea, is a staple in Iraq, the native home of the founders: brother-and-sister team Ahmed and Reem Rahim. The company incorporates the quadruple bottom line (people, planet, product, and profit) into their business model with organic tea that is completely natural and ethically and environmentally sourced. In reaching their shared goals, the founders quickly learned that effective communication is a vital component. Having different communication styles, Ahmed taught Reem to be more outspoken with her ideas and criticisms, while Reem taught Ahmed the value of listening to others and considering their opinions.

They translated these lessons externally to build partnerships with various Fair Trade organizations to extend their reach. As a result, Numi became one of the world's leaders in importing Fair Trade–certified organic tea and achieved annual sales of more than $20 million with a presence in almost 40 countries. Face-to-face communication is heavily emphasized by the company. The founders frequently travel to the farms where the tea leaves are sourced to make sure farmers are receiving competitive compensation and Fair Trade standards are met.

Their values are also apparent in their packaging. Numi became the first company to receive verification of its packaging and tea bags by the Non-GMO Project with its all-natural, completely recyclable, and biodegradable hemp-based tea bags that are printed with soy-based inks. Many companies, especially in the United States, make packaging and tea bags from genetically modified materials such as genetically modified corn and petroleum-based nylon.[29]

---

automobile industry have used quality circles to shift the organization to a more participative culture. The use of teams to address quality issues will no doubt continue to increase throughout the business world.

自主工作团队

Self-directed Work Teams. A **self-directed work team (SDWT)** is a group of employees responsible for an entire work process or segment that delivers a product to an internal or external customer.[30] SDWTs permit the flexibility to change rapidly to meet the competition or respond to customer needs. The defining characteristic of an SDWT is the extent to which it is empowered or given authority to make and implement work decisions. Thus, SDWTs are designed to give employees a feeling of "ownership" of a whole job. Employees at 3M as well as an increasing number of companies encourage employees to be active to perform a function or operational task. With shared team responsibility for work outcomes, team members often have broader job assignments and cross-train to master other jobs, thus permitting greater team flexibility.

自主工作团队
self-directed work team (SDWT)
a group of employees responsible for an entire work process or segment that delivers a product to an internal or external customer

组织中的沟通

Communicating in Organizations

LO 4-6

Communication within an organization can flow in a variety of directions and from a number of sources, each using both oral and written forms of communication. The success of communication systems within the organization has a tremendous effect on the overall success of the firm. Communication mistakes can lower productivity and morale.

Alternatives to face-to-face communications—such as meetings—are growing, thanks to technology such as voice-mail, e-mail, social media, and online newsletters. Many companies use internal networks called intranets

DID YOU KNOW? A survey of managers and executives found that they feel 28 percent of meetings are a waste of time and that information could be communicated more effectively using other methods.[31]

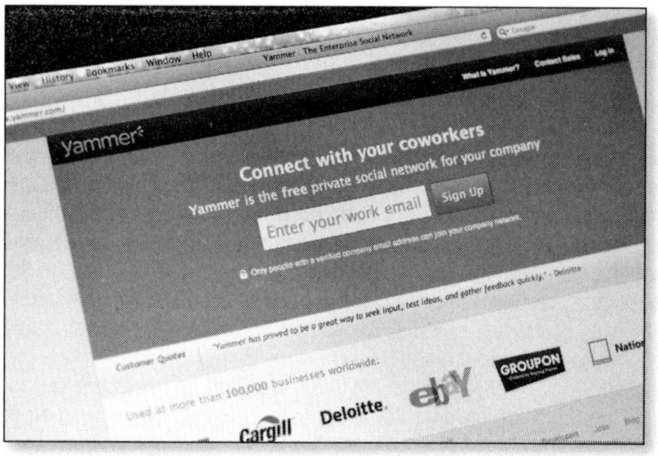

Yammer is a social network that companies can use to connect employees with one another.

to share information with employees. Intranets increase communication across different departments and levels of management and help with the flow of everyday business activities. Another innovative approach is cloud computing. Rather than using physical products, companies using cloud computing technology can access computing resources and information over a network. Cloud computing allows companies to have more control over computing resources and can be less expensive than hardware or software. Salesforce.com uses cloud computing in its customer relationship management solutions.[32] Companies can even integrate aspects of social media into their intranets, allowing employees to post comments and pictures, participate in polls, and create group calendars. However, increased access to the Internet at work has also created many problems, including employee abuse of company email and Internet access.[33]

正式沟通

Formal Communication

Formal channels of communication are intentionally defined and designed by the organization. They represent the flow of communication within the formal organizational structure, as shown on organizational charts. Traditionally, formal communication patterns were classified as vertical and horizontal, but with the increased use of teams and matrix structures, formal communication may occur in a number of patterns (Figure 4.8).

Upward communication flows from lower to higher levels of the organization and includes information such as progress reports, suggestions for improvement, inquiries, and grievances. *Downward communication* refers to the traditional flow of

FIGURE 4.8
The Flow of Communication in an Organizational Hierarchy

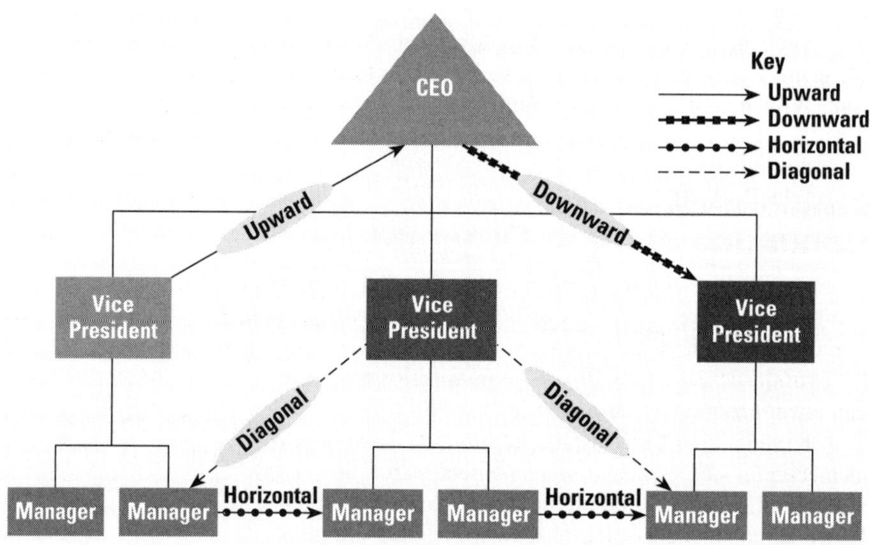

information from upper organizational levels to lower levels. This type of communication typically involves directions, the assignment of tasks and responsibilities, performance feedback, and certain details about the organization's strategies and goals. Speeches, policy and procedures manuals, employee handbooks, company leaflets, telecommunications, and job descriptions are examples of downward communication.

Horizontal communication involves the exchange of information among colleagues and peers on the same organizational level, such as across or within departments. Horizontal information informs, supports, and coordinates activities both within the department and with other departments. At times, the business will formally require horizontal communication among particular organizational members, as is the case with task forces or project teams.

With more and more companies downsizing and increasing the use of self-managed work teams, many workers are being required to communicate with others in different departments and on different levels to solve problems and coordinate work. When these individuals from different units and organizational levels communicate, it is *diagonal communication.*

非正式沟通渠道
Informal Communication Channels

Along with the formal channels of communication shown on an organizational chart, all firms communicate informally as well. Communication between friends, for instance, cuts across department, division, and even management–subordinate boundaries. Such friendships and other nonwork social relationships comprise the *informal organization* of a firm, and their impact can be great.

小道消息
grapevine
an informal channel of communication, separate from management's formal, official communication channels

The most significant informal communication occurs through the **grapevine,** an informal channel of communication, separate from management's formal, official communication channels. Grapevines exist in all organizations. Information passed along the grapevine may relate to the job or organization, or it may be gossip and rumors unrelated to either. The accuracy of grapevine information has been of great concern to managers.

Additionally, managers can turn the grapevine to their advantage. Using it as a "sounding device" for possible new policies is one example. Managers can obtain valuable information from the grapevine that could improve decision making. Some organizations use the grapevine to their advantage by floating ideas, soliciting feedback, and reacting accordingly. People love to gossip, and managers need to be aware that grapevines exist in every organization. Managers who understand how the grapevine works also can use it to their advantage by feeding it facts to squelch rumors and incorrect information.

对沟通的监控
Monitoring Communications

Technological advances and the increased use of electronic communication in the workplace have made monitoring its use necessary for most companies. Failing to monitor employees' use of e-mail, social media, and the Internet can be costly. Many companies require that employees sign and follow a policy on appropriate Internet use. These agreements often require that employees will use corporate computers only for work-related activities. Additionally, several companies use software programs to monitor employee computer usage.[34] Instituting practices that show respect for employee privacy but do not abdicate employer responsibility are increasingly necessary in today's workplace. Several websites provide model policies and detailed guidelines for conducting electronic monitoring, including the Model Electronic Privacy Act on the American Civil Liberties Union site.

提高沟通效率
Improving Communication Effectiveness

Without effective communication, the activities and overall productivity of projects, groups, teams, and individuals will be diminished. Communication is an important area for a firm to address at all levels of management. Apple supplier Foxconn is one example of how essential communication is to a firm. Despite criticisms of unfair labor conditions, the Fair Labor Association determined that Foxconn had formal procedures in place at its factories to prevent many major accidents. However, it concluded that the firm had a communication problem. These procedures were not being communicated to the factory workers, contributing to unsafe practices and two tragic explosions.[35]

One of the major issues of effective communication is in obtaining feedback. If feedback is not provided, then communication will be ineffective and can drag down overall performance. Managers should always encourage feedback, including concerns and challenges about issues. Listening is a skill that involves hearing, and most employees listen much more than they actively communicate to others. Therefore, managers should encourage employees to provide feedback—even if it is negative. This will allow the organization to identify strengths and weaknesses and make adjustments when needed. At the same time, strong feedback mechanisms help to empower employees as they feel that their voices are being heard.

Interruptions can be a serious threat to effective communication. Various activities can interrupt the message. For example, interjecting a remark can create discontinuance in the communication process or disrupt the uniformity of the message. Even small interruptions can be a problem if the messenger cannot adequately understand or interpret the communicator's message. One suggestion is to give the communicator space or time to make another statement rather than quickly responding or making your own comment.

Strong and effective communication channels are a requirement for companies to distribute information to different levels of the company. Businesses have several channels for communication, including face-to-face, e-mail, phone, and written communication (for example, memos). Each channel has advantages and disadvantages, and some are more appropriate to use than others. For instance, a small task requiring little instruction might be communicated through a short memo or e-mail. An in-depth task would most likely require a phone conversation or face-to-face contact. E-mail has become especially helpful for businesses, and both employees and managers are increasingly using e-mail rather than memos or phone conversations. However, it is important that employees use e-mail correctly. It is quite easy to send the wrong e-mail to the wrong person, and messages sent over e-mail can be misinterpreted. Inappropriate e-mails can be forwarded without a second thought, and employees have gotten in trouble for sending personal e-mails in the workplace. It is therefore important for companies to communicate their e-mail policies throughout the organization. Communicators using e-mail, whether managers or employees, must exert caution before pushing that "Send" button.

Communication is necessary in helping every organizational member understand what is expected of him or her. Many business problems can be avoided if clear communication exists within the company. Even the best business strategies are of little use if those who will oversee them cannot understand what is intended. Communication might not seem to be as big of a concern to management as finances, human resources, and marketing, but in reality it can make the difference between successful implementation of business activities or failure.

So You Want a Job in Managing Organizational Culture, Teamwork, and Communication

Jobs dealing with organizational culture and structure are usually at the top of the organization. If you want to be a CEO or high-level manager, you will help shape these areas of business. On the other hand, if you are an entrepreneur or small-business person, you will need to make decisions about assigning tasks, departmentalization, and assigning responsibility. Even managers in small organizations have to make decisions about decentralization, span of management, and forms of organizational structure. While these decisions may be part of your job, there are usually no job titles dealing with these specific areas. Specific jobs that attempt to improve organizational culture could include ethics and compliance positions as well as those who are in charge of communicating memos, manuals, and policies that help establish the culture. These positions will be in communications, human resources, and positions that assist top organizational managers.

Teams are becoming more common in the workplace, and it is possible to become a member of a product development group or quality assurance team. There are also human resource positions that encourage teamwork through training activities. The area of corporate communications provides lots of opportunities for specific jobs that facilitate communication systems. Thanks to technology, there are job positions to help disseminate information through online newsletters, intranets, or internal computer networks to share information to increase collaboration. In addition to the many advances using electronic communications, there are technology concerns that create new job opportunities. Monitoring workplace communications such as the use of e-mail and the Internet has created new industries. There have to be internal controls in the organization to make sure that the organization does not engage in any copyright infringement. If this is an area of interest, there are specific jobs that provide an opportunity to use your technological skills to assist in maintaining appropriate standards in communicating and using technology.

If you go to work for a large company with many divisions, you can expect a number of positions dealing with the tasks discussed here. If you go to work for a small company, you will probably engage in most of these tasks as a part of your position. Organizational flexibility requires individual flexibility, and those employees willing to take on new domains and challenges will be the employees who survive and prosper in the future.

Review Your Understanding

Define organizational structure, and relate how organizational structures develop.

Structure is the arrangement or relationship of positions within an organization; it develops when managers assign work activities to work groups and specific individuals and coordinate the diverse activities required to attain organizational objectives. Organizational structure evolves to accommodate growth, which requires people with specialized skills.

Describe how specialization and departmentalization help an organization achieve its goals.

Structuring an organization requires that management assign work tasks to specific individuals and groups. Under specialization, managers break labor into small, specialized tasks and assign employees to do a single task, fostering efficiency. Departmentalization is the grouping of jobs into working units (departments, units, groups, or divisions). Businesses may departmentalize by function, product, geographic region, or customer, or they may combine two or more of these.

Distinguish between groups and teams, and identify the types of groups that exist in organizations.

A group is two or more persons who communicate, share a common identity, and have a common goal. A team is a small group whose members have complementary skills, a common purpose, goals, and approach and who hold themselves mutually accountable. The major distinction is that individual performance is most important in groups, while collective work group performance counts most in teams. Special kinds of groups include task forces, committees, project teams, product-development teams, quality-assurance teams, and self-directed work teams.

Determine how organizations assign responsibility for tasks and delegate authority.

Delegation of authority means assigning tasks to employees and giving them the power to make commitments, use resources, and take whatever actions are necessary to accomplish the tasks. It lays responsibility on employees to carry out assigned tasks satisfactorily and holds them accountable to a superior for the proper execution of their assigned work. The extent to which authority is delegated throughout an organization determines its degree of centralization. Span of management refers to the number of subordinates who report to a particular manager. A wide span of management occurs in flat organizations; a narrow one exists in tall organizations.

Compare and contrast some common forms of organizational structure.

Line structures have direct lines of authority that extend from the top manager to employees at the lowest level of the organization. The line-and-staff structure has a traditional line relationship between superiors and subordinates, and specialized staff managers are available to assist line managers. A multidivisional structure gathers departments into larger groups called divisions. A matrix, or project-management, structure sets up teams from different departments, thereby creating two or more intersecting lines of authority.

Describe how communication occurs in organizations.

Communication occurs both formally and informally in organizations. Formal communication may be downward, upward, horizontal, and even diagonal. Informal communication takes place through friendships and the grapevine.

Analyze a business's use of teams.

"Solve the Dilemma" on page 228 introduces a firm attempting to restructure to a team environment. Based on the material presented in this chapter, you should be able to evaluate the firm's efforts and make recommendations for resolving the problems that have developed.

Revisit the World of Business

1. How does CarMax encourage employees to put customer needs first?
2. How has CarMax developed a decentralized culture?
3. Describe some ways that CarMax empowers its employees.

Learn the Terms

accountability
centralized organization
committee
customer departmentalization
decentralized organization
delegation of authority
departmentalization
functional departmentalization
geographical departmentalization
grapevine
group
line-and-staff structure
line structure
matrix structure
multidivisional structure
organizational chart
organizational culture
organizational layers
product departmentalization
product-development teams
project teams
quality-assurance teams (or quality circles)
responsibility
self-directed work team (SDWT)
span of management
specialization
structure
task force
team

Check Your Progress

1. Identify four types of departmentalization and give an example of each type.
2. Explain the difference between groups and teams.
3. What are self-managed work teams and what tasks might they perform that traditionally are performed by managers?
4. Explain how delegating authority, responsibility, and accountability are related.
5. Distinguish between centralization and decentralization. Under what circumstances is each appropriate?
6. Define span of management. Why do some organizations have narrow spans and others wide spans?
7. Discuss the different forms of organizational structure. What are the primary advantages and disadvantages of each form?
8. Discuss the role of the grapevine within organizations. How can managers use it to further the goals of the firm?
9. How have technological advances made electronic oversight a necessity in many companies?
10. Discuss how an organization's culture might influence its ability to achieve its objectives. Do you think that managers can "manage" the organization's culture?

Get Involved

1. Explain, using a specific example (perhaps your own future business), how an organizational structure might evolve. How would you handle the issues of specialization, delegation of authority, and centralization? Which structure would you use? Explain your answers.
2. Interview the department chairperson in charge of one of the academic departments in your college or university. Using Table 4.2 as a guideline, explore whether the professors function more like a group or a team. Contrast what you find here with what you see on your school's basketball, football, or baseball team.

Build Your Skills

Teamwork

Background

Think about all the different kinds of groups and teams you have been a member of or been involved with. Here's a checklist to help you remember them—with "Other" spaces to fill in ones not listed. Check all that apply.

School Groups/Teams	Community Groups/Teams	Employment Groups/Teams
☐ Sports teams	☐ Fund-raising groups	☐ Problem-solving teams
☐ Cheerleading squads	☐ Religious groups	☐ Work committees
☐ Musical groups	☐ Sports teams	☐ Project teams
☐ Hobby clubs	☐ Political groups	☐ Labor union groups
☐ Foreign language clubs	☐ Boy/Girl Scout troops	☐ Work crews
☐ Study groups	☐ Volunteer organizations	☐ Other ____
☐ Other ____	☐ Other ____	

Task

1. Of those you checked, circle those that you would categorize as a "really great team."
2. Examine the following table[36] and circle those characteristics from columns two and three that were represented in your "really great" team experiences.

Indicator	Good Team Experience	Not-So-Good Team Experience
Members arrive on time?	Members are prompt because they know others will be.	Members drift in sporadically, and some leave early.
Members prepared?	Members are prepared and know what to expect.	Members are unclear what the agenda is.
Meeting organized?	Members follow a planned agenda.	The agenda is tossed aside, and free-wheeling discussion ensues.
Members contribute equally?	Members give each other a chance to speak; quiet members are encouraged.	Some members always dominate the discussion; some are reluctant to speak their minds.
Discussions help members make decisions?	Members learn from others' points of view, new facts are discussed, creative ideas evolve, and alternatives emerge.	Members reinforce their belief in their own points of view, or their decisions were made long before the meeting.

Indicator	Good Team Experience	Not-So-Good Team Experience
Any disagreement?	Members follow a conflict-resolution process established as part of the team's policies.	Conflict turns to argument, angry words, emotion, blaming.
More cooperation or more conflict?	Cooperation is clearly an important ingredient.	Conflict flares openly, as well as simmering below the surface.
Commitment to decisions?	Members reach consensus before leaving.	Compromise is the best outcome possible; some members don't care about the result.
Member feelings after team decision?	Members are satisfied and are valued for their ideas.	Members are glad it's over, not sure of results or outcome.
Members support decision afterward?	Members are committed to implementation.	Some members second-guess or undermine the team's decision.

3. What can you take with you from your positive team experiences and apply to a work-related group or team situation in which you might be involved? ______________________________

Solve the Dilemma LO 4-7

Quest Star in Transition

Quest Star (QS), which manufactures quality stereo loudspeakers, wants to improve its ability to compete against Japanese firms. Accordingly, the company has launched a comprehensive quality-improvement program for its Iowa plant. The QS Intracommunication Leadership Initiative (ILI) has flattened the layers of management. The program uses teams and peer pressure to accomplish the plant's goals instead of multiple management layers with their limited opportunities for communication. Under the initiative, employees make all decisions within the boundaries of their responsibilities, and they elect team representatives to coordinate with other teams. Teams are also assigned tasks ranging from establishing policies to evaluating on-the-job safety.

However, employees who are not self-motivated team players are having difficulty getting used to their peers' authority within this system. Upper-level managers face stress and frustration because they must train workers to supervise themselves.

Discussion Questions

1. What techniques or skills should an employee have to assume a leadership role within a work group?
2. If each work group has a team representative, what problems will be faced in supervising these representatives?
3. Evaluate the pros and cons of the system developed by QS.

Build Your Business Plan

Organization, Teamwork, and Communication

Developing a business plan as a team is a deliberate move of your instructor to encourage you to familiarize yourself with the concept of teamwork. You need to realize that you are going to spend a large part of your professional life working with others. At this point in time, you are working on the business plan for a grade, but after graduation, you will be "teaming" with coworkers and the success of your endeavor may determine whether you get a raise or a bonus. It is important that you be comfortable as soon as possible with working with others and holding them accountable for their contributions.

Some people are natural "leaders," and leaders often feel that if team members are not doing their work, they take it upon themselves to "do it all." This is not leadership, but rather micro-managing.

Leadership means holding members accountable for their responsibilities. Your instructor may provide ideas on how this could be implemented, possibly by utilizing peer reviews. Remember, you are not doing a team member a favor by doing their work for them.

If you are a "follower" (someone who takes directions well) rather than a leader, try to get into a team where others are hard workers and you will rise to their level. There is nothing wrong with being a follower; not everyone can be a leader!

See for Yourself Videocase

Zappos Creates Organizational Structure and Culture with Teams

Zappos began in 1999 as an online shoe retailer but has expanded into many product categories since then. The company has always taken pride in its focus on employees and customers and, as a result, has adopted a team structure to reinforce the kind of organizational culture for which it aims. Jeanne Markel, the director of the Downtown Team, states that the managerial goal "is to drive the culture within Zappos." As Zappos began incorporating more product categories, the teams grew both in size and number. This helped to reduce the complexity of company growth and establish a basis for success. Many companies utilize functional departmentalization as a structure to organize their activities. Zappos' many teams serve this same purpose but are described as teams rather than departments. This means that there is a team for each function under each product category, and if the product category is large enough, there will be teams for product subcategories.

While the company is run by teams in every department, one of the most important teams is the merchandising team, because team members are responsible for purchasing all inventory on the Zappos website. This team has approximately 200 people and is led by the Vice President of Merchandising. Under the VP is a Senior Director of Clothing and a General Manager of Footwear, who lead the directors responsible for each purchasing category, including clothing, fashion, and couture and accessories, as well as private-label, performance, and casual lifestyle categories. A team that encompasses such a large and integral responsibility to Zappos' business model will likely change structure to accommodate growth. For example, over the course of seven years, Jeanne Markel saw her team grow from 4 people to 27.

Each purchasing category is composed of its own team as well. The casual lifestyle category, for instance, is led by the Director of Merchandising, who manages four directors responsible for separate subcategories, including kids, comfort, size and width, and home and luggage. There is also a Lead Buyer for each subcategory. From here, the subcategories are divided into further categories. The kids category has a kids footwear merchandising team. The structure of this team begins with entry level Merchandising Assistants, who work closely with the next level of Assistant Buyers to learn the industry and the trade. Assistant Buyers are responsible for mentoring Merchandising Assistants as well as handling up to 15 brands and making decisions on purchases. The next level consists of Buyers, who manage the Assistant Buyers and govern a group of brands. As an employee reaches higher levels in the team, his or her responsibility shifts more from buying activities to mentoring, training, and building the team. This is a core characteristic of Zappos' structure. The company strives to empower employees from the bottom up so that when they are hired as an entry-level employee, within five to seven years they have the opportunity to move up to leadership positions. The top-level positions on this team are the Lead Buyers, who manage the largest one or two brands on the team or on the company's website, and the Director, who rarely ever buys and only mentors and manages.

Because Zappos is an online company, most of the communication that occurs is via e-mail. However in order to ensure that teams function properly and work to reinforce their strong organizational culture, the company encourages face-to-face meetings. Formal meetings between the directors and the various levels on their teams will occur once per month. CEO Tony Hsieh also calls for directors to spend 20 percent of their time with their teams outside of work and gives them an allowance of $50 per month in order to do this. These kinds of activities strengthen the teams by making them more invested in collaboration and instilling trust among team members, as well as with other teams outside of their specific functional area. This serves as a valuable relationship building activity that allows entry-level employees to engage with all levels of the company in a casual manner, promotes brainstorming that results in creative solutions to challenges the team might be facing, and offers all employees a different perspective of their team members and the company they work for.

The most recent development the company has made in terms of organizational structure and teamwork is the adoption of Holacracy. This is a management structure that focuses on the type and amount of work that needs to be accomplished rather than on titles and hierarchy. This seems to be a natural transition for a company whose structure is highlighted by the use of teams and was instituted to avoid rigid structure that leads to inflexibility. The effects of this emerging management style are not fully known; however, it leaves Zappos with an opportunity to show others how it can be successful.[37]

Discussion Questions

1. Why do companies like Zappos incorporate the use of teams into their organizational structure?
2. How does the use of teams contribute to the organizational culture?
3. How does a focus on the work to be accomplished versus the institution of titles relate to the concept of teamwork?

You can find the related video in the Video Library in Connect. Ask your instructor how you can access Connect.

Team Exercise

Assign the responsibility of providing the organizational structure for a company one of your team members has worked for. Was your organization centralized or decentralized in terms of decision making? Would you consider the span of control to be wide or narrow? Were any types of teams, committees, or task forces utilized in the organization? Report your work to the class.

5

Managing Service and Manufacturing Operations 服务与生产运营管理

Learning Objectives

After reading this chapter, you will be able to:

LO 5-1 Define operations management, and differentiate between operations and manufacturing.

LO 5-2 Explain how operations management differs in manufacturing and service firms.

LO 5-3 Describe the elements involved in planning and designing an operations system.

LO 5-4 Specify some techniques managers may use to manage the logistics of transforming inputs into finished products.

LO 5-5 Assess the importance of quality in operations management.

LO 5-6 Evaluate a business's dilemma and propose a solution.

Chapter Outline

Introduction
The Nature of Operations Management
- *The Transformation Process*
- *Operations Management in Service Businesses*

Planning and Designing Operations Systems
- *Planning the Product*
- *Designing the Operations Processes*
- *Planning Capacity*
- *Planning Facilities*
- *Sustainability and Manufacturing*

Managing the Supply Chain
- *Purchasing*
- *Managing Inventory*
- *Outsourcing*
- *Routing and Scheduling*

Managing Quality
- *International Organization for Standardization (ISO)*
- *Inspection*
- *Sampling*

Integrating Operations and Supply Chain Management

进入商业世界

Enter the World of Business

制造厂商采用远程监控系统发现问题

Manufacturers Use Remote Monitoring Systems to Detect Problems

When something breaks at a manufacturing plant, an engineer or manager comes in to fix the problem. Often, these problems happen after work hours, including the middle of the night. Loss of sleep and stress can profoundly affect these employees, particularly as factories are facing a shortage of skilled workers to handle manufacturing malfunctions. This has created an opportunity for global suppliers of factory automation equipment to expand into remote monitoring.

For instance, ABB Ltd. works with Bayer AG to remotely monitor equipment at its plant in Berkeley, California, for signs that would indicate a problem with Bayer's equipment. This monitoring helps factory employees detect a potential problem and correct it before it becomes an issue. ABB's factory-automation gear also creates greater efficiencies, removing the likelihood for error. International Paper has a similar system with Rockwell Automation. Rockwell monitors International Paper's factory in Ticonderoga, New York, from its location in Cleveland. If a problem is detected at International Paper's factory, Rockwell engineers will contact International Paper and provide recommendations on how to fix the problem.

Some organizations have found it beneficial to offer 24-hour monitoring services. Mitsubishi Power Systems, for instance, provides 24-hour remote monitoring services for turbine operators. Eaton technicians use a remote monitoring system to detect issues with the battery systems of clients. However, there are risks associated with allowing an outside supplier complete access to information about manufacturing processes. Protecting their manufacturing processes is important for manufacturers to retain their competitive advantage. For this reason, some organizations such as Bayer are allowing remote monitoring of its systems only when the company requires help fixing problems.[1]

引言
Introduction

All organizations create products—goods, services, or ideas—for customers. Thus, organizations as diverse as Toyota, Campbell Soup, UPS, and a public hospital share a number of similarities relating to how they transform resources into the products we consume. Most hospitals use similar admission procedures, while online social media companies, like Facebook and Twitter, use their technology and operating systems to create social networking opportunities and sell advertising. Such similarities are to be expected. But even organizations in unrelated industries take similar steps in creating goods or services. The check-in procedures of hotels and commercial airlines are comparable, for example. The way Subway assembles a sandwich and the way GMC assembles a truck are similar (both use automation and an assembly line). These similarities are the result of operations management, the focus of this chapter.

Here, we discuss the role of production or operations management in acquiring and managing the resources necessary to create goods and services. Production and operations management involves planning and designing the processes that will transform those resources into finished products, managing the movement of those resources through the transformation process, and ensuring that the products are of the quality expected by customers.

运营管理的本质
The Nature of Operations Management

LO 5-1

运营管理
operations management (OM)
the development and administration of the activities involved in transforming resources into goods and services

Operations management (OM), the development and administration of the activities involved in transforming resources into goods and services, is of critical importance. Operations managers oversee the transformation process and the planning and designing of operations systems, managing logistics, quality, and productivity. Quality and productivity have become fundamental aspects of operations management because a company that cannot make products of the quality desired by consumers, using resources efficiently and effectively, will not be able to remain in business. OM is the "core" of most organizations because it is responsible for the creation of the organization's goods and services. Some organizations like General Motors produce tangible products, but service is an important part of the total product for the customer.

制造
manufacturing
the activities and processes used in making tangible products; also called production

生产
production
the activities and processes used in making tangible products; also called manufacturing

运营
operations
the activities and processes used in making both tangible and intangible products

Historically, operations management has been called "production" or "manufacturing" primarily because of the view that it was limited to the manufacture of physical goods. Its focus was on methods and techniques required to operate a factory efficiently. The change from "production" to "operations" recognizes the increasing importance of organizations that provide services and ideas. Additionally, the term *operations* represents an interest in viewing the operations function as a whole rather than simply as an analysis of inputs and outputs.

Today, OM includes a wide range of organizational activities and situations outside of manufacturing, such as health care, food service, banking, entertainment, education, transportation, and charity. Thus, we use the terms **manufacturing** and **production** interchangeably to represent the activities and processes used in making *tangible* products, whereas we use the broader term **operations** to describe those processes used in the making of *both tangible and intangible products.* Manufacturing provides tangible products such as Hewlett-Packard's latest printer, and operations provides intangibles such as a stay at Wyndham Hotels and Resorts.

转化过程
The Transformation Process

At the heart of operations management is the transformation process through which **inputs** (resources such as labor, money, materials, and energy) are converted into **outputs** (goods, services, and ideas). The transformation process combines inputs in predetermined ways using different equipment, administrative procedures, and technology to create a product (Figure 5.1). To ensure that this process generates quality products efficiently, operations managers control the process by taking measurements (feedback) at various points in the transformation process and comparing them to previously established standards. If there is any deviation between the actual and desired outputs, the manager may take some sort of corrective action. All adjustments made to create a satisfying product are a part of the transformation process.

Transformation may take place through one or more processes. In a business that manufactures oak furniture, for example, inputs pass through several processes before being turned into the final outputs—furniture that has been designed to meet the desires of customers (Figure 5.2). The furniture maker must first strip the oak trees of their bark and saw them into appropriate sizes—one step in the transformation process. Next, the firm dries the strips of oak lumber, a second form of transformation. Third, the dried wood is routed into its appropriate shape and made smooth. Fourth, workers assemble and treat the wood pieces, then stain or varnish the piece of assembled furniture. Finally, the completed piece of furniture is stored until it can be shipped to customers at the appropriate time. Of course, many businesses choose to eliminate some of these stages by purchasing already processed materials—lumber, for example—or outsourcing some tasks to third-party firms with greater expertise.

投入
inputs
the resources—such as labor, money, materials, and energy—that are converted into outputs

产出
outputs
the goods, services, and ideas that result from the conversion of inputs

connect

Need help understanding the Transformation Process for Goods and Services? Visit your Connect ebook video tab for a brief animated explanation.

服务型企业的运营管理
Operations Management in Service Businesses

LO 5-2

Different types of transformation processes take place in organizations that provide services, such as airlines, colleges, and most nonprofit organizations. An airline transforms inputs such as employees, time, money, and equipment through processes such as booking flights, flying airplanes, maintaining equipment, and training crews. The

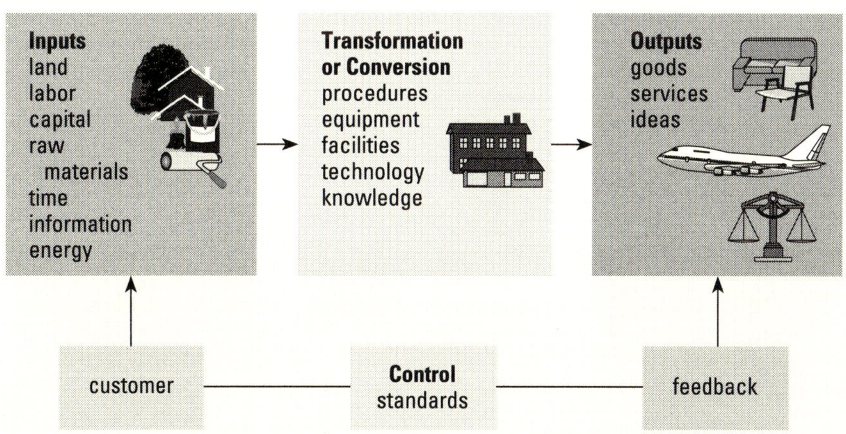

FIGURE 5.1
The Transformation Process of Operations Management

Entrepreneurship in Action

Celebrity Auto Group Provides Unique Service—Matching Customized Cars to Celebrities

Celebrity Auto Group
Founder: Conor Delaney
Founded: 2006, in Sarasota, Florida
Success: With annual revenue of $16 million, Celebrity Auto Group has grown 4,745 percent in the last three years.

Conor Delaney learned from his days as a professional tennis athlete that celebrities, especially professional basketball players, buy about 2 to 12 cars every year at an average price of $150,000 each. They usually customize their vehicles by style, features, or comfort. This inspired Delaney to retire from tennis and open Celebrity Auto Group—a service operation that finds cars for celebrities, customizes them, transports them, and sells them when the celebrities no longer want them. Customization is an important component in attracting celebrities. For instance, one of its cars included a Rolls-Royce Phantom with built-in iPads.

Delaney has been successful because of his personal involvement and the trust he has built with clients. Delaney promises never to reveal the names of the celebrities. Because he does not reveal the identity of the previous owner, Delaney sells the vehicles for less than he would be able to if he disclosed this information. This kind of trust allows Delaney to create and maintain long-term relationships with customers. Their loyalty is reinforced because Delaney sells them vehicles for less than other dealers.[2]

---

output of these processes is flying passengers and/or packages to their destinations. In a nonprofit organization like Habitat for Humanity, inputs such as money, materials, information, and volunteer time and labor are used to transform raw materials into homes for needy families. In this setting, transformation processes include fundraising and promoting the cause in order to gain new volunteers and donations of supplies, as well as pouring concrete, raising walls, and setting roofs. Transformation processes occur in all organizations, regardless of what they produce or their objectives. For most organizations, the ultimate objective is for the produced outputs to be worth more than the combined costs of the inputs.

Unlike tangible goods, services are effectively actions or performances that must be directed toward the consumers who use them. Thus, there is a significant customer-contact component to most services. Examples of high-contact services include health care, real estate, tax preparation, and food service. At the Inn at Little Washington in Washington, Virginia, for example, food servers are critical to delivering the perfect dining experience expected by the most discriminating diners. Wait staff are expected not only to be courteous, but also to demonstrate a detailed knowledge of the

FIGURE 5.2
Inputs, Outputs, and Transformation Processes in the Manufacture of Oak Furniture

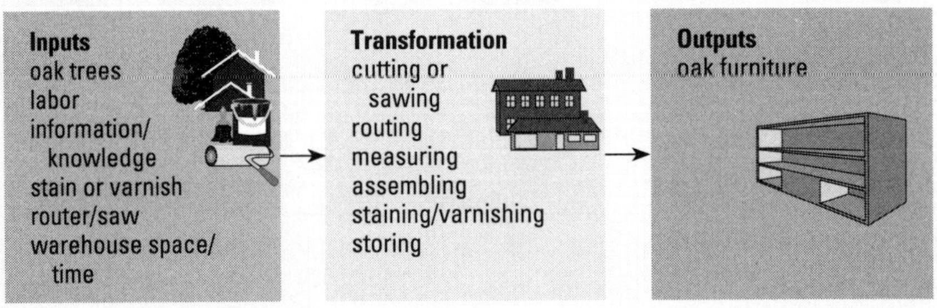

restaurant's offerings, and even to assess the mood of guests in order to respond to diners appropriately.[3] Low-contact services, such as online auction services like eBay, often have a strong high-tech component.

Regardless of the level of customer contact, service businesses strive to provide a standardized process, and technology offers an interface that creates an automatic and structured response. The ideal service provider will be high-tech and high-touch. JetBlue, for example, strives to maintain an excellent website; friendly, helpful customer contact; and satellite TV service at every seat on each plane. Thus, service organizations must build their operations around good execution, which comes from hiring and training excellent employees, developing flexible systems, customizing services, and maintaining adjustable capacity to deal with fluctuating demand.[4]

Another challenge related to service operations is that the output is generally intangible and even perishable. Few services can be saved, stored, resold, or returned.[5] A seat on an airline or a table in a restaurant, for example, cannot be sold or used at a later date. Because of the perishability of services, it can be extremely difficult for service providers to accurately estimate the demand in order to match the right supply of a service. If an airline overestimates demand, for example, it will still have to fly each plane even with empty seats. The flight costs the same regardless of whether it is 50 percent full or 100 percent full, but the former will result in much higher costs per passenger. If the airline underestimates demand, the result can be long lines of annoyed customers or even the necessity of bumping some customers off of an overbooked flight.

Businesses that manufacture tangible goods and those that provide services or ideas are similar yet different. For example, both types of organizations must make design and operating decisions. Most goods are manufactured prior to purchase, but most services are performed after purchase. Flight attendants at Southwest Airlines, hotel service personnel, and even the New York Giants football team engage in performances that are a part of the total product. Though manufacturers and service providers often perform similar activities, they also differ in several respects. We can classify these differences in five basic ways.

产出的本质和消费方式

Nature and Consumption of Output. First, manufacturers and service providers differ in the nature and consumption of their output. For example, the term *manufacturer* implies a firm that makes tangible products. A service provider, on the other hand, produces more intangible outputs such as U.S. Postal Service delivery of priority mail or a business stay in a Hyatt hotel. As mentioned earlier, the very nature of the service provider's product requires a higher degree of customer contact. Moreover, the actual performance of the service typically occurs at the point of consumption. At the Hyatt, the business traveler may evaluate in-room communications and the restaurant. Automakers, on the other hand, can separate the production of a car from its actual use, but the service dimension requires closer contact with the consumer. Manufacturing, then, can occur in an isolated environment, away from the customer. However, service providers, because of their need for customer contact, are often more limited than manufacturers in selecting work methods, assigning jobs, scheduling work, and exercising control over operations. For this reason, Freddie Mac implemented the Quality Control Information Manager (QCIM) system, a secure, web-based system that allows lenders access to the status of quality control loan file requests. The system makes it easier to control this important aspect of lending.[6] The quality of the service experience is often controlled by a service contact employee. However, some hospitals are studying the manufacturing processes and quality control mechanisms applied in

Subway's inputs are sandwich components such as bread, tomatoes, and lettuce, while its outputs are customized sandwiches.

the automotive industry in an effort to improve their service quality. By analyzing work processes to find unnecessary steps to eliminate and using teams to identify and address problems as soon as they occur, these hospitals are slashing patient waiting times, decreasing inventories of wheelchairs, readying operating rooms sooner, and generally moving patients through their hospital visit more quickly, with fewer errors, and at a lower cost.[7]

投入的一致程度

Uniformity of Inputs. A second way to classify differences between manufacturers and service providers has to do with the uniformity of inputs. Manufacturers typically have more control over the amount of variability of the resources they use than do service providers. For example, each customer calling Fidelity Investments is likely to require different services due to differing needs, whereas many of the tasks required to manufacture a Ford Focus are the same across each unit of output. Consequently, the products of service organizations tend to be more "customized" than those of their manufacturing counterparts. Consider, for example, a haircut versus a bottle of shampoo. The haircut is much more likely to incorporate your specific desires (customization) than is the bottle of shampoo.

产出的一致程度

Uniformity of Output. Manufacturers and service providers also differ in the uniformity of their output, the final product. Because of the human element inherent in providing services, each service tends to be performed differently. Not all grocery checkers, for example, wait on customers in the same way. If a barber or stylist performs 15 haircuts in a day, it is unlikely that any two of them will be exactly the same. Consequently, human and technological elements associated with a service can result in a different day-to-day or even hour-to-hour performance of that service. The service experience can even vary at McDonald's or Burger King despite the fact that the two chains employ very similar procedures and processes. Moreover, no two customers are exactly alike in their perception of the service experience. Health care offers another excellent example of this challenge. Every diagnosis, treatment, and surgery varies because every individual is different. In manufacturing, the high degree of automation available allows manufacturers to generate uniform outputs and, thus, the operations are more effective and efficient. For example, we would expect every TAG Heuer or Rolex watch to maintain very high standards of quality and performance.

所需人力

Labor Required. A fourth point of difference is the amount of labor required to produce an output. Service providers are generally more labor-intensive (require more labor) because of the high level of customer contact, perishability of the output (must be consumed immediately), and high degree of variation of inputs and outputs (customization). For example, Adecco provides temporary support personnel. Each temporary worker's performance determines Adecco's product quality. A manufacturer, on the other hand, is likely to be more capital-intensive because of the machinery and technology used in the mass production of highly similar goods. For instance, it would take a considerable investment for Ford to make an electric car that has batteries with a longer life.

生产率的测量

Measurement of Productivity. The final distinction between service providers and manufacturers involves the measurement of productivity for each output produced. For manufacturers, measuring productivity is fairly straightforward because of the tangibility of the output and its high degree of uniformity. For the service provider, variations in demand (for example, higher demand for air travel in some seasons than in others), variations in service requirements from job to job, and the intangibility of the product make productivity measurement more difficult. Consider, for example, how much easier it is to measure the productivity of employees involved in the production of Intel computer processors as opposed to serving the needs of Prudential Securities' clients.

It is convenient and simple to think of organizations as being either manufacturers or service providers as in the preceding discussion. In reality, however, most organizations are a combination of the two, with both tangible and intangible qualities embodied in what they produce. For example, Porsche provides customer services such as toll-free hotlines and warranty protection, while banks may sell checks and other tangible products that complement their primarily intangible product offering. Thus, we consider "products" to include both tangible physical goods and intangible service offerings. It is the level of tangibility of its principal product that tends to classify a company as either a manufacturer or a service provider. From an OM standpoint, this level of tangibility greatly influences the nature of the company's operational processes and procedures.

运营系统的规划和设计

Planning and Designing Operations Systems

LO 5-3

Before a company can produce any product, it must first decide what it will produce and for what group of customers. It must then determine what processes it will use to make these products as well as the facilities it needs to produce them. These decisions comprise operations planning. Although planning was once the sole realm of the production and operations department, today's successful companies involve all departments within an organization, particularly marketing and research and development, in these decisions.

产品规划

Planning the Product

Before making any product, a company first must determine what consumers want and then design a product to satisfy that want. Most companies use marketing research to determine the kinds of goods and services to provide and the features they must possess. Twitter and Facebook provide new opportunities for businesses to discover what consumers want, then design the product accordingly. For instance,the hamburger restaurant chain Red Robin used the social network Yammer to solicit customer and employee feedback. It has become extremely popular among employees and restaurant owners. When Red Robin introduced its new Tavern Double Burger, restaurant servers and regional managers posted comments they had heard from customers. Based on these comments, Red Robin was able to make immediate changes to its recipe to satisfy its customer needs. This process, which traditionally takes 6 to 12 months, took four weeks using social media.[8] Marketing research can also help gauge the demand for a product and how much consumers are willing to pay for it. But when a market's environment changes, firms have to be flexible.

Developing a product can be a lengthy, expensive process. For example, in the automobile industry, developing the new technology for night vision, parking assist systems, and a satellite service that locates and analyzes car problems has been a lengthy, expensive process. Most companies work to reduce development time and costs. The University of Leicester and Polytec UK joined together to build the Advanced Structural Dynamics Evaluation Centre (ASDEC), which reduces new product development time for the automotive and engineered systems industries.[9] Once management has developed an idea for a product that customers will buy, it must then plan how to produce the product.

Within a company, the engineering or research and development department is charged with turning a product idea into a workable design that can be produced economically. In smaller companies, a single individual (perhaps the owner) may be solely responsible for this crucial activity. Regardless of who is responsible for product design, planning does not stop with a blueprint for a product or a description of a service; it must also work out efficient production of the product to ensure that enough is available to satisfy consumer demand. How does a lawn mower company transform steel, aluminum, and other materials into a mower design that satisfies consumer and environmental requirements? Operations managers must plan for the types and quantities of materials needed to produce the product, the skills and quantity of people needed to make the product, and the actual processes through which the inputs must pass in their transformation to outputs.

运营流程的设计
Designing the Operations Processes

Before a firm can begin production, it must first determine the appropriate method of transforming resources into the desired product. Often, consumers' specific needs and desires dictate a process. Customer needs, for example, require that all 3/4-inch bolts have the same basic thread size, function, and quality; if they did not, engineers and builders could not rely on 3/4-inch bolts in their construction projects. A bolt manufacturer, then, will likely use a standardized process so that every 3/4-inch bolt produced is like every other one. On the other hand, a bridge often must be customized so that it is appropriate for the site and expected load; furthermore, the bridge must be constructed on site rather than in a factory. Typically, products are designed to be manufactured by one of three processes: standardization, modular design, or customization.

标准化

Standardization. Most firms that manufacture products in large quantities for many customers have found that they can make them cheaper and faster by standardizing designs. **Standardization** is making identical, interchangeable components or even complete products. With standardization, a customer may not get exactly what he or she wants, but the product generally costs less than a custom-designed product. Television sets, ballpoint pens, and tortilla chips are standardized products; most are manufactured on an assembly line. Standardization speeds up production and quality control and reduces production costs. And, as in the example of the 3/4-inch bolts, standardization provides consistency so that customers who need certain products to function uniformly all the time will get a product that meets their expectations. Standardization becomes more complex on a global scale because different countries have different standards for quality. To help solve this problem, the International Organization for Standardization (ISO) has developed a list of global standards that companies can adopt to assure stakeholders that they are complying with the highest quality, environmental, and managerial guidelines.

标准化
standardization
the making of identical interchangeable components or products

模块设计

Modular Design. **Modular design** involves building an item in self-contained units, or modules, that can be combined or interchanged to create different products. IKEA furniture, for example, embodies a modular design with several components.

模块设计
modular design
the creation of an item in self-contained units, or modules, that can be combined or interchanged to create different products

This allows for customers to mix and match components for customized design. Because many modular components are produced as integrated units, the failure of any portion of a modular component usually means replacing the entire component. Modular design allows products to be repaired quickly, thus reducing the cost of labor, but the component itself is expensive, raising the cost of repair materials. Many automobile manufacturers use modular design in the production process. Manufactured homes are built on a modular design and often cost about one-fourth the cost of a conventionally built house.

客户化

Customization. **Customization** is making products to meet a particular customer's needs or wants. Products produced in this way are generally unique. Such products include repair services, photocopy services, custom artwork, jewelry, and furniture, as well as large-scale products such as bridges, ships, and computer software. For instance, bicycles are popular products to customize. A company called Breadwinner Cycles designs eight models of bicycles in such a way that riders can customize various features and sizes to fit their specific needs.[10] Mass customization relates to making products that meet the needs or wants of a large number of individual customers. The customer can select the model, size, color, style, or design of the product. Dell can customize a computer with the exact configuration that fits a customer's needs. Services such as fitness programs and travel packages can also be custom designed for a large number of individual customers. For both goods and services, customers get to make choices and have options to determine the final product.

客户化
customization
making products to meet a particular customer's needs or wants

产能规划

Planning Capacity

Planning the operational processes for the organization involves two important areas: capacity planning and facilities planning. The term **capacity** basically refers to the maximum load that an organizational unit can carry or operate. The unit of measurement may be a worker or machine, a department, a branch, or even an entire plant. Maximum capacity can be stated in terms of the inputs or outputs provided. For example, an electric plant might state plant capacity in terms of the maximum number of kilowatt-hours that can be produced without causing a power outage, while a restaurant might state capacity in terms of the maximum number of customers who can be effectively—comfortably and courteously—served at any one particular time.

产能
capacity
the maximum load that an organizational unit can carry or operate

Efficiently planning the organization's capacity needs is an important process for the operations manager. Capacity levels that fall short can result in unmet demand, and consequently, lost customers. On the other hand, when there is more capacity available than needed, operating costs are driven up needlessly due to unused and often expensive resources. To avoid such situations, organizations must accurately forecast demand and then plan capacity based on these forecasts. Another reason for the importance of efficient capacity planning has to do with long-term commitment of resources. Often, once a capacity decision—such as factory size—has been implemented, it is very difficult to change the decision without incurring substantial costs. Large companies have come to realize that although change can be expensive, not adjusting to future demand and stakeholder desires will be more expensive in the long run. For this reason, Honda has begun to adopt ISO 14001 guidelines for environmental management systems in its factories. These systems help firms monitor their impact on the environment. Thirteen of Honda's 14 North American factories have received certification.[12]

DID YOU KNOW? **Hershey's has the production capacity to make more than 80 million chocolate kisses per day.**[11]

设施规划

Planning Facilities

Once a company knows what process it will use to create its products, it then can design and build an appropriate facility in which to make them. Many products are manufactured in factories, but others are produced in stores, at home, or where the product ultimately will be used. Companies must decide where to locate their operations facilities, what layout is best for producing their particular product, and even what technology to apply to the transformation process.

Many firms are developing both a traditional organization for customer contact and a virtual organization. Charles Schwab Corporation, a securities brokerage and investment company, maintains traditional offices and has developed complete telephone and Internet services for customers. Through its website, investors can obtain personal investment information and trade securities over the Internet without leaving their home or office.

设施选址

Facility Location. Where to locate a firm's facilities is a significant question because, once the decision has been made and implemented, the firm must live with it due to the high costs involved. When a company decides to relocate or open a facility at a new location, it must pay careful attention to factors such as proximity to market, availability of raw materials, availability of transportation, availability of power, climatic influences, availability of labor, community characteristics (quality of life),

Apple stores are designed to make the most efficient use of space. The layout of the stores allows customers to test its products before purchasing.

and taxes and inducements. Inducements and tax reductions have become an increasingly important criterion in recent years. To increase production and to provide incentives for small startups, many states are offering tax inducements for solar companies. State governments are willing to forgo some tax revenue in exchange for job growth, getting in on a burgeoning industry as well as the good publicity generated by the company. In a very solar-friendly state like Colorado, companies may get tax reductions for starting production, and consumers receive additional rebates for installing solar systems in their homes and businesses.[13] Apple has followed the lead of other major companies by locating its manufacturing facilities in Asia to take advantage of lower labor and production costs. The facility-location decision is complex because it involves the evaluation of many factors, some of which cannot be measured with precision. Because of the long-term impact of the decision, however, it is one that cannot be taken lightly.

设施布局

Facility Layout. Arranging the physical layout of a facility is a complex, highly technical task. Some industrial architects specialize in the design and layout of certain types of businesses. There are three basic layouts: fixed-position, process, and product.

A company using a **fixed-position layout** brings all resources required to create the product to a central location. The product—perhaps an office building, house, hydroelectric plant, or bridge—does not move. A company using a fixed-position layout may be called a **project organization** because it is typically involved in large, complex projects such as construction or exploration. Project organizations generally make a unique product, rely on highly skilled labor, produce very few units, and have high production costs per unit.

Firms that use a **process layout** organize the transformation process into departments that group related processes. A metal fabrication plant, for example, may have a cutting department, a drilling department, and a polishing department. A hospital may have an X-ray unit, an obstetrics unit, and so on. These types of organizations are sometimes called **intermittent organizations,** which deal with products of a lesser magnitude than do project organizations, and their products are not necessarily unique but possess a significant number of differences. Doctors, makers of custom-made cabinets, commercial printers, and advertising agencies are intermittent organizations because they tend to create products to customers' specifications and produce relatively few units of each product. Because of the low level of output, the cost per unit of product is generally high.

The **product layout** requires that production be broken down into relatively simple tasks assigned to workers, who are usually positioned along an assembly line. Workers remain in one location, and the product moves from one worker to another. Each person in turn performs his or her required tasks or activities. Companies that use assembly lines are usually known as **continuous manufacturing organizations,** so named because once they are set up, they run continuously, creating products with many similar characteristics. Examples of products produced on assembly lines are automobiles, television sets, vacuum cleaners, toothpaste, and meals from a cafeteria. Continuous manufacturing organizations using a product layout are characterized by the standardized product they produce, the large number of units produced, and the relatively low unit cost of production.

Many companies actually use a combination of layout designs. For example, an automobile manufacturer may rely on an assembly line (product layout) but may also use a process layout to manufacture parts.

定位式布局
fixed-position layout
a layout that brings all resources required to create the product to a central location

项目型组织
project organization
a company using a fixed-position layout because it is typically involved in large, complex projects such as construction or exploration

流程式布局
process layout
a layout that organizes the transformation process into departments that group related processes

间歇型组织
intermittent organizations
organizations that deal with products of a lesser magnitude than do project organizations; their products are not necessarily unique but possess a significant number of differences

产品式布局
product layout
a layout requiring that production be broken down into relatively simple tasks assigned to workers, who are usually positioned along an assembly line

连续制造型组织
continuous manufacturing organizations
companies that use continuously running assembly lines, creating products with many similar characteristics

科技

Technology. Every industry has a basic, underlying technology that dictates the nature of its transformation process. The steel industry continually tries to improve steelmaking techniques. The health care industry performs research into medical technologies and pharmaceuticals to improve the quality of health care service. Two developments that have strongly influenced the operations of many businesses are computers and robotics.

计算机辅助设计
computer-assisted design (CAD)
the design of components, products, and processes on computers instead of on paper

计算机辅助制造
computer-assisted manufacturing (CAM)
manufacturing that employs specialized computer systems to actually guide and control the transformation processes

Computers have been used for decades and on a relatively large scale since IBM introduced its 650 series in the late 1950s. The operations function makes great use of computers in all phases of the transformation process. **Computer-assisted design (CAD),** for example, helps engineers design components, products, and processes on the computer instead of on paper. CAD is used in 3D printing. CAD software is used to develop a 3D image. Then, the CAD file is sent to the printer. The printer is able to use layers of liquid, powder, paper, or metal to construct a 3D model.[14] **Computer-assisted manufacturing (CAM)** goes a step further, employing specialized computer systems to actually guide and control the transformation processes. Such systems can monitor the transformation process, gathering information about the equipment used to produce the products and about the product itself as it goes from one stage of the transformation process to the next. The computer provides information to an operator who may, if necessary, take corrective action. In some highly automated systems, the computer itself can take corrective action. At Dell's OptiPlex Plant, electronic instructions are sent to double-decker conveyor belts that speed computer components to assembly stations. Two-member teams are told by computers which PC or server to build, with initial assembly taking only three to four minutes. Then more electronic commands move the products to a finishing area to be customized, boxed, and sent to waiting delivery trucks.

柔性制造
flexible manufacturing
the direction of machinery by computers to adapt to different versions of similar operations

Using **flexible manufacturing,** computers can direct machinery to adapt to different versions of similar operations. For example, with instructions from a computer, one machine can be programmed to carry out its function for several different versions of an engine without shutting down the production line for refitting.

Robots are also becoming increasingly useful in the transformation process. These "steel-collar" workers have become particularly important in industries such as nuclear power, hazardous-waste disposal, ocean research, and space construction and maintenance, in which human lives would otherwise be at risk. Robots are used in numerous applications by companies around the world. Many assembly operations—cars, television sets, telephones, stereo equipment, and numerous other products—depend on industrial robots. The Robotic Industries Association estimates that about 228,000 robots are now at work in U.S. factories, making the United States one of the two largest users of robotics, second only to Japan. Researchers continue to make more sophisticated robots, extending their use beyond manufacturing and space programs to various industries, including laboratory research, education, medicine, and household activities. Projections for the next few years indicate that these emerging markets will account for the use of 22 million robots. There are many advantages in using robotics, such as more successful surgeries, re-shoring manufacturing activities back to America, energy conservation, and safer work practices.[15]

计算机集成制造
computer-integrated manufacturing (CIM)
a complete system that designs products, manages machines and materials, and controls the operations function

When all these technologies—CAD/CAM, flexible manufacturing, robotics, computer systems, and more—are integrated, the result is **computer-integrated manufacturing (CIM),** a complete system that designs products, manages machines and materials, and controls the operations function. Companies adopt CIM to boost productivity and quality and reduce costs. Such technology, and computers in particular, will continue to make strong inroads into operations on two fronts—one dealing with

Responding to Business Challenges

Lenovo Gains a Competitive Advantage through Manufacturing

Lenovo, a Chinese computer company and one of the largest PC manufacturers in the world, has defied the state of the personal computer market by experiencing rapid growth and increase in market share. In 2013, the company completed a 240,000-square-foot manufacturing facility in Whitsett, North Carolina, where it previously had a logistics center, customer solutions center, and national returns center. This expansion will enable it to become even larger, which is necessary for its next venture.

While the company specializes in PCs, Lenovo is preparing to enter the U.S. mobile phone market. The market is highly competitive, with Apple and Samsung holding 70 percent of the market. Despite the intense competition, however, Lenovo's manufacturing plant could help it gain a competitive advantage. For instance, the manufacturing plant could be used to increase the range of Lenovo's product lines. The company also achieves efficiencies in manufacturing that may help it save costs and meet changing market conditions. Lenovo sets itself apart from others in the industry by having all parts of the production process in-house. It does not outsource any activities, unlike many other companies in the industry. This allows the firm to keep up with the changes in innovation by better understanding and controlling inventory, matching supply with demand, and handling fast inventory turnover.[16]

Discussion Questions

1. Despite the decline in PCs, Lenovo has surpassed most of its competitors in the computer market. Do you think it can do the same in the mobile phone industry?
2. Describe some of the ways Lenovo sets itself apart from competitors.
3. How might keeping the production process in-house help Lenovo?

the technology involved in manufacturing and one dealing with the administrative functions and processes used by operations managers. The operations manager must be willing to work with computers and other forms of technology and to develop a high degree of computer literacy

可持续发展与制造
Sustainability and Manufacturing

Manufacturing and operations systems are moving quickly to establish environmental sustainability and minimize negative impact on the natural environment. Sustainability deals with conducting activities in such a way as to provide for the long-term well-being of the natural environment, including all biological entities. Sustainability issues are becoming increasingly important to stakeholders and consumers, as they pertain to the future health of the planet. Some sustainability issues include pollution of the land, air, and water, climate change, waste management, deforestation, urban sprawl, protection of biodiversity, and genetically modified foods.

For example, Biogen Idec, the world's oldest biotechnology company, set a goal in 2009 to increase sustainability of operations in water, energy, and materials usage by 15 percent in 2015. The company reached this goal in 2012 by using an internally developed tool called Risk-Weighted Environmental Index to measure the impact of its operations on the environment. As a result, the company was awarded a spot on the Dow Jones Sustainability World Index. Biogen Idec is the first American biotechnology company to be awarded this honor.[17]

New Belgium Brewing is another company that illustrates green initiatives in operations and manufacturing. New Belgium was the first brewery to adopt 100 percent wind-powered electricity, reducing carbon emissions by 1,800 metric tons a year. It uses a steam condenser to capture hot water to be reused for boiling the next batch of barley and hops. Then the steam is redirected to heat the floor tiles and de-ice the loading docks

The outdoor clothing company Patagonia is always looking for a greener way to design, produce, and recycle its products. The company's mission statement: *Build the best product, cause no unnecessary harm, and use business to inspire and implement solutions to the environmental crisis.*

in cold Colorado weather. Used barley and hops are given to local farmers to feed cattle. The company is moving to aluminum cans because they can be recycled an infinite number of times, and recycling one can save enough electricity to run a television for three hours or save a half gallon of gasoline.

Biogen Idec and New Belgium Brewing demonstrate that reducing waste, recycling, conserving, and using renewable energy not only protect the environment, but can also gain the support of stakeholders. Green operations and manufacturing can improve a firm's reputation along with customer and employee loyalty, leading to improved profits.

Much of the movement to green manufacturing and operations is the belief that global warming and climate change must decline. The McKinsey Global Institute (MGI) says that just by investing in existing technologies, the world's energy use could be reduced by 50 percent by the year 2020. Creating green buildings and higher mileage cars could yield $900 billion in savings per year by 2020.[18] Companies like General Motors and Ford are adapting to stakeholder demands for greater sustainability by producing smaller and more fuel-efficient cars. Tesla has taken sustainability even further by making a purely electric vehicle that also ranks at the top in safety. The company also makes sure that its manufacturing facilities operate sustainably by installing solar panels and other renewable sources of energy. Green products produced through green operations and manufacturing are our future. A report authored by the Center for American Progress cites ways that cities and local governments can play a role. For example, Los Angeles plans to save the city utility costs by retrofitting hundreds of city buildings while creating a green careers training program for low-income residents. Newark, New Jersey, and Richmond, California, also have green jobs training programs.[19] Government initiatives provide space for businesses to innovate their green operations and manufacturing.

供应链管理
Managing the Supply Chain

LO 5-4

供应链管理
supply chain management connecting and integrating all parties or members of the distribution system in order to satisfy customers

A major function of operations is **supply chain management,** which refers to connecting and integrating all parties or members of the distribution system in order to satisfy customers.[20] Also called logistics, supply chain management includes all the activities involved in obtaining and managing raw materials and component parts, managing finished products, packaging them, and getting them to customers. UPS implemented a cloud-based supply chain management system to better control international operations. This allowed for more accuracy and on-time delivery of shipments, better management and coordination of suppliers, and real-time shipment status of packages.[21] The supply chain integrates firms such as raw material suppliers, manufacturers, retailers, and ultimate consumers into a seamless flow of information and products.[22] In this section, we look at purchasing, managing inventory, outsourcing, and scheduling, which are vital tasks in the transformation of raw materials into finished goods. To illustrate logistics, consider a hypothetical small business—we'll call it Rushing Water Canoes Inc.—that manufactures aluminum canoes, which it sells primarily to sporting goods stores and river-rafting expeditions. Our company also makes paddles and helmets, but the focus of the following discussion is the manufacture of the company's quality canoes as they proceed through the logistics process.

采购
Purchasing

Purchasing, also known as procurement, is the buying of all the materials needed by the organization. The purchasing department aims to obtain items of the desired quality in the right quantities at the lowest possible cost. Rushing Water Canoes, for example, must procure not only aluminum and other raw materials, and various canoe parts and components, but also machines and equipment, manufacturing supplies (oil, electricity, and so on), and office supplies in order to make its canoes. People in the purchasing department locate and evaluate suppliers of these items. They must constantly be on the lookout for new materials or parts that will do a better job or cost less than those currently being used. The purchasing function can be quite complex and is one area made much easier and more efficient by technological advances.

采购
purchasing
the buying of all the materials needed by the organization; also called procurement

Not all companies purchase all of the materials needed to create their products. Oftentimes, they can make some components more economically and efficiently than can an outside supplier. Zara, a Spanish fast fashion retailer, manufactures the majority of the clothes it sells.[23] On the other hand, firms sometimes find that it is uneconomical to make or purchase an item, and instead arrange to lease it from another organization. Some airlines, for example, lease airplanes rather than buy them. Whether to purchase, make, or lease a needed item generally depends on cost, as well as on product availability and supplier reliability.

库存管理
Managing Inventory

Once the items needed to create a product have been procured, some provision has to be made for storing them until they are needed. Every raw material, component, completed or partially completed product, and piece of equipment a firm uses—its **inventory**—must be accounted for, or controlled. There are three basic types of inventory. *Finished-goods inventory* includes those products that are ready for sale, such as a fully assembled automobile ready to ship to a dealer. *Work-in-process inventory* consists of those products that are partly completed or are in some stage of the transformation process. At McDonald's, a cooking hamburger represents work-in-process inventory because it must go through several more stages before it can be sold to a customer. *Raw materials inventory* includes all the materials that have been purchased to be used as inputs for making other products. Nuts and bolts are raw materials for an automobile manufacturer, while hamburger patties, vegetables, and buns are raw materials for the fast-food restaurant. Our fictional Rushing Water Canoes has an inventory of materials for making canoes, paddles, and helmets, as well as its inventory of finished products for sale to consumers. **Inventory control** is the process of determining how many supplies and goods are needed and keeping track of quantities on hand, where each item is, and who is responsible for it.

库存
inventory
all raw materials, components, completed or partially completed products, and pieces of equipment a firm uses

库存控制
inventory control
the process of determining how many supplies and goods are needed and keeping track of quantities on hand, where each item is, and who is responsible for it

Operations management must be closely coordinated with inventory control. The production of televisions, for example, cannot be planned without some knowledge of the availability of all the necessary materials—the chassis, picture tubes, color guns,

Operations managers are concerned with managing inventory to ensure that there is enough inventory in stock to meet demand.

and so forth. Also, each item held in inventory—any type of inventory—carries with it a cost. For example, storing fully assembled televisions in a warehouse to sell to a dealer at a future date requires not only the use of space, but also the purchase of insurance to cover any losses that might occur due to fire or other unforeseen events.

Inventory managers spend a great deal of time trying to determine the proper inventory level for each item. The answer to the question of how many units to hold in inventory depends on variables such as the usage rate of the item, the cost of maintaining the item in inventory, future costs of inventory and other procedures associated with ordering or making the item, and the cost of the item itself. For example, the price of copper has fluctuated between $1.50 and $3 a pound over the past five years.[24] Firms using copper wiring for construction, copper pipes for plumbing, and other industries requiring copper have to analyze the trade-offs between inventory costs and expected changes in the price of copper. Several approaches may be used to determine how many units of a given item should be procured at one time and when that procurement should take place.

经济订货批量模型

The Economic Order Quantity Model. To control the number of items maintained in inventory, managers need to determine how much of any given item they should order. One popular approach is the **economic order quantity (EOQ) model,** which identifies the optimum number of items to order to minimize the costs of managing (ordering, storing, and using) them.

经济订货批量模型
economic order quantity (EOQ) model
a model that identifies the optimum number of items to order to minimize the costs of managing (ordering, storing, and using) them

准时制库存管理
just-in-time (JIT) inventory management
a technique using smaller quantities of materials that arrive "just in time" for use in the transformation process and therefore require less storage space and other inventory management expense

准时制库存管理

Just-in-Time Inventory Management. An increasingly popular technique is **just-in-time (JIT) inventory management,** which eliminates waste by using smaller quantities of materials that arrive "just in time" for use in the transformation process and therefore require less storage space and other inventory management expense. JIT minimizes inventory by providing an almost continuous flow of items from suppliers to the production facility. Many U.S. companies, including Hewlett-Packard, IBM, and Harley Davidson, have adopted JIT to reduce costs and boost efficiency.

Let's say that Rushing Water Canoes uses 20 units of aluminum from a supplier per day. Traditionally, its inventory manager might order enough for one month at a time: 440 units per order (20 units per day times 22 workdays per month). The expense of such a large inventory could be considerable because of the cost of insurance coverage, recordkeeping, rented storage space, and so on. The just-in-time approach would reduce these costs because aluminum would be purchased in smaller quantities, perhaps in lot sizes of 20, which the supplier would deliver once a day. Of course, for such an approach to be effective, the supplier must be extremely reliable and relatively close to the production facility.

On the other hand, there are some downsides to just-in-time inventory management that marketers must take into account. When the earthquake and tsunami hit Japan, resulting in a nuclear reactor crisis, several Japanese companies halted their operations. Some multinationals relied so much upon their Japanese suppliers that their supply chains were also affected. In the case of natural disasters, having only enough inventory to meet current needs could create delays in production and hurt the company's bottom line. For this reason, many economists suggest that businesses store components that are essential for production and diversify their supply chains. That way, if a natural disaster knocks out a major supplier, the company can continue to operate.[25]

物料需求计划

Material-requirements Planning. Another inventory management technique is **material-requirements planning (MRP),** a planning system that schedules the precise quantity of materials needed to make the product. The basic components of MRP are a master production schedule, a bill of materials, and an inventory status file. At Rushing Water Canoes, for example, the inventory-control manager will look at the production schedule to determine how many canoes the company plans to make. He or she will then prepare a bill of materials—a list of all the materials needed to make that quantity of canoes. Next, the manager will determine the quantity of these items that RWC already holds in inventory (to avoid ordering excess materials) and then develop a schedule for ordering and accepting delivery of the right quantity of materials to satisfy the firm's needs. Because of the large number of parts and materials that go into a typical production process, MRP must be done on a computer. It can be, and often is, used in conjunction with just-in-time inventory management.

物料需求计划
material-requirements planning (MRP)
a planning system that schedules the precise quantity of materials needed to make the product

外包
Outsourcing

Increasingly, outsourcing has become a component of supply chain management in operations. Outsourcing refers to the contracting of manufacturing or other tasks to independent companies, often overseas. Many companies elect to outsource some aspects of their operations to companies that can provide these products more efficiently, at a lower cost, and with greater customer satisfaction. Globalization has put pressure on supply chain managers to improve speed and balance resource against competitive pressures. Companies outsourcing to China, in particular, face heavy regulation, high transportation costs, inadequate facilities, and unpredictable supply chain execution. Therefore, suppliers need to provide useful, timely, and accurate information about every aspect of the quality requirements, schedules, and solutions to dealing with problems. Companies that hire suppliers must also make certain that their suppliers are following company standards; failure to do so could lead to criticism of the parent company. For example, Tesco, a British grocery chain, had to reevaluate its supply chain after some meat sold in its stores was found to have traces of horse meat. Some changes include sourcing meat from closer locations and conducting DNA testing on meat.[26]

Many high-tech firms have outsourced the production of chips, computers, and telecom equipment to Asian companies. The hourly labor costs in countries such as China, India, and Vietnam are far less than in the United States, Europe, or even Mexico. These developing countries have improved their manufacturing capabilities, infrastructure, and technical and business skills, making them more attractive regions for global sourcing. For instance, Nike outsources almost all of its production to Asian countries such as China and Vietnam. On the other hand, the cost of outsourcing halfway around the world must be considered in decisions. While information technology

Going Green

Automakers Look toward Hydrogen Fuel Vehicles

In order to meet the California government's clean air requirements, automakers have been investing millions of dollars into research and development for clean vehicle technology. Electric vehicles are becoming more popular, but a lack of infrastructure, the range of charge, and high prices are impacting widespread adoption. Automakers are investigating other forms of cleaner energy, including hydrogen fuel.

Investments into hydrogen fuel-cell technology have proved promising as the costs have significantly fallen and vehicles can travel 250 miles on a single tank. However, there is still the service problem due to lack of infrastructure. Extracting hydrogen can be a difficult and time-consuming process. Additionally, hydrogen vehicles will require cities to build hydrogen fueling stations. Hydrogen fuel cars require high capital costs, which have led many automakers to conclude that wide-scale manufacturing of these cars will not be feasible until about 2020.

On the other hand, Toyota is not allowing these challenges to hinder its production. Toyota plans to release its first hydrogen fuel car in 2015. Honda has already begun selling hydrogen-fuel electric cars in California. Additionally, California announced plans to install 68 hydrogen fueling stations by the end of 2015. Whether automakers plan to introduce hydrogen fuel-cell vehicles in a few years or in another decade, it seems clear that auto companies are very interested in this alternative fuel technology.[27]

Discussion Questions

1. Why are automakers attempting to develop more eco-friendly vehicles?
2. What are some of the challenges in the manufacturing and adoption of hydrogen fuel cars?
3. Why do you think Toyota is willing to expend resources in developing hydrogen vehicles despite the high costs of capital involved?

is often outsourced today, transportation, human resources, services, and even marketing functions can be outsourced. Our hypothetical Rushing Water Canoes might contract with a local janitorial service to clean its offices and with a local accountant to handle routine bookkeeping and tax-preparation functions.

Outsourcing, once used primarily as a cost-cutting tactic, has increasingly been linked with the development of competitive advantage through improved product quality, speeding up the time it takes products to get to the customer, and overall supply-chain efficiencies. Table 5.1 provides the world's top five outsourcing providers that assist mainly in information technology. Outsourcing allows companies to free up time and resources to focus on what they do best and to create better opportunities to focus on customer satisfaction. Many executives view outsourcing as an innovative way to boost productivity and remain competitive against low-wage offshore factories. However, outsourcing may create conflict with labor and negative public opinion when it results in U.S. workers being replaced by lower-cost workers in other countries.

TABLE 5.1
The World's Top Five Outsourcing Providers

Company	Services
ISS	Facility services
Accenture	Management consulting, technology, and outsourcing
Wipro	Global information technology, consulting, and outsourcing
CBRE	Commercial real estate services
Infosys	Business consulting, IT services, and product engineering

Source: International Association of Outsourcing, "The 2013 Global Outsourcing 100".

生产路径和日程安排
Routing and Scheduling

After all materials have been procured and their use determined, managers must then consider the **routing,** or sequence of operations through which the product must pass. For example, before employees at Rushing Water Canoes can form aluminum sheets into a canoe, the aluminum must be cut to size. Likewise, the canoe's flotation material must be installed before workers can secure the wood seats. The sequence depends on the product specifications developed by the engineering department of the company.

生产路径
routing
the sequence of operations through which the product must pass

Once management knows the routing, the actual work can be scheduled. **Scheduling** assigns the tasks to be done to departments or even specific machines, workers, or teams. At Rushing Water, cutting aluminum for the company's canoes might be scheduled to be done by the "cutting and finishing" department on machines designed especially for that purpose.

日程安排
scheduling
the assignment of required tasks to departments or even specific machines, workers, or teams

Many approaches to scheduling have been developed, ranging from simple trial and error to highly sophisticated computer programs. One popular method is the *Program Evaluation and Review Technique (PERT),* which identifies all the major activities or events required to complete a project, arranges them in a sequence or path, determines the critical path, and estimates the time required for each event. Producing a McDonald's Big Mac, for example, involves removing meat, cheese, sauce, and vegetables from the refrigerator; grilling the hamburger patties; assembling the ingredients; placing the completed Big Mac in its package; and serving it to the customer (Figure 5.3). The cheese, pickles, onions, and sauce cannot be put on before the hamburger patty is completely grilled and placed on the bun. The path that requires the longest time from start to finish is called the *critical path* because it determines the minimum amount of time in which the process can be completed. If any of the activities on the critical path for production of the Big Mac fall behind schedule, the sandwich will not be completed on time, causing customers to wait longer than they usually would.

FIGURE 5.3 **A Hypothetical PERT Diagram for a McDonald's Big Mac**

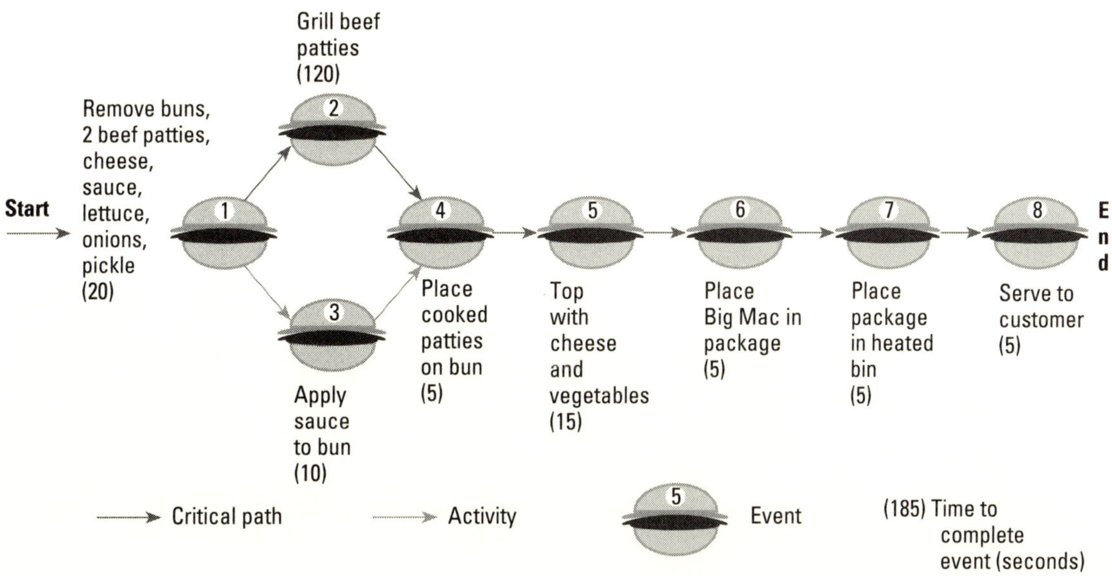

质量管理
Managing Quality

LO 5-5

Quality, like cost and efficiency, is a critical element of operations management, for defective products can quickly ruin a firm. Quality reflects the degree to which a good or service meets the demands and requirements of customers. Customers are increasingly dissatisfied with the quality of service provided by many airlines. Table 5.2 gives the rankings of U.S. airlines in certain operational areas. Determining quality can be difficult because it depends on customers' perceptions of how well the product meets or exceeds their expectations. For example, customer satisfaction on airlines can vary wildly depending on individual customers' perspectives. However, the airline industry is notorious for its dissatisfied customers. Flight delays are a common complaint from airline passengers; 30 percent of all flights arrive late. However, most passengers do not select an airline based on how often flights arrive on time.[28]

The fuel economy of an automobile or its reliability (defined in terms of frequency of repairs) can be measured with some degree of precision. Although automakers rely on their own measures of vehicle quality, they also look to independent sources such as the J.D. Power & Associates annual initial quality survey for confirmation of their quality assessment as well as consumer perceptions of quality for the industry, as indicated in Figure 5.4.

It is especially difficult to measure quality characteristics when the product is a service. A company has to decide exactly which quality characteristics it considers important and then define those characteristics in terms that can be measured. The inseparability of production and consumption and the level of customer contact

TABLE 5.2
2013 Airline Scorecard (Best to Worst)

Rank	Overall Rank	On-Time Arrival	Cancelled Flights	Baggage Handling	Bumping Passengers	Customer Complaints
1	Alaska	Alaska	Delta	Virgin America	JetBlue	Southwest
2	Delta	Delta	Frontier	JetBlue	Virgin America	Alaska
3	Virgin America	Virgin America	Virgin America	Delta	Alaska	Delta
4	Southwest	US Airways	Alaska	Frontier	American Airlines	JetBlue
5	JetBlue	United	Southwest	US Airways	US Airways	Virgin America
6	US Airways	American Airlines	JetBlue	Alaska	Delta	US Airways
7	Frontier	Southwest	US Airways	American Airlines	Frontier	American Airlines
8	American Airlines	JetBlue	United	United	Southwest	United
9	United	Frontier	American Airlines	Southwest	United	Frontier

Sources: FlightStats; U.S. Department of Transportation.

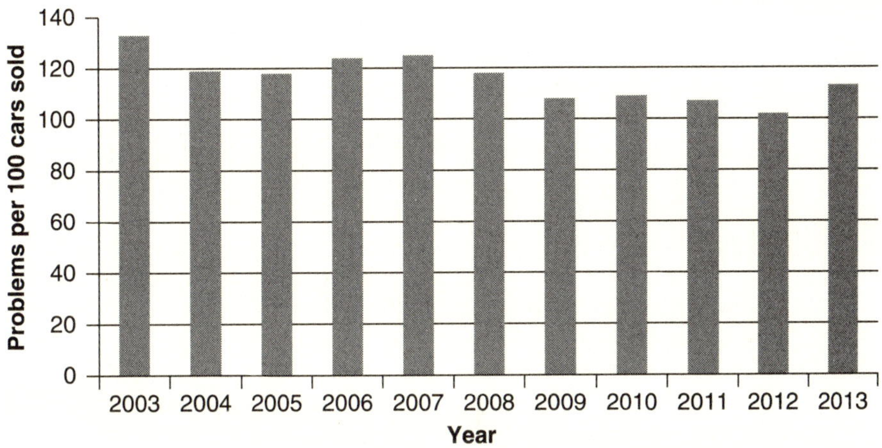

FIGURE 5.4
J.D. Power and Associates Initial Automobile Quality Study

Source: J.D. Power and Associates, "2013 U.S. Initial Quality Study," June 19, 2013.

influence the selection of characteristics of the service that are most important. Employees in high-contact services such as hairstyling, education, legal services, and even the barista at Starbucks are an important part of the product.

The Malcolm Baldrige National Quality Award is given each year to companies that meet rigorous standards of quality. The Baldrige criteria are (1) leadership, (2) information and analysis, (3) strategic planning, (4) human resource development and management, (5) process management, (6) business results, and (7) customer focus and satisfaction. The criteria have become a worldwide framework for driving business improvement. Three organizations won the award in 2013, representing two different categories: Pewaukee School District, Pewaukee, Wisconsin (education); Baylor Regional Medical Center at Plano, Plano, Texas (health care); and Sutter Davis Hospital, Davis, California (health care).[29]

Quality is so important that we need to examine it in the context of operations management. **Quality control** refers to the processes an organization uses to maintain its established quality standards. Kia recognized the importance of quality control when it sought to revamp its image. For years, Kia vehicles were seen as low quality. To change consumer perceptions of the Kia brand, the company had its quality-control managers provide final approval for its products instead of sales executives, implemented benchmarks for improving product quality, developed strong marketing campaigns promoting the brand, and cut dealers that they did not feel were supporting the Kia franchise. Kia's quality efforts were largely successful; its overall sales grew 27 percent in a one-year period.[30] Quality has become a major concern in many organizations, particularly in light of intense foreign competition and increasingly demanding customers. To regain a competitive edge, a number of firms have adopted a total quality management approach. **Total quality management (TQM)** is a philosophy that uniform commitment to quality in all areas of the organization will promote a culture that meets customers' perceptions of quality. It involves coordinating efforts to improve customer satisfaction, increasing employee participation, forming and strengthening supplier partnerships, and facilitating an organizational culture of continuous quality improvement. TQM requires constant improvements in all areas of the company as well as employee empowerment.

质量控制
quality control
the processes an organization uses to maintain its established quality standards

全面质量管理
total quality management (TQM)
a philosophy that uniform commitment to quality in all areas of an organization will promote a culture that meets customers' perceptions of quality

Continuous improvement of an organization's goods and services is built around the notion that quality is free; by contrast, *not* having high-quality goods and services can be very expensive, especially in terms of dissatisfied customers.[31] A primary tool of the continuous improvement process is *benchmarking,* the measuring and evaluating of the quality of the organization's goods, services, or processes as compared with the quality produced by the best-performing companies in the industry.[32] Benchmarking lets the organization know where it stands competitively in its industry, thus giving it a goal to aim for over time. Now that online digital media are becoming more important in businesses, companies such as Compuware Corporation offer benchmarking tools so companies can monitor and compare the success of their websites. Such tools allow companies to track traffic to the site versus competitors' sites. Studies have shown a direct link between website performance and online sales, meaning this type of benchmarking is important.[33]

Companies employing TQM programs know that quality control should be incorporated throughout the transformation process, from the initial plans to the development of a specific product through the product and production-facility design processes to the actual manufacture of the product. In other words, they view quality control as an element of the product itself, rather than as simply a function of the operations process. When a company makes the product correctly from the outset, it eliminates the need to rework defective products, expedites the transformation process itself, and allows employees to make better use of their time and materials. One method through which many companies have tried to improve quality is **statistical process control,** a system in which management collects and analyzes information about the production process to pinpoint quality problems in the production system.

统计过程控制
statistical process control
a system in which management collects and analyzes information about the production process to pinpoint quality problems in the production system

国际标准化组织
International Organization for Standardization (ISO)

Regardless of whether a company has a TQM program for quality control, it must first determine what standard of quality it desires and then assess whether its products meet that standard. Product specifications and quality standards must be set so the company can create a product that will compete in the marketplace. Rushing Water Canoes, for example, may specify that each of its canoes has aluminum walls of a specified uniform thickness, that the front and back be reinforced with a specified level of steel, and that each contain a specified amount of flotation material for safety. Production facilities must be designed that can produce products with the desired specifications.

Intel has adopted ISO 9000 quality standards to ensure consistent quality throughout its global operations.

Quality standards can be incorporated into service businesses as well. A hamburger chain, for example, may establish standards relating to how long it takes to cook an order and serve it to customers, how many fries are in each order, how thick the burgers are, or how many customer complaints might be acceptable. Once the desired quality characteristics, specifications, and standards have been stated in measurable terms, the next step is inspection.

The International Organization for Standardization (ISO) has created a series of quality management standards—**ISO 9000**—designed to ensure the customer's quality standards are met. The standards provide a framework for documenting how a certified business keeps records, trains employees, tests products, and fixes defects. To obtain ISO 9000 certification, an independent auditor must verify that a business's factory, laboratory, or office meets the quality standards spelled out by the International Organization for Standardization. The certification process can require significant investment, but for many companies, the process is essential to being able to compete. Thousands of companies have been certified, including General Electric Analytical Instruments, which has applied ISO standards to everything from the design to the manufacturing practices of its global facilities.[34] Certification has become a virtual necessity for doing business in Europe in some high-technology businesses. ISO 9002 certification was established for service providers. **ISO 14000** is a comprehensive set of environmental standards that encourages a cleaner and safer world. ISO 14000 is a valuable standard because currently considerable variation exists between the regulations in different nations, and even regions within a nation. These variations make it difficult for organizations committed to sustainability to find acceptable global solutions to problems. The goal of the ISO 14000 standards is to promote a more uniform approach to environmental management and to help companies attain and measure improvements in their environmental performance.

ISO 9000 质量标准

ISO 9000
a series of quality assurance standards designed by the International Organization for Standardization (ISO) to ensure consistent product quality under many conditions

ISO 14000 环境管理系列标准

ISO 14000
a comprehensive set of environmental standards that encourages companies to conduct business in a cleaner, safer, and less wasteful way; ISO 14000 provides a uniform set of standards globally

检查
Inspection

Inspection reveals whether a product meets quality standards. Some product characteristics may be discerned by fairly simple inspection techniques—weighing the contents of cereal boxes or measuring the time it takes for a customer to receive his or her hamburger. As part of the ongoing quality assurance program at Hershey Foods, all wrapped Hershey Kisses are checked, and all imperfectly wrapped kisses are rejected. Other inspection techniques are more elaborate. Automobile manufacturers use automated machines to open and close car doors to test the durability of latches and hinges. The food-processing and pharmaceutical industries use various chemical tests to determine the quality of their output. Rushing Water Canoes might use a special device that can precisely measure the thickness of each canoe wall to ensure that it meets the company's specifications.

Organizations normally inspect purchased items, work-in-process, and finished items. The inspection of purchased items and finished items takes place after the fact; the inspection of work-in-process is preventive. In other words, the purpose of inspection of purchased items and finished items is to determine what the quality level is. For items that are being worked on—an automobile moving down the assembly line or a canoe being assembled—the purpose of the inspection is to find defects before the product is completed so that necessary corrections can be made.

抽样
Sampling

An important question relating to inspection is how many items should be inspected. Should all canoes produced by Rushing Water be inspected or just some of them? Whether to inspect 100 percent of the output or only part of it is related to the cost of the inspection process, the destructiveness of the inspection process (some tests last until the product fails), and the potential cost of product flaws in terms of human lives and safety.

Some inspection procedures are quite expensive, use elaborate testing equipment, destroy products, and/or require a significant number of hours to complete. In such cases, it is usually desirable to test only a sample of the output. If the sample passes inspection, the inspector may assume that all the items in the lot from which the sample was drawn would also pass inspection. By using principles of statistical inference, management can employ sampling techniques that ensure a relatively high probability of reaching the right conclusion—that is, rejecting a lot that does not meet standards and accepting a lot that does. Nevertheless, there will always be a risk of making an incorrect conclusion—accepting a population that *does not* meet standards (because the sample was satisfactory) or rejecting a population that *does* meet standards (because the sample contained too many defective items).

Sampling is likely to be used when inspection tests are destructive. Determining the life expectancy of lightbulbs by turning them on and recording how long they last would be foolish: There is no market for burned-out lightbulbs. Instead, a generalization based on the quality of a sample would be applied to the entire population of lightbulbs from which the sample was drawn. However, human life and safety often depend on the proper functioning of specific items, such as the navigational systems installed in commercial airliners. For such items, even though the inspection process is costly, the potential cost of flawed systems—in human lives and safety—is too great not to inspect 100 percent of the output.

运营和供应链管理的整合
Integrating Operations and Supply Chain Management

Managing operations and supply chains can be complex and challenging due to the number of independent organizations that must perform their responsibilities in creating product quality. Managing supply chains requires constant vigilance and the ability to make quick tactical changes. Even Apple Inc., the most admired company in the world, has had supply chain problems. Reports of forced overtime, underage workers, and dangerous conditions at some of its supplier factories have resulted in negative publicity for the company.[35] Therefore, managing the various partners involved in supply chains and operations is important because many stakeholders hold the firm responsible for appropriate conduct related to product quality. This requires that the company exercise oversight over all suppliers involved in producing a product. Encouraging suppliers to report problems, issues, or concerns requires excellent communication systems to obtain feedback. Ideally, suppliers will report potential problems before they reach the next level of the supply chain, which reduces damage.

Despite the challenges of monitoring global operations and supply chains, there are steps businesses can take to manage these risks. All companies who work with global suppliers should adopt a Global Supplier Code of Conduct and ensure that it is effectively communicated. Additionally, companies should encourage compliance and procurement employees to work together to find ethical suppliers at reasonable costs. Those in procurement are concerned with the costs of obtaining materials for the company. As a result, supply chain and procurement managers must work together to make operational decisions to ensure the selection of the best suppliers from an ethical and cost-effective standpoint. Businesses must also work to make certain that their supply chains are diverse. Having only a few suppliers in one area can disrupt operations should a disaster strike. Finally, companies must perform regular audits on its suppliers and take action against those found to be in violation of company standards.[36]

So You Want a Job in Operations Management

While you might not have been familiar with terms such as *supply chain* or *logistics* or *total quality management* before taking this course, careers abound in the operations management field. You will find these careers in a wide variety of organizations—manufacturers, retailers, transportation companies, third-party logistics firms, government agencies, and service firms. Approximately $1.3 trillion is spent on transportation, inventory, and related logistics activities, and logistics alone accounts for more than 9.5 percent of U.S. gross domestic product.[37] Closely managing how a company's inputs and outputs flow from raw materials to the end consumer is vital to a firm's success. Successful companies also need to ensure that quality is measured and actively managed at each step.

Supply chain managers have a tremendous impact on the success of an organization. These managers are engaged in every facet of the business process, including planning, purchasing, production, transportation, storage and distribution, customer service, and more. Their performance helps organizations control expenses, boost sales, and maximize profits.

Warehouse managers are a vital part of manufacturing operations. A typical warehouse manager's duties include overseeing and recording deliveries and pickups, maintaining inventory records and the product tracking system, and adjusting inventory levels to reflect receipts and disbursements. Warehouse managers also have to keep in mind customer service and employee issues. Warehouse managers can earn up to $60,000 in some cases.

Operations management is also required in service businesses. With more than 80 percent of the U.S. economy in services, jobs exist for services operations. Many service contact operations require standardized processes that often use technology to provide an interface that provides an automatic quality performance. Consider jobs in health care, the travel industry, fast food, and entertainment. Think of any job or task that is a part of the final product in these industries. Even an online retailer such as Amazon.com has a transformation process that includes information technology and human activities that facilitate a transaction. These services have a standardized process and can be evaluated based on their level of achieved service quality.

Total quality management is becoming a key attribute for companies to ensure that quality pervades all aspects of the organization. Quality assurance managers make a median salary of $79,500. These managers monitor and advise on how a company's quality management system is performing and publish data and reports regarding company performance in both manufacturing and service industries.[38]

Review Your Understanding

Define operations management, and differentiate between operations and manufacturing.

Operations management (OM) is the development and administration of the activities involved in transforming resources into goods and services. Operations managers oversee the transformation process and the planning and designing of operations systems, managing logistics, quality, and productivity. The terms *manufacturing* and *production* are used interchangeably to describe the activities and processes used in making tangible products, whereas *operations* is a broader term used to describe the process of making both tangible and intangible products.

Explain how operations management differs in manufacturing and service firms.

Manufacturers and service firms both transform inputs into outputs, but service providers differ from manufacturers in several ways: They have greater customer contact because the service typically occurs at the point of consumption; their inputs and outputs are more variable than manufacturers', largely because of the human element; service providers are generally more labor intensive; and their productivity measurement is more complex.

Describe the elements involved in planning and designing an operations system.

Operations planning relates to decisions about what product(s) to make, for whom, and what processes and facilities are needed to produce them. OM is often joined by marketing and research and development in these decisions. Common facility layouts include fixed-position layouts, process layouts, or product layouts. Where to locate operations facilities is a crucial decision that depends on proximity to the market, availability of raw materials, availability of transportation, availability of power, climatic influences, availability of labor, and community characteristics. Technology is also vital to operations, particularly computer-assisted design, computer-assisted manufacturing, flexible manufacturing, robotics, and computer-integrated manufacturing.

Specify some techniques managers may use to manage the logistics of transforming inputs into finished products.

Logistics, or supply chain management, includes all the activities involved in obtaining and managing raw materials and component parts, managing finished products, packaging them, and getting them to customers. The organization must first make or purchase (procure) all the materials it needs. Next, it must control its inventory by determining how many supplies and goods it needs and keeping track of every raw material, component, completed or partially completed product, and piece of equipment, how many of each are on hand, where they are, and who has responsibility for them. Common approaches to inventory control include the economic order quantity (EOQ) model, the just-in-time (JIT) inventory concept, and material-requirements planning (MRP). Logistics also includes routing and scheduling processes and activities to complete products.

Assess the importance of quality in operations management.

Quality is a critical element of OM because low-quality products can hurt people and harm the business. Quality control refers to the processes an organization uses to maintain its established quality standards. To control quality, a company must establish what standard of quality it desires and then determine whether its products meet that standard through inspection.

Evaluate a business's dilemma and propose a solution.

Based on this chapter and the facts presented in "Solve the Dilemma" on page 258, you should be able to evaluate the business's problem and propose one or more solutions for resolving it.

Revisit the World of Business

1. Describe how suppliers of factory automation equipment are helping manufacturers to solve or prevent factory malfunctions.
2. How might these remote monitoring systems create greater efficiencies at factories?
3. What are some of the risks associated with continual monitoring by a third-party supplier?

Learn the Terms

capacity
computer-assisted design (CAD)
computer-assisted manufacturing (CAM)
computer-integrated manufacturing (CIM)
continuous manufacturing organizations
customization
economic order quantity (EOQ) model
fixed-position layout
flexible manufacturing
inputs
intermittent organizations
inventory
inventory control
ISO 9000
ISO 14000
just-in-time (JIT) inventory management
manufacturing
material-requirements planning (MRP)
modular design
operations
operations management (OM)
outputs
process layout
product layout
production
project organization
purchasing
quality control
routing
scheduling
standardization
statistical process control
supply chain management
total quality management (TQM)

Check Your Progress

1. What is operations management?
2. Differentiate among the terms *operations, production,* and *manufacturing.*
3. Compare and contrast a manufacturer versus a service provider in terms of operations management.
4. Who is involved in planning products?

5. In what industry would the fixed-position layout be most efficient? The process layout? The product layout? Use real examples.
6. What criteria do businesses use when deciding where to locate a plant?
7. What is flexible manufacturing? How can it help firms improve quality?
8. Define supply chain management and summarize the activities it involves.
9. Describe some of the methods a firm may use to control inventory.
10. When might a firm decide to inspect a sample of its products rather than test every product for quality?

Get Involved

1. Compare and contrast OM at McDonald's with that of Honda of America. Compare and contrast OM at McDonald's with that of a bank in your neighborhood.
2. Find a real company that uses JIT, either in your local community or in a business journal. Why did the company decide to use JIT? What have been the advantages and disadvantages of using JIT for that particular company? What has been the overall effect on the quality of the company's goods or services? What has been the overall effect on the company's bottom line?
3. Interview someone from your local Chamber of Commerce and ask him or her what incentives the community offers to encourage organizations to locate there. (See if these incentives relate to the criteria firms use to make location decisions.)

Build Your Skills

Reducing Cycle Time

Background

An important goal of production and operations management is reducing cycle time—the time it takes to complete a task or process. The goal in cycle time reduction is to reduce costs and/or increase customer service.[39] Many experts believe that the rate of change in our society is so fast that a firm must master speed and connectivity.[40] Connectivity refers to a seamless integration of customers, suppliers, employees, and organizational, production, and operations management. The use of the Internet and other telecommunications systems helps many organizations connect and reduce cycle time.

Task

Break up into pairs throughout the class. Select two businesses (local restaurants, retail stores, etc.) that both of you frequent, are employed by, and/or are fairly well acquainted with. For the first business, one of you will role-play the "manager" and the other will role-play the "customer." Reverse roles for the second business you have selected. As managers at your respective businesses, you are to prepare a list of five questions you will ask the customer during the role-play. The questions you prepare should be designed to get the customer's viewpoint on how good the cycle time is at your business. If one of the responses leads to a problem area, you may need to ask a follow-up question to determine the nature of the dissatisfaction. Prepare one main question and a follow-up, if necessary, for each of the five dimensions of cycle time:

1. **Speed**—the delivery of goods and services in the minimum time; efficient communications; the elimination of wasted time.
2. **Connectivity**—all operations and systems in the business appear connected with the customer.
3. **Interactive relationships**—a continual dialog exists among operations units, service providers, and customers that permits the exchange of feedback on concerns or needs.
4. **Customization**—each product is tailored to the needs of the customer.
5. **Responsiveness**—the willingness to make adjustments and be flexible to help customers and to provide prompt service when a problem develops.

Begin the two role-plays. When it is your turn to be the manager, listen carefully when your partner answers your prepared questions. You need to elicit information on how to improve the cycle time at your business. You will achieve this by identifying the problem areas (weaknesses) that need attention.

After completing both role-play situations, fill out the form on the next page for the role-play when you were the manager. You may not have gathered enough information to fill in all the boxes.

For example, for some categories, the customer may have had only good things to say; for others, the comments may all be negative. Be prepared to share the information you gain with the rest of the class.

I role-played the manager at (business). After listening carefully to the customer's responses to my five questions, I determined the following strengths and weaknesses as they relate to the cycle time at my business:

Dimension	Strength	Weakness
Speed		
Connectivity		
Interactive relationships		
Customization		
Responsiveness		

Solve the Dilemma LO 5-6

Planning for Pizza

McKing Corporation operates fast-food restaurants in 50 states, selling hamburgers, roast beef and chicken sandwiches, french fries, and salads. The company wants to diversify into the growing pizza business. Six months of tests revealed that the ideal pizza to sell was a 16-inch pie in three varieties: cheese, pepperoni, and deluxe (multiple toppings). Research found the size and toppings acceptable to families as well as to individuals (single buyers could freeze the leftovers), and the price was acceptable for a fast-food restaurant ($7.99 for cheese, $8.49 for pepperoni, and $9.99 for deluxe).

Marketing and human resources personnel prepared training manuals for employees, advertising materials, and the rationale to present to the restaurant managers (many stores are franchised). Store managers, franchisees, and employees are excited about the new plan. There is just one problem: The drive-through windows in current restaurants are too small for a 16-inch pizza to pass through. The largest size the present windows can accommodate is a 12-inch pie. The managers and franchisees are concerned that if this aspect of operations has been overlooked, perhaps the product is not ready to be launched. Maybe there are other problems yet to be uncovered.

Discussion Questions

1. What mistake did McKing make in approaching the introduction of pizza?
2. How could this product introduction have been coordinated to avoid the problems that were encountered?
3. If you were an executive at McKing, how would you proceed with the introduction of pizza into the restaurants?

Build Your Business Plan

Managing Service and Manufacturing Operations

For your business, you need to determine if you are providing raw materials that will be used in further production, or if you are a reseller of goods and services, known as a retailer. If you are the former, you need to determine what processes you go through in making your product.

The text provides ideas of breaking the process into inputs, transformation processes, and outputs. If you are a provider of a service or a link in the supply chain, you need to know exactly what your customer expectations are. Services are intangible, so it is all the more important to better understand what exactly the customer is looking for in resolving a problem or filling a need.

See for Yourself Videocase

Home Run Inn's Operational Excellence Propels It to Top Spot

It's not often that frozen pizza is compared favorably with fresh pizzas served in restaurants. Home Run Inn is the exception to the rule. Home Run Inn's frozen cheese pizza is considered tastier than the fresh deep dish and original pizzas from Domino's and Pizza Hut. In 2013, *Consumer Reports* named Home Run Inn as number one in the frozen pizza category. Its popularity is evident as it has become one of the fastest-growing frozen pizza companies in the nation. Today, Home Run Inn distributes pizza in 28 states and sells almost as much as DiGiorno and Tombstone brands combined.

Home Run Inn is a family-run business with headquarters in Chicago. The inspiration for the name happened after a baseball from a nearby sandlot crashed through Mary and Vincent Grittani's window of their new restaurant in 1923. More than 20 years later, in 1947 the Grittanis' son-in-law Nick Perinno partnered with Mary Grittani to develop the recipe for the company's all-natural Home Run Inn pizza. This pizza would place the restaurant on the map.

During the 1950s, the business chose to expand into the frozen pizza business. In the 1980s, Nick's son Joe Perrino, currently the president and CEO of the business, realized that they needed to expand if they wanted to grow. He began to look at ways to improve the organization's operations through automation. "We started very basically with conveyers and ovens, and we then proceeded with different presses," he said.

Soon, demand for Home Run Inn pizzas began to eclipse supply. Home Run Inn was unable to meet this demand with its current capacity due to manufacturing limitations. Cooking the pizzas and freezing them with conventional freezing methods was complex and placed constraints on how much the company could produce. As a result, Perrino decided to purchase a cryogenic freezer that freezes using CO_2 gas. The equipment cost $250,000, which was approximately what it would cost to purchase a restaurant. However, the result was far worth the money spent. Perrino states, "We were able to produce pizzas three, four times as fast as we were currently doing with fewer people, so that really set a light bulb off in our heads."

Two years later, the company built a new facility to keep up with demand. The major reason for this high demand is the quality of the pizza. Home Run Inn guarantees that its frozen pizzas are just as good as the pizzas it serves in its restaurants (it currently has nine restaurant locations). The company does this by controlling quality in-house. Home Run Inn pizza uses all-natural ingredients and its homemade sauce, sausage, and cheese. These all-natural ingredients have enabled the company to differentiate its products, allowing it to have higher prices compared to competitors and still retain high demand.

In 2002, Home Run Inn decided to go a step further. The company partnered with former Kraft CEO Jay Williams to self-distribute its pizzas. Until then, Home Run Inn frozen pizzas were stored in warehouses and then distributed to retailers. Self-distribution required the company to have its own fleet of trucks to deliver the pizzas to the retailers. This requires Home Run Inn to keep careful track of inventory in the stores. It was a significant investment for Home Run Inn, but it also allowed the company to control its supply chain and ensure that quality was maintained from manufacturing all the way to the finished product on the shelf. According to Perrino, this move helped the firm grow from 8 percent market share to 28 percent market share.

Thanks to quality operation processes, strong supply chain control, and careful monitoring of inventory, Home Run Inn pizza has secured its place as a top-quality frozen pizza business. Despite its high price compared to rivals, customers are eager to purchase Home Run Inn frozen pizza because they know the value is worth the price.[41]

Discussion Questions

1. Describe how taking risks to increase its operational capacity turned Home Run Inn pizza into the top player in the frozen pizza industry.
2. Why is Home Run Inn able to compete at prices higher than its rivals'?
3. Why has self-distribution been so beneficial for Home Run Inn? Do you think it would be successful for every manufacturing company?

You can find the related video in the Video Library in Connect. Ask your instructor how you can access Connect.

Team Exercise

Form groups and assign the responsibility of finding companies that outsource their production to other countries. What are the key advantages of this outsourcing decision? Do you see any drawbacks or weaknesses in this approach? Why would a company not outsource when such a tactic can be undertaken to cut manufacturing costs? Report your findings to the class.

Notes 注释

Chapter 1

1. Emily Chasan and Maxwell Murphy, "Activist Investors Go Big," *The Wall Street Journal*, October 1, 2013, p. B6; Michael J. De La Merced, "How Elliot and Hess Settled a Bitter Proxy Battle," *The New York Times*, May 16, 2013; Heidi Moore, "Activist Investor David Einhorn Drops 'iPref' Lawsuit against Apple," *The Guardian*, March 1, 2013.
2. The Entrepreneurs' Help Page; Kent Hoover, "Startups Down for Women Entrepreneurs, Up for Men," *SanFrancisco Business Times*, May 2, 2008.
3. Maggie Overfelt, "Start-Me-Up: How the Garage Became a Legendary Place to Rev Up Ideas," *Fortune Small Business*, September 1, 2003.
4. Forbes, "Barrett Business Services," October 2013. BBSI, "Our Solutions".
5. Bruce Horovitz, "Smashburger Thinks Outside Box to Compete," *USA Today*, August 19, 2013, p. 3B; Michael Thrasher, "Smashburger Founder Attributes Success to Unorthodox Marketing Strategy," *Business Insider*, August 8, 2013; "Smashburger Lands on the Inc. 500," Smashburger, 2011.
6. Webco, "Webco's General Partnership".
7. Crimson Renewable website; Stephanie Paul, "LLC or LP: What's Best for Your Business?" Legal Zoom, February 2011; Celia Lamb, "Biodiesel Company Eyes Port of Sacramento for Manufacturing, Storage Facility," *Sacramento Business Journal*, July 13, 2008.
8. Julie Triedman, "The Am Law 100, the Early Numbers: Profits Spike at Davis Polk," *American Lawyer*, February 28, 2014.
9. Bill Orben, "uBreakiFix Launches Franchise Unit, Sets Sights on 125 Stores This Year," *Orlando Business Journal*, February 20, 2013.
10. PwC, "Facts and Figures," 2013.
11. Henry Blodget, "Come On, Snapchat, Here's What Your Ousted Co-Founder Deserves—Settle This Lawsuit and Move On," *Business Insider*, November 22, 2013; Alyson Shantell, "Snapchat Has Tried Twice to Settle Its Lawsuit with Ousted Co-Founder Reggie Brown," *Business Insider*, December 18, 2013.
12. Warren Buffett's Berkshire Hathaway Letter to Shareholders.
13. "America's Largest Private Companies," *Forbes*, December 31, 2013.
14. "America's Largest Private Companies," *Forbes*, December 31, 2013; Carla Zanetos Scully, "2014 Global Top 100: Candy Industry's Exclusive List of the Top 100 Confectionery Companies in the World!" *Candy Industry*, January 31, 2014.
15. Deborah Orr, "The Secret World of Mars," Forbes, April 28, 2008.
16. "America's Largest Private Companies."
17. David Streitfeld, "Amazon's Revenue Soars, but No Profit Is in Sight," *New York Times*, October 24, 2013.
18. Liz Hoffman, "Moelis Founder to Keep Control after IPO," *Money Beat*, March 4, 2014.
19. Forbes Corporate Communications, "Forbes 2013 10th Annual Global 2000: The World's Biggest Public Companies," *Forbes*, April 17, 2013.
20. Ibid.; Scott DeCarlo, "The World's Biggest Companies," *Forbes*, April 17, 2013.
21. Ingrid Lunden, "Big Data Analytics Specialist Tableau Software Raises $254M in IPO, Shares Close 64% Up; Marketo's First Day Up 78% to $23.10," *Tech Crunch*, May 17, 2013; Chris Preston, "Rocket Fuel Headlines Huge Week for IPOs," *Yahoo! Finance*, September 25, 2013; Josh Costine, "Veeva Systems' Life Science Cloud IPO Is a Hit, Raising $217M and Closing up 85%," *Tech Crunch*, October 16, 2013.
22. Brendan Marasco, "3 Reasons Dell Went Private," *The Motley Fool*, November 1, 2013.
23. O. C. Ferrell, John Fraedrich, and Linda Ferrell, *Business Ethics: Ethical Decision Making and* Cases, 8th ed. (Mason, OH: South-Western Cengage Learning, 2011), p. 109.
24. Chris Burritt and Jeffrey McCracken, "Best Buy Says It Got No Offer from Founder Schulze," *Bloomberg*, March 1, 2013; Abram Brown, "Best Buy Founder Schulze Returns as Chairman Emeritus after Failed LBO," *Forbes*, March 25, 2013.
25. Diane Brady, "Cozy Corporate Directors Raise Their Pay to $1,000 an Hour," *Bloomberg Businessweek*, May 30, 2013.
26. P&G, "Board Composition," 2013.
27. Joseph Nathan Kane, *Famous First Facts*, 4th ed. (New York: The H.W. Wilson Company, 1981), p. 202.
28. Reuters, "Venezuela Launches Joint Venture with Samsung Electronics," November 20, 2013.
29. Robert D. Hisrich and Michael P. Peters, *Entrepreneurship*, 5th ed. (Boston: McGraw-Hill, 2002), pp. 315–16.
30. SEC, "List of Companies".
31. Coop Directory, "Coop Directory Service Listing".
32. David Gelles, "For Once-Mighty Sears, Pictures of Decay," *The New York Times*, October 13, 2013, pp. B1, B5; Sears, "Sears History"; Brigid Sweeney, "Sears—Where America Shopped," Crane's Chicago Business, April 23, 2012; Associated Press, "Kmart to Acquire Sears in $11 Billion Deal," *NBC News*, November 17, 2004.
33. Aaron Tilley, "Google Acquires Smart Thermostat Maker Nest for $3.2 Billion," *Forbes*, January 13, 2014.

34. Eric Savitz, "Did Google Buy a Lemon? Motorola Mobility Whiffs Q4," Forbes, January 8, 2012; Brian Womack, "Google Discloses $151 Million Price Tag for Zagat Service," *Bloomberg Businessweek*, October 26, 2011.
35. Andrew Edgecliffe-Johnson, "News Corp Adopts 'Poison Pill' Share Plan to Protect Divisions," *Financial Times*, May 24, 2013.
36. "Company Overview of PODS Enterprises, Inc.," *Bloomberg Businessweek*; "PODS Taking a Chunk Out of Moving and Storage Market," *USA Today*, August 4, 2006; Consortium Media Services, "PODS Recognized as One of the Nation's Best Service Providers by Professional Organizing Association," *Yahoo!® Voices*, February 28, 2011.

Chapter 2

1. Megan Durisin, "Chobani CEO: Our Success Has Nothing to Do With Yogurt," *Business Insider*, May 3, 2013; Deveon Pendleton, "Hidden Chobani Billionaire Emerges as Greek Yogurt Soars," *Bloomberg*, September 14, 2012; Maria Bartiromo, "A Conversation with the 'Steve Jobs of Yogurt,'" *USA Today*, June 17, 2013, p. 3B; Kimberly Weisul, "Even Chobani Can't Stay Independent Forever: Yogurtmaker Looks to Raise $500 Million," *Inc.*, March 11, 2014.
2. Small Business Administration Department of Advocacy, "Frequently Asked Questions," March 2014.
3. Joshua Yaffa, "Signs of a Russian Thaw (Toward Business)," *The New York Times*, December 28, 2013.
4. Dinah Eng and Dal LaMagna, "The Rise of the Tweezerman," *Fortune*, January 13, 2014, pp. 23–26.
5. Small Business Administration Department of Advocacy, "Frequently Asked Questions."
6. National Association of Women Business Owners Indianapolis, "Women-Owned Businesses Key Facts".
7. U.S. Census Bureau, "2007 Survey of Business Owners Summaries of Findings".
8. Marie Gray, "From the Frontier to Fashion's Peak," *Fortune*, November 18, 2013, pp. 29–32.
9. Small Business Administration Department of Advocacy, "Frequently Asked Questions."
10. "Statistics of U.S. Businesses (SUSB)," *Statistics of U.S. Businesses*.
11. "Bittersweet Synergy: Domestic Outsourcing in India," *The Economist*, October 22, 2009, p. 74.
12. John Tozzi, "Innovation: Tap to Unlock," *Bloomberg Businessweek*, June 13, 2013, p. 42.
13. "Small Biz Stats & Trends," SCORE®.
14. Business Insurance Quotes, "10 Mom-and-Pop Businesses That Turned Into Empires," Business Insurance.
15. Michael Wolff, "Uber: Tech Company of the Year," *USA Today*, December 23, 2013, pp. 1B, 3D.
16. Dinah Eng and Patrick Leon Esquerré, "Even Texans Can Love Quiche," *Fortune*, September 2, 2013, pp. 27–30.
17. Dinah Eng, "Soft Pretzels Out of Hard Times," *Fortune*, July 22, 2013, pp. 23–26; Auntie Anne's, "National News," Auntie Anne's website; Auntie Anne's, "About Us," Auntie Anne's website.
18. Christine Birkner, "Southern Sweet Spot," *Marketing News*, January 2014, pp. 16–17.
19. Small Business Administration Department of Advocacy, "Frequently Asked Questions." 20. Lev Grossman, "Head Trip," *Time*, April 7, 2014, pp. 36–41.
21. Jefferson Graham, "Start-Up Cooks Up a Future for Food," *USA Today*, December 23, 2013, p. 4B.
22. Small Business Administration Department of Advocacy, "Frequently Asked Questions."
23. Jeff Bercovici, "Why (Some) Psychopaths Make Great CEOs," *Forbes*, June 14, 2011; Sebastian Bailey, "What Do Entrepreneurs, U.S. Presidents and Psychopaths Have in Common?" *Forbes*, August 29, 2012; Alexander Stein, "What Entrepreneurs and Con Men Have in Common," *Inc.*, June 2013, p. 58.
24. Eric Butterman, "Shark Tank-Like Business Plan Competition Helps Launch Rutgers Business Ideas," Rutgers Business School.
25. Danielle Kucera, "Stitch Fix Nabs $12 Million From Benchmark to Customize Commerce," *Bloomberg*, October 17, 2013; Nicole Laporte, "Getting Their Fix," *Fast Company*, March 2014, pp. 44–46.
26. Josh Hyatt, "An Idea Up His Sleeve," *Fortune*, January/February 2013, pp. 41–42; Kelly Kearsley, "What I Gave Up to Start My Business," *CNN Money*, June 12, 2013; ReFleece website.
27. Thomas W. Zimmerer and Norman M. Scarborough, *Essentials of Entrepreneurship and Small Business Management*, 6th ed. (Upper Saddle River, NJ: Pearson Prentice Hall, 2005), pp. 118–24.
28. Ibid.
29. "The SCORE Association Media Fact Sheet," *SCORE*.
30. Adapted from "Tomorrow's Entrepreneur," *Inc. State of Small Business*, 23, no. 7 (2001), pp. 80–104.
31. Dan Barry, "Boomers Hit New Self-Absorption Milestone: Age 65," *International New York Times*, December 21, 2010.
32. Molly Smith, "Managing Generation Yas They Change the Workforce," *Reuters*, January 8, 2008.
33. Jeffrey Passal and D'Vera Cohn, "Immigration to Play Lead Role in Future U.S. Growth," Pew Research, February 11, 2008; U.S. Bureau of the Census, *Statistical Abstract of the United States, 2011*.
34. "How Imgur Became a Photo-Sharing Hit," *Bloomberg Businessweek*, January 23, 2013, pp. 31–32.
35. Gifford Pinchott III, *Intrapreneuring* (New York: Harper & Row, 1985), p. 34.
36. Paul Brown, "How to Cope with Hard Times," *The New York Times*, June 10, 2008.
37. Adapted from Carol Kinsey Gorman, *Creativity in Business: A Practical*

Guide for Creative Thinking, Crisp Publications Inc., 1989, pp. 5–6. © Crisp Publications Inc., 1200 Hamilton Court, Menlo Park, CA 94025.

38. Sam Oches, "Top 50 Unit Breakdown Sorted by 2010 Total Units," *QSR*, August 2011; "About Sonic Beach," *Sonic Beach*; Sonic website; "Strictly Speaking," Sonic website.

Chapter 3

1. Rachel Feintzeig, "Building Middle-Manager Morale," *The Wall Street Journal*, April 7, 2013; Melissa Korn and Anita Hofschneider, "How to Get Ahead as a Middle Manager: Try These Tips," *The Wall Street Journal*, August 7, 2013; "Managers by the Numbers," *The Wall Street Journal*, August 6, 2013; Melissa Korn, "How I Survived Life as a Middle Manager," The Wall Street Journal, August 5, 2013; Melissa Korn, "What It's Like Being a Middle Manager Today," *The Wall Street Journal*, August 5, 2013; "Using Their Own Words, Middle Managers Describe the Nature of Their Jobs," *The Wall Street Journal*.
2. Pete Pachal, "Samsung Bets Big on Curved TVs," *Mashable*, March 20, 2014; Brian X. Chen, "Television Sales Look Grim Again This Year," *The New York Times*, November 6, 2013.
3. Barbara Thau, "New Toys 'R' Us CEO Reveals 'Diagnosis,' Treatment Plan for Ailing Chain," *Forbes*, March 27, 2014; Suzanne Kapner, "Toys 'R' Us CEO Sets Revamp Plan to Return to Profitability," *The Wall Street Journal*, March 26, 2014.
4. "Seventh Generation: Ethosolution Go Green Products and All Natural Cleaners," EthoSolutions.
5. Stephanie Strom, "CVS Vows to Quit Selling Tobacco Products," *The New York Times*, February 5, 2014; Kyle Stock, "The Strategy Behind CVS's No-Smoking Campaign," *Bloomberg Businessweek*, February 5, 2014.
6. Jayson Derrick, "Nike's 2017 Objective: $36 Billion Revenue," *The Motley Fool*, October 20, 2014.
7. Eric Pfanner, "After Losses, Yet Another Overhaul for Sony," *The New York Times*, February 6, 2014; Jackie Northam, "As Overseas Costs Rise, More U.S. Companies Are 'Reshoring,'" *NPR*, January 27, 2014.
8. G. Tomas, M. Hult, David W. Cravens, and Jagdish Sheth, "Competitive Advantage in the Global Marketplace: A Focus on Marketing Strategy," *Journal of Business Research* 51 (January 2001), p. 1.
9. Michigan Department of Natural Resources Fisheries Division, "Tactical Plan," October 24, 2013.
10. Dennis McCafferty, "The Ten Commandments of Disaster Recovery," May 13, 2013.
11. Tamara Lytle, "Rising for the Rubble," *Society for Human Resource Management*, 56, no. 9 (September 1, 2011).
12. Mariko Yasu, "Panasonic Plans to Eliminate 17,000 Jobs in Reorganization," *Bloomberg Businessweek*, April 28, 2011.
13. PRWeb, "Collabera Named 2014 'Best Staffing Firm to Work For' by Staffing Industry Analysts for Record Third Consecutive Year," *PRWeb*, March 25, 2014; Collabera, "Home".
14. "Labor Force Statistics from the Current Population Survey," Bureau of Labor Statistics.
15. C. O. Trevor, and A. J. Nyberg, "Keeping Your Headcount When All About You Are Losing Theirs: Downsizing, Voluntary Turnover Rates, and the Moderating Role of HR Practices," *Academy of Management Journal*, 51 (2008), pp. 259–76.
16. Jon Kaufman and Rob Markey, "Who Keeps You Jazzed About Your Job?" *Forbes*, February 11, 2014.
17. Liz Welch, "The Way I Work: Ken Grossman, Sierra Nevada," *Inc.*, April 24, 2013; Bryan Carey, "Sierra Nevada Brewery Tops $200 Million Mark," *The Examiner*, September 11, 2013; Tip Top, "Beyond the Pale: The Story of Sierra Nevada Brewing Co.," *Beer Spot*, August 27, 2013.
18. International Association of Privacy Professionals, "About IAPP".
19. Catalyst, "Women CEOs of the Fortune 1000," Catalyst, January 15, 2014.
20. Ross Kerber, "Growth in Compensation for U.S. CEOs May HaveSslowed," *Reuters*, March 17, 2014.
21. DiversityInc, "The DiversityInc Top 50 Companies for Diversity," *DiversityInc*, 2014; Diversity Best Practices Staff, "Inside Diversity Structure at Sodexo, Johnson & Johnson, and Rockwell Automation," *Diversity Best Practices*, January 29, 2013.
22. Laura Nichols, "Agencies Called to Step Up the Pace on Diversity Efforts," *PRWeek*, February 7, 2014.
23. Clay Latimer, "Philip Pillsbury's Treats Turned Into Tasty Sales," *Investor's Business Daily*, August 1, 2013, p. A3; Funding Universe, "The Pillsbury Company History," *International Directory of Company Histories*, Vol. 62, St. James Press, 2004; Walter Waggoner, "Philip Pillsbury of Minnesota; Led Food Products Concern," *The New York Times*, June 16, 1984; Constance L. Hays and Andrew Ross Sorkin, "General Mills Is Seen in a $10.5 Billion Deal for Pillsbury," *The New York Times*, July 17, 2000.
24. Del Jones, "Autocratic Leadership Works—Until It Fails," *USA Today*, June 5, 2003.
25. George Manning and Kent Curtis, *The Art of Leadership* (New York: McGraw-Hill, 2003), p. 125.
26. Joann S. Lublin and Dana Mattioli, "Penney CEO Out, Old Boss Back In," *The Wall Street Journal*, April 8, 2013.
27. Bruce J. Avolio and William L. Gardner, "Authentic Leadership Development: Getting to the Root of Positive Forms of Leadership," *The Leadership Quarterly*, 2005, pp. 315–38.
28. John P. Kotter, "What Leaders Really Do," *Harvard Business Review*, December 2001.
29. Lisa Baertlein, "McDonald's CEO Jim Skinner to Retire," *Reuters*, March 22, 2012.
30. C. L. Pearce and C. C. Manz, "The

New Silver Bullets of Leadership: The Importance of Self-and Shared Leadership in Knowledge Work," *Organizational Dynamics*, 34, no. 2 (2005), pp. 130–40.

31. Deborah Harrington-Mackin, *The Team Building Tool Kit* (New York: New Directions Management, 1994); Joseph P. Folger, Marshall Scott Poole, and Randall K. Stutman, *Working through Conflict: Strategies for Relationships, Groups, and Organizations*, 6th ed. (Upper Saddle River, NJ: Pearson Education, 2009).
32. Leigh Buchanan, "Between Venus and Mars," *Inc.*, June 2013, pp. 64–74; Leigh Buchanan, "What a Leader Needs Now: 7 'Feminine' Qualities," *Inc.*, June 2013.
33. Kerrie Unsworth, "Unpacking Creativity," *Academy of Management Review*, 26 (April 2001), pp. 289–97.
34. Pallavi Gogoi, "A Bittersweet Deal or Wrigley," *BusinessWeek*, May 12, 2008, p. 341 "About Us," Wrigley.
35. *Harvard Business Review* 60 (November–December 1982), p. 160.
36. Dan Schwabel, "5 Reasons Why Your Online Presence Will Replace Your Resume in 10 Years," *Forbes*, February 21, 2012.
37. "Salary After Taxes," *Employment Spot*.
38. Bureau of Labor Statistics, "May 2013 National Occupational Employment and Wage Estimates United States".
39. Ford, "Our Strategy," 2011–2012; Mark Vaughn, "2013 Ford Fusion Drive Review," *Autoweek*, September 21, 2012; Lawrence Ulrich, "A Hybrid Done Right, but Not Without Glitches," *The New York Times*, November 2, 2012.

Chapter 4

1. Erika Fry, "How CarMax Cares," *Fortune*, April 8, 2013, p. 21; CarMax website, "CarMax Culture and Values"; Michael Myser, "The Wal-Mart of Used Cars," *CNN Money*, October 2, 2006.
2. Horace Dediu, "Understanding Apple's Organizational Structure," Asymco, July 3, 2013; Sam Grobart, "How Samsung Became the World's No. 1 Smartphone Maker," *Bloomberg Businessweek*, March 28, 2013; Jay Yarow, "Apple's New Organizational Structure Could Help It Move Faster," *Business Insider*, May 1, 2013.
3. Reed Hastings, "How to Set Your Employees Free: Reed Hastings," *Bloomberg Businessweek*, April 12, 2012; Dan Lyons, "Advice on Corporate Culture From Netfl ix's Former Chief Talent Officer," *HubSpot*, May 7, 2013.
4. "A New Future for Toms Shoes, Tweed Shire and Room to Read," *Reputation Report*, August 7, 2009; "Our Movement," TOMS Shoes.
5. "Best Companies to Work For: Happy Campers," *CNNMoney*; Christopher Palmeri, "Zappos Retails Its Culture," *Bloomberg Businessweek*, December 30, 2009.
6. Rachel Emma Sullivan, "When Water-Cooler Chats Aren't Enough," *The Wall Street Journal*, May 1, 2013, p. B6; Max Nisen, "Zappos to Build Intentionally Inconvenient Office in Las Vegas, Arch Daily, March 28, 2013; Ben Kesling and James R. Hagerty, "Say Goodbye to the Office Cubicle," *The Wall Street Journal*, April 2, 2013.
7. Joe Light, "Finance and Tech Signal Bold Attitudes on Ethics," *The Wall Street Journal*, March 7, 2011.
8. Lisa Magloff, "Examples of Transformational Change," *Chron*; Nokia, "The Nokia Story".
9. Adam Smith, *Wealth of Nations* (New York: Modern Library, 1937; originally published in 1776).
10. Malcolm Moore, "What Has Triggered the Suicide Cluster at Foxconn?" *The Telegraph*, May 16, 2010.
11. Unilever, "Annual Report and Accounts 2013".
12. PepsiCo Inc., *The New York Times*, March 31, 2014. PepsiCo Inc., "Global Business Units".
13. Diageo, "Regions".
14. Procter & Gamble, "P&G Organizes Global Business Units into Industry-Based Sectors," *P&G Corporate Newsroom*, June 5, 2013.
15. Micah Solomon, "Take These Two Steps to Rival Nordstrom's Customer Service Experience," *Forbes*, March 15, 2014.
16. Kerry Hannon, "The Write Stuff," *Money*, October 2013, pp. 29–30; Nota Bene, "About Us"; "Nota Bene,"*Whirl Magazine*, June 9, 2010; "Shopping Guide," *Pittsburgh Magazine*.
17. Julie Jargon, "Burger King Joins Crowd in India," *The Wall Street Journal*, November 19, 2014; Lily Kuo, "Why Burger King Should Sell Pizza at Its New Restaurants in India," *Quartz*, November 21, 2013.
18. "Why Work Here?"
19. PR Newswire, "PepsiCo Unveils New Organizational Structure, Names CEOs of Three Principle Operating Units," November 5, 2007; "The PepsiCo Family," PepsiCo.
20. Jon R. Katzenbach and Douglas K. Smith, "The Discipline of Teams," *Harvard Business Review*, 71 (March–April 1993), p. 19.
21. Ibid.
22. John Baldoni, "The Secret to Team Collaboration: Individuality," *Inc.*, January 18, 2012.
23. Gregory Ciotti, "Why Remote Teams Are the Future (and How to Make Them Work)," *Help Scout*, October 23, 2013.
24. Esther Shein, "Making the Virtual Team Real," *The Network*, April 2, 2008.
25. Patrick Kiger, "Task Force Training Develops New Leaders, Solves Real Business Issues and Helps Cut Costs," *Workforce*, September 7, 2011; Duane D. Stanford, "Coca-Cola Woman Board Nominee Bucks Slowing Diversity Trend," *Bloomberg*, February 22, 2013.
26. Jerry Useem, "What's That Spell? TEAMWORK," *Fortune*, June 12, 2006, p. 66.
27. Jia Lynnyang, "The Power of Number 4.6," *Fortune*, June 12, 2006, p. 122.
28. Natasha Singer, "Intel's Sharp-Eyed Social Scientist," *The New York Times*, February 15, 2014.
29. Catherine Dunn, "Brother-and-Sister

Brewer," *Fortune*, November 18, 2013; Esha Chhabra, "Fair Trade Crucial Ingredient in Numi Organic Teas," *SF Gate*, December 30, 2011; Certified B Corporation, "Numi Organic Tea"; Kristen, "Numi Organic Tea Brews 'Pure Tea' Precedent with Non-GMO Verification," *The Shelby Report*, August 27, 2012.

30. Richard S. Wellins, William C. Byham, and Jeanne M. Wilson, *Empowered Teams: Creating Self-Directed Work Groups That Improve Quality, Productivity, and Participation* (San Francisco: Jossey-Bass Publishers, 1991), p. 5.
31. Matt Krumrie, "Are Meetings a Waste of Time? Survey Says Yes," *Minneapolis Workplace Examiner*, May 12, 2009.
32. Peter Mell and Timothy Grance, "The NIST Definition of Cloud Computing," National Institute of Standards and Technology, Special Publication 800-145, September 2011.
33. Michael Christian, "Top 10 Ideas: Making the Most of Your Corporate Intranet," April 2, 2009.
34. Kim Komando, "Why You Need a Company Policy on Internet Use".
35. PBSNewsHour, "Apple Supplier Foxconn Pledges Better Working Conditions, but Will It Deliver?" *YouTube*.
36. Michael D. Maginn, *Effective Teamwork*, 1994, p. 10. © 1994 Richard D. Irwin, a Times Mirror Higher Education Group Inc. Company.
37. Tony Hsieh, "Zappos CEO: Training, Mentorship at the Core of Our Employee 'Pipeline Strategy,'" *The Huffington Post*, January 21, 2011; Eleanor Bloxham, "Zappos and the Search for a Better Way to Run a Business," *CNN Money*, January 29, 2014.

Chapter 5

1. James R. Hagerty, "Keeping Plants Running from Afar," *The Wall Street Journal*, September 5, 2013, p. B8; ABB Communications Services, "ABB Integrates Plant, Stops Batch Rejects," 2004; "Turbine Remote Monitoring Service Allows for Scalability," *Automation World*, September 17, 2012; Eaton, "eNotify RemoteMonitoring".
2. Reshma Memon Yaqub, "Matching Stars to Their Dream Cars," *Inc.*, September 2013; Celebrity Auto Group; "Celebrity Auto Group Rolls-Royce Phantom with Build-in iPads," GTSpirit.com, November 14, 2012.
3. Rina Rapuano, "Check Please!" *The Washingtonian Blog*, February 18, 2010.
4. Leonard L. Berry, *Discovering the Soul of Service* (New York: The Free Press, 1999), pp. 86–96.
5. Valerie A. Zeithaml and Mary Jo Bitner, *Services Marketing*, 3rd ed. (Boston: McGraw-Hill Irwin, 2003), pp. 3, 22.
6. Chris Mock, "Quality Control in 2014," *Freddie Mac*, February 10, 2014.
7. Bernard Wysocki Jr., "To Fix Health Care, Hospitals Take Tips from the Factory Floor," *The Wall Street Journal*, April 9, 2004.
8. Tim Mullaney, "Social Media Is Reinventing How Business Is Done," *USA Today*, May 16, 2012; David Lavenda, "How Red Robin Transformed Its Business with Yammer," *Fast Company*, February 6, 2014.
9. Matthew Peach, "UK's First Laser Vibrometry Test Facility Opening in Early 2014," Optics.org, October 29, 2013.
10. Christina Cooke, "America's Rebel Band of Custom-Bike Builders," *The Atlantic*, April 3, 2014.
11. Marie Singer, "The Hershey Company—Company Information," Market Business News, April 14, 2014.
12. Honda, "Honda to Build New Automobile Plant in Mexico for Production of Subcompact Vehicles, Starting in 2014," *Business Wire*, August 12, 2011.
13. "Top 10 Solar Friendly States," *Cooler Planet*.
14. Ross Toro, "How 3D Printers Work (Infographic)," *Live Science*, June 18, 2013.
15. Robotic Industries Association, "North American Robotics Shipments Grow in 2013 While New Orders Contract," Robotics Online, February 4, 2014; Sian Harris, "Will Robots Be the Answer to Our Next Manufacturing Revolution?" *E&T*, January 20, 2014. Elisabeth Eitel, "Technology forecast 2014: Robots Priced for the Masses," *Machine Design*, January 8, 2014.
16. Tiffany Kaiser, "Lenovo Launches Its First U.S. PC Manufacturing Line in North Carolina," *Daily Tech*, June 6, 2013; Shane McGlaun, "Lenovo Eyes Smartphone Push in the U.S.," *Daily Tech*, May 27, 2013; Loretta Chao, "As Rivals Outsource, Lenovo Keeps Production In-House," *The Wall Street Journal*, July 9, 2012; Simon Montlake, The Middle Way: Inside Lenovo's Bid to Build a Better Tablet," *Forbes*, November 18, 2013.
17. Biogen Idec, "Corporate Citizenship Report," 2012; Business Wire via The Motley Fool, "Biogen Idec Becomes First U.S.-Based Biotech Named to Dow Jones Sustainability World Index," *Daily Finance*, September 24, 2013.
18. Bryan Walsh, "Why Green Is the New Red, White and Blue," *Time*, April 28, 2008, p. 53.
19. Megan Kamerick, "How To Go Green," *New Mexico Business Weekly*, May 23–29, 2008, p. 3.
20. O. C. Ferrell and Michael D. Hartline, *Marketing Strategy* (Mason, OH: South Western, 2011), p. 215.
21. Keisha A. Simmons, "UPS Introduces New Cloud-Based Technology Platform to Improve International Supply Chain Management," *UPS*, November 13, 2012.
22. Ferrell and Hartline, *Marketing Strategy*, p. 215.
23. Susan Berfield and Manuel Baigorri, "Zara's Fast-Fashion Edge," *Bloomberg Businessweek*, November 14, 2013.
24. Investment Mine, "Historical Copper Prices and Price Chart," April 8, 2014.

25. "Broken Links," *The Economist*, March 31, 2011.
26. Jez Fredenburgh, "Horsemeat: Tesco's Pledges, One Year On," *Farmer's Weekly*, February 21, 2014.
27. Brian Dumaine, "Fill 'Er Up with Hydrogen?" *Fortune*, September 2, 2013, p. 23; Sarah Zielinski, "George W. Bush vs. Elon Musk: Who Was Right about the Future of Hydrogen Cars?" *Slate*, August 27, 2013; "Hobbled by High Cost, Hydrogen Fuel Cells Will Be a Modest $3 Billion Market in 2020," Lux Research, January 8, 2013; Alissa Priddle, "Toyota to Start Selling Hydrogen Fuel-Cell Car in 2015," USA Today, August 8, 2012.
28. Susan Carey, "Airlines Play Up Improvements in On-Time Performance," *The Wall Street Journal*, February 10, 2010, p. B6; U.S. Department of Transportation, "Air Travel Consumer Report," March 2014.
29. Michael E. Newman, "Three U.S. Organizations Honored with the 2013 Baldrige National Quality Award," Baldridge Performance Excellence Program, November 13, 2013.
30. Roger Yu, "Kia Looks to Buff Image with Value, New Designs," *USA Today*, June 29, 2011; Jonathon Ramsey, "Kia Using Quality and Technology to Increase Sales and Brand Prestige," *AutoBlog*, April 11, 2013.
31. Philip B. Crosby, *Quality Is Free: The Art of Making Quality Certain* (New York: McGraw-Hill, 1979), pp. 9–10.
32. Nigel F. Piercy, *Market-Led Strategic Change* (Newton, MA: Butterworth-Heinemann, 1992), pp. 374–85.
33. Bloomberg LLP, "Compuware Gomez Introduces Free Web Performance Benchmarking Tool," *Bloomberg*, February 16, 2010.
34. "ISO 9001 Certification," GE Power & Water.
35. Charles Duhigg and David Barboza, "In China, Human Costs Are Built into an iPad," *The New York Times*, January 25, 2012.
36. "Monitoring and Auditing Global Supply Chains Is a Must," *Ethisphere*, 2011, Q3, pp. 38–45.
37. "Employment Opportunities," Careers in Supply Chain Management.
38. "Best Jobs in America," *CNN Money*.
39. James Wetherbe, "Principles of Cycle Time Reduction," *Cycle Time Research*, 1995, p. iv.
40. Stan Davis and Christopher Meyer, *Blur: The Speed of Change in the Connected Economy* (Reading, MA: Addison-Wesley, 1998), p. 5.
41. "Home Run Inn," *CBS Chicago*, January 4, 2012; Home Run Inn, *Home Run Inn All-Star Catering*; "Consumer Reports Names Home Run Inn Best Frozen Pizza," August 20, 2013; HomeRun Inn, "Frozen Pizza".

Glossary 术语表

A

accountability the principle that employees who accept an assignment and the authority to carry it out are answerable to a superior for the outcome.

acquisition the purchase of one company by another, usually by buying its stock.

administrative managers those who manage an entire business or a major segment of a business; they are not specialists but coordinate the activities of specialized managers.

agenda a calendar, containing both specific and vague items, that covers short-term goals and long-term objectives.

analytical skills the ability to identify relevant issues, recognize their importance, understand the relationships between them, and perceive the underlying causes of a situation.

articles of partnership legal documents that set forth the basic agreement between partners.

B

board of directors a group of individuals, elected by the stockholders to oversee the general operation of the corporation, who set the corporation's long-range objectives.

business plan a precise statement of the rationale for a business and a step-by-step explanation of how it will achieve its goals.

C

capacity the maximum load that an organizational unit can carry or operate.

centralized organization a structure in which authority is concentrated at the top, and very little decision-making authority is delegated to lower levels.

commitee a permanent, formal group that performs a specific task.

common stock stock whose owners have voting rights in the corporation, yet do not receive preferential treatment regarding dividends.

computer-assisted design (CAD) the design of components, products, and processes on computers instead of on paper.

computer-assisted manufacturing (CAM) manufacturing that employs specialized computer systems to actually guide and control the transformation processes.

computer-integrated manufacturing (CIM) a complete system that designs products, manages machines and materials, and controls the operations function.

conceptual skills the ability to think in abstract terms and to see how parts fit together to form the whole.

continuous manufacturing organizations companies that use continuously running assembly lines, creating products with many similar characteristics.

controlling the process of evaluating and correcting activities to keep the organization on course.

cooperative (co-op) an organization composed of individuals or small businesses that have banded together to reap the benefits of belonging to a larger organization.

corporate charter a legal document that the state issues to a company based on information the company provides in the articles of incorporation.

corporation a legal entity, created by the state, whose assets and liabilities are separate from its owners.

crisis management (contingency planning) an element in planning that deals with potential disasters such as product tampering, oil spills, fire, earthquake, computer virus, or airplane crash.

customer departmentalization the arrangement of jobs around the needs of various types of customers.

customization making products to meet a particular customer's needs or wants.

D

decentralized organization an organization in which decision-making authority is delegated as far down the chain of command as possible.

delegation of authority giving employees not only tasks, but also the power to make commitments, use resources, and take whatever actions are necessary to carry out those tasks.

departmentalization the grouping of jobs into working units usually called departments, units, groups, or divisions.

directing motivating and leading employees to achieve organizational objectives.

dividends profits of a corporation that are distributed in the form of cash payments to stockholders.

downsizing the elimination of a significant number of employees from an organization.

E

economic order quantity (EOQ) model a model that identifies the optimum number of items to order to minimize the costs of managing (ordering, storing, and using) them.

employee empowerment when employees are provided with the ability to take on responsibilities and make decisions about their jobs.

entrepreneurship the process of creating and managing a business to achieve desired objectives.

F

financial managers those who focus on obtaining needed funds for the successful operation of an organization and using those funds to further organizational goals.

first-line managers those who supervise both workers and the daily operations of an organization.

fixed-position layout a layout that brings all resources required to create the product to a central location.

flexible manufacturing the direction of machinery by computers to adapt to different versions of similar operations.

franchise a license to sell another's products or to use another's name in business, or both.

franchisee the purchaser of a franchise.

franchiser the company that sells a franchise.

functional departmentalization the grouping of jobs that perform similar functional activities, such as finance, manufacturing, marketing, and human resources.

G

general partnership a partnership that involves a complete sharing in both the management and the liability of the business.

geographical departmentalization the grouping of jobs according to geographic location, such as state, region, country, or continent.

grapevine an informal channel of communication, separate from management's formal, official communication channels.

group two or more individuals who communicate with one another, share a common identity, and have a common goal.

H

human relations skills the ability to deal with people, both inside and outside the organization.

human resources managers those who handle the staffing function and deal with employees in a formalized manner.

I

information technology (IT) managers those who are responsible for implementing, maintaining, and controlling technology applications in business, such as computer networks.

initial public offering (IPO) selling a corporation's stock on public markets for the first time.

inputs the resources—such as labor, money, materials, and energy—that are converted into outputs.

intermittent organizations organizations that deal with products of a lesser magnitude than do project organizations; their products are not necessarily unique but possess a significant number of differences.

intrapreneurs individuals in large firms who take responsibility for the development of innovations within the organizations.

inventory all raw materials, components, completed or partially completed products, and pieces of equipment a firm uses.

inventory control the process of determining how many supplies and goods are needed and keeping track of quantities on hand, where each item is, and who is responsible for it.

ISO 9000 a series of quality assurance standards designed by the International Organization for Standardization (ISO) to ensure consistent product quality under many conditions.

ISO 14000 a comprehensive set of environmental standards that encourages a cleaner and safer world by promoting a more uniform approach to environmental management and helping companies attain and measure improvements in their environmental performance.

J

joint venture a partnership established for a specific project or for a limited time.

just-in-time (JIT) inventory management a technique using smaller quantities of materials that arrive "just in time" for use in the transformation process and therefore require less storage space and other inventory management expense.

L

leadership the ability to influence employees to work toward organizational goals.

leveraged buyout (LBO) a purchase in which a group of investors borrows money from banks and other institutions to acquire a company (or a division of one), using the assets of the purchased company to guarantee repayment of the loan.

limited liability company (LLC) form of ownership that provides limited liability and taxation like a partnership but places fewer restrictions on members.

limited partnership a business organization that has at least one general partner, who assumes unlimited liability, and at least one limited partner, whose liability is limited to his or her investment in the business.

line-and-staff structure a structure having a traditional line relationship between superiors and subordinates and also specialized managers—called staff managers—who are available to assist line managers.

line structure the simplest organizational structure, in which direct lines of authority extend from the top manager to the lowest level of the organization.

M

management a process designed to achieve an organization's objectives by using its resources effectively and efficiently in a changing environment.

managers those individuals in organizations who make decisions about the use of resources and who are concerned with planning, organizing, staffing, directing, and controlling the organization's activities to reach its objectives.

manufacturing the activities and processes used in making tangible products; also called production.

marketing managers those who are responsible for planning, pricing, and promoting products and making them available to customers.

material-requirements planning (MRP) a planning system that schedules the precise quantity of materials needed to make the product.

matrix structure a structure that sets up teams from different departments, thereby creating two or more intersecting lines of authority; also called a projectmanagement structure.

merger the combination of two companies (usually corporations) to form a new company.

middle managers those members of an organization responsible for the tactical planning that implements the general guidelines established by top management.

mission the statement of an organization's fundamental purpose and basic philosophy.

modular design the creation of an item in self-contained units, or modules, that can be combined or interchanged to create different products.

multidivisional structure a structure that organizes departments into larger groups called divisions.

N

networking the building of relationships and sharing of information with colleagues who can help managers achieve the items on their agendas.

nonprofit corporations corporations that focus on providing a service rather than earning a profit but are not owned by a government entity.

O

operational plans very short-term plans that specify what actions individuals, work groups, or departments need to accomplish in order to achieve the tactical plan and ultimately the strategic plan.

operations the activities and processes used in making both tangible and intangible products.

operations management (OM) the development and administration of the activities involved in transforming resources into goods and services.

organizational chart a visual display of the organizational structure, lines of authority (chain of command), staff relationships, permanent committee arrangements, and lines of communication.

organizational culture a firm's shared values, beliefs, traditions, philosophies, rules, and role models for behavior.

organizational layers the levels of management in an organization.

organizing the structuring of resources and activities to accomplish objectives in an efficient and effective manner.

outputs the goods, services, and ideas that result from the conversion of inputs.

P

partnership a form of business organization defined by the Uniform Partnership Act as "an association of two or more persons who carry on as co-owners of a business for profit."

planning the process of determining the organization's objectives and deciding how to accomplish them; the first function of management.

preferred stock a special type of stock whose owners, though not generally having a say in running the company, have a claim to profits before other stockholders do.

private corporation a corporation owned by just one or a few people who are closely involved in managing the business.

process layout a layout that organizes the transformation process into departments that group related processes.

product departmentalization the organization of jobs in relation to the products of the firm.

product layout a layout requiring that production be broken down into relatively simple tasks assigned to workers, who are usually positioned along an assembly line.

product-development teams a specific type of project team formed to devise, design, and implement a new product.

production the activities and processes used in making tangible products; also called manufacturing.

production and operations managers those who develop and administer the activities involved in transforming resources into goods, services, and ideas ready for the marketplace.

project organization a company using a fixed-position layout because it is typically involved in large, complex projects such as construction or exploration.

project teams groups similar to task forces that normally run their operation and have total control of a specific work project.

public corporation a corporation whose stock anyone may buy, sell, or trade.

purchasing the buying of all the materials needed by the organization; also called procurement.

Q

quality control the processes an organization uses to maintain its established quality standards.

quality-assurance teams (or quality circles) small groups of workers brought together from throughout the organization to solve specific quality, productivity, or service problems.

quasi-public corporations corporations owned and operated by the federal, state, or local government.

R

responsibility the obligation, placed on employees through delegation, to perform assigned tasks satisfactorily and be held accountable for the proper execution of work.

routing the sequence of operations through which the product must pass.

S

S corporation corporation taxed as though it were a partnership with restrictions on shareholders.

scheduling the assignment of required tasks to departments or even specific machines, workers, or teams.

self-directed work team (SDWT) a group of employees responsible for an entire work process or segment that delivers a product to an internal or external customer.

small business any independently owned and operated

business that is not dominant in its competitive area and does not employ more than 500 people.

Small Business Administration (SBA) an independent agency of the federal government that offers managerial and financial assistance to small businesses.

sole proprietorships businesses owned and operated by one individual; the most common form of business organization in the United States.

span of management the number of subordinates who report to a particular manager.

specialization the division of labor into small, specific tasks and the assignment of employees to do a single task.

staffing the hiring of people to carry out the work of the organization.

standardization the making of identical interchangeable components or products.

statistical process control a system in which management collects and analyzes information about the production process to pinpoint quality problems in the production system.

stock shares of a corporation that may be bought or sold.

strategic plans those plans that establish the long-range objectives and overall strategy or course of action by which a firm fulfills its mission.

structure the arrangement or relationship of positions within an organization.

supply chain management connecting and integrating all parties or members of the distribution system in order to satisfy customers.

T

tactical plans short-range plans designed to implement the activities and objectives specified in the strategic plan.

task force a temporary group of employees responsible for bringing about a particular change.

team a small group whose members have complementary skills; have a common purpose, goals, and approach; and hold themselves mutually accountable.

technical expertise the specialized knowledge and training needed to perform jobs that are related to particular areas of management.

top managers the president and other top executives of a business, such as the chief executive officer (CEO), chief financial officer (CFO), and chief operations officer (COO), who have overall responsibility for the organization.

total quality management (TQM) a philosophy that uniform commitment to quality in all areas of an organization will promote a culture that meets customers' perceptions of quality.

U

undercapitalization the lack of funds to operate a business normally.

V

venture capitalists persons or organizations that agree to provide some funds for a new business in exchange for an ownership interest or stock.

Photo Credits 图片版权

Chapter 1 Opener: © Scott Eells/Bloomberg via Getty Images; p. 6: © Ariel Skelley/Blend Images LLC; p. 7: © PhotoLink/Getty Images; p. 10: © Ben Margot/AP Images; p. 18: © Stockbyte/Getty Images; p. 20: © Mikhail Pochuyev/ZUMA Press/Newscom; p. 22: © AlphaAndOmega/Alamy; p. 25: © Konrad Fiedler/Bloomberg via Getty Images.

Chapter 2 Opener: © McGraw-Hill Education/Mark A.S. Dierker, photographer; p. 37: © dov makabaw/Alamy; p. 38: © Richard Cummins/Alamy; p. 42: © Wendell and Carolyn/Getty Images; p. 45: © Ariel Skelley/Getty Images; p. 46: © DreamPictures/Blend Images/Corbis; p. 50: © Maria Teijeiro/Getty Images.

Chapter 3 Opener: © kali9/iStock; p. 62: © Bill Pugliano/Getty Images; p. 64: © Joe Harpring/AP Images; p. 65: © Patrick Fallon/Bloomberg/Getty Images; p. 68: © McGraw-Hill Education/Mark A.S. Dierker, photographer; p. 70: © David Maxwell/Bloomberg via Getty Images; p. 76: © NAN104/iStock; p. 77: © Sakchai Lalit/AP Images; p. 81: © Mutlu Kurtbas/Getty Images; p. 83: © Ingvar Björk/Alamy.

Chapter 4 Opener: © Zuma Press/Newscom; p. 93: © Michael Orrell/The El Dorado News-Times/AP Images; p. 96: © Ulrich Baumgarten/Getty Images; p. 108: © Stuart Isett/Polaris/Newscom; p. 110: © NetPhotos/Alamy.

Chapter 5 Opener: © Roger Bamber/Alamy; p. 124: © Brent Lewin/Bloomberg via Getty Images; p. 128: © Mark Lennihan/AP Images; p. 132: © ZUMA Press/Alamy; p. 134: © Andersen Ross/Digital Vision/Getty Images; p. 140: © Justin Sullivan/Getty Images.